COME AND SEE

Catholic Bible Study

The Synoptics
On the Gospels of Matthew, Mark, Luke

by

Monsignor Jan Majernik, S.T.D.

Father Joseph Ponessa, S.S.D

and

Laurie Watson Manhardt, Ph.D.

Emmaus Road Publishing
827 North Fourth Street
Steubenville, OH 43952

Library of Congress Control Number: 2005926393
ISBN: 1-931018-31-6
ISBN 13: 978-1-931018-31-9

Cover design and layout by
Jacinta Calcut/Image Graphics & Design

Cover artwork:
Raphael (1483–1520), The Miraculous Draught of Fishes

For additional information on the "Come and See"
Catholic Bible Study series, visit www.CatholicBibleStudy.net

The Synoptics
On the Gospels of Matthew, Mark, and Luke

PRAYER TO
THE HOLY SPIRIT

O Holy Spirit,
Beloved of my soul,
I adore You,
enlighten, guide, strengthen
and console me.
Tell me what I ought to say and do
and command me to do it.
I promise to be submissive in
everything You will ask of me
and to accept all that You
permit to happen to me,
only show me what is Your will.

Amen

Introduction

**It is written, "Man shall not live by bread alone,
but by every word that proceeds from the mouth of God." (Matthew 4:4)**

**May God set His Word in your heart
and fill you with everlasting joy.**

"Come and See" Catholic Bible Study ~*The Synoptics* embraces the fullness of God's Word as described in the Book of Hebrews: "For the word of God is living and active, sharper than any two-edged sword, piercing to the division of soul and spirit, of joints and marrow, and discerning the thoughts and intentions of the heart" (Hebrews 4:12). Ponder God's interest in the human heart. The prophet Isaiah reveals, "The Lord longs to be gracious to you" (Isaiah 30:18). God draws the human soul to Himself by pouring His love into our hearts by the Holy Spirit. The discerning person responds by diligently studying God's revelation in salvation history recorded for us in the Bible.

The Catholic Church invites the faithful to study God's Word for very important reasons:

1. Faith is enhanced by our knowledge of God. His Word is the primary source of information about the Lord Himself. In the language of the Church, we learn that God's Word is *norma normans non normata* (the norm without need of reform). The Gospels offer us the most valuable information about the person and words of Jesus Christ, which will remain true even when heaven and earth pass away (Matthew 24:35).

2. The more we know God's Word, the more we can know and understand ourselves, especially in relationship to God and other people. Our faith frees us to serve our brothers and sisters. The study of the Gospels helps us to know Jesus Christ better and model our lives after Him. We become more loving and caring, imitating the example of Christ in the midst of our world for the greater honor and glory of God and the good of His Church. Through this effort, we believe God will save our souls.

"Synoptics" (the Greek *syn* means "with" and *optics* means "to look") considers the life and ministry of Jesus of Nazareth through the eyewitnesses of Matthew, Mark, and Luke. Their accounts can be put alongside each other to compare events in Christ's life. This study will not attempt to determine the precise nature of the relationship between these accounts (called "the Synoptic problem" by biblical scholars) although to study a number of oral traditions and written sources may help discover additional information about Jesus. Rather, we will focus directly on the beauty of God's Word expressed in the theological outlook of the final text of each Synoptic Gospel transmitted to us from the Tradition of the Church.

The method used for this Bible study will differ somewhat from previous studies in this series. Because of the vast material contained in the Synoptic Gospels, quite familiar to most Christians, we have chosen some themes in the life of our Lord Jesus Christ, from the preparation for His birth and public teaching to His Passion, death and Resurrection. We focus whenever possible on what Saint Jerome (347–420 AD) calls *pellegrinatio*—"pilgrimage" through the holy places associated with the proclamation of the Gospel passage for the first time by the Lord Jesus. We invite you to enter into the culture on pilgrimage to the Holy Land.

Further emphasis is placed on the traditional interpretation of the early Church Fathers on the Synoptic Gospels to show how the text was understood in the early Church and matured throughout the Church's history. Key topics will be outlined and studied in light of the Old Testament tradition, along with the archeological discoveries and geographical backgrounds.

Selected passages of the Gospels will be viewed in light of the Church's teaching summarized in the *Catechism of the Catholic Church* (CCC). For this study, we recommend a Bible text closest to the original manuscripts, such as the Revised Standard Version Catholic Edition (RSVCE). A guide to the Holy Land, such as the classical *Guide to the Holy Land* by Eugene Hoade, issued by the Franciscans in Jerusalem, or a modern scientific guide, *The Holy Land,* by Jerome Murphy-O'Connor, O.P. will show the places where the Gospels originated. Perhaps, later, you can travel to the Holy Land, explore the roots of your faith, and walk in the footsteps of Jesus. Also, please pray for the plight of the small number of Christians remaining in the Holy Land.

The serious Catholic, while becoming intimately acquainted with the Gospel passages, will also want to learn how to pray with God's Word and how to study the biblical text to grasp its moral and spiritual implications for his everyday life. Jesus' prayer in Gethsemane (Luke 22:41–44) illustrates this. Jesus prays with abandonment, giving Himself over entirely to the will of His Father. Jesus prays in silence, privately withdrawing from the presence of His disciples, on His knees and with deep concentration. Later, Jesus invites the disciples to join Him in prayer (Luke 22:46). The format of this Bible study encourages you to go to prayer and personal study first and then join a small group in your home or parish to pray and share with others.

For your personal prayer and Bible study, try to create an atmosphere for prayer which allows for personal purification in God's presence. In silence, invoke the presence of the Lord, asking forgiveness for sins and the grace to forgive others. Start with prayer, perhaps the Our Father and the Prayer to the Holy Spirit, asking to be conformed to the will of our heavenly Father.

You might sit or kneel, breathing calmly. Pray at a time when there will be the least interruptions, perhaps early in the morning or when children are napping. A firm resolve and exercise in concentration helps to avoid distractions and mind wandering. Use your imagination to reconstruct the scene, countryside, people, their actions, and words during this process of meditation. You might also read the passage aloud; aware that behind every word the Lord speaks personally to you. Keep a pen nearby to jot down thoughts prompted by the Holy Spirit. Ask the Lord about His will and any opportunities to be at the disposal of divine Providence. Ask God to help your memory and understanding. Application to your personal life enables you to show gratitude to God, adore Him, and love and serve others.

Conclude each meditation on God's Word with thanksgiving and trust in the guidance of the Holy Spirit. Such a process of prayer and study leads the soul to experience the everlasting presence of God's love in your life. It is not necessary to pray with the passage too long. Try to remain with the passage long enough to experience the fullness of what God wants to share.

Concentrate on interior joy, peace, and consolation during the interaction with God's Word. Meditation should lead to greater intimacy with the Lord. More precious than the study is the interior experience of God's presence and His work in your heart.

Personal Home Study

Seek a quiet place for prayer and study. Adoration of the Blessed Sacrament may enable you to do Bible study and meditate in the presence of our Lord. Or find a place at home for daily prayer and study. Set aside time to pray and study God's Word. 1) Pray, 2) Read the Bible passages and commentary, and then 3) Write answers to the questions using the Bible and *Catechism*. This year, you will read the familiar Gospel passages that you hear at every Holy Mass. You will be able to compare the insights of Saint Matthew, Saint Mark and Saint Luke at various stages throughout the life, ministry, Passion, death, and Resurrection of our Lord Jesus Christ. Bible tabs can help you move back and forth through these books quickly and easily.

Getting Started

- **Pray to the Holy Spirit.** Ask God for wisdom on when to have Bible study, whom to study with, and when and where to meet.
- **Invite neighbors and friends** to a "get acquainted coffee" and find out who will make a commitment to meet for 60–90 minutes once a week for group Bible study.
- **Determine a day of the week** and time of day to meet.
- **Find an appropriate location.** Start in someone's home and then, as your group becomes larger, see if you could meet in church or school facilities.
- **Hire a baby-sitter** for young mothers and share the cost among everyone.
- **Consider a cooperative arrangement** in which each woman takes a turn caring for and teaching the young children.
- **Gather a small prayer group** to pray regularly for your Bible study and for your specific needs and challenges. Pray to discern God's will, brainstorm, and make plans.

Pray that God will anoint faithful, practicing Catholics to lead your study.

- **Teachers ~** take overall responsibility to read commentaries and prepare a 20–30 minute wrap-up lecture after the small group discussions each week.
- **Prayer Leaders ~** begin with a prayer and ask someone to prepare a short five minute opening devotional each week. This could be an answer to prayer or personal testimony.
- **Children's Leaders ~** hire baby-sitters, prepare lessons and teach preschool children who attend Bible study with their mothers.
- **Coordinators ~** communicate with parish personnel about needs for space and use of facilities. Put invitations in church bulletins. Make sure rooms are left in good condition.

Small group facilitators will be needed for each small group. Find two good, practicing Catholics who are excellent listeners to serve together as small group leaders for each group. Small group facilitators share the following responsibilities for their small sharing group:

✝ Pray for each member of the small group each day. Make a nametag for each one.
✝ Meet before the study to pray with other leaders.
✝ Make sure that each person in the group shares each week. Ask each person to read a question and have the first chance to answer it.
✝ You might just go around in a circle, so that each person can look forward to his or her turn. After reading the question others should feel free to offer answers as well.
✝ Ensure that no one person dominates the discussion, including *you!*
✝ Keep the discussion positive and focused on this week's lesson.
✝ Speak kindly and charitably. Steer conversations away from any negative or uncharitable speech, gossip, or griping. Don't badmouth anyone, any group, or any church.
✝ Listen well! Keep your eyes and ears open. Give your full attention to the one speaking.
✝ Look at people while they are speaking. Get comfortable with silence and pauses in the discussion. Be patient. Encourage quieter people to share first. Ask questions.
✝ If questions, misunderstandings, or disagreements arise, refer them to the question box for a teacher or the parish priest to research and discuss later.
✝ Arrange for a social activity at intervals as offered in this book.

Invite and Welcome Priests and Religious

Invite your pastor and associate priests, deacons, and religious to visit Bible study whenever they can. Ask for their blessing. Invite them to come and pray with the Bible study members. See if they would like to come and answer some written questions from the question box periodically. Accept whatever they can offer to the Bible study. However, don't expect anything from them. Appreciate that they may be very busy and don't add additional burdens on them.

Some Practical Considerations

✝ Jesus chose a group of twelve apostles. So, perhaps small groups should be about twelve or thirteen people. When you get too big, break up into two groups.
✝ Women share best with women and men with men. If you plan a mixed Bible study, organize separate men's groups, led by men, and women's groups, led by women.
✝ Offer a married couples' group if two married couples are willing to act as small group facilitators and come together to every single class meeting. Each person should have his or her own book and share his or her own home study answers.
✝ You may also want to consider a nursing mothers' group in which mothers can bring their infants with them and hold the babies while they share their home study work.

- A group of teenagers or young adults could be led by a youth minister.
- Family groups can work together on the home study questions on a given night of the week, with older children or parents helping younger children to find the answers.
- Share the overall goal that *each person* in each group shares aloud *each time* the group meets. Everyone should contribute every time Bible study meets!
- Sit next to the most talkative person in the group and across from the quietest. Use eye contact to encourage quiet members to speak up. Evaluate each week: Am I a good listener? Did I really hear what others shared? Did I affirm others? Did I talk too much?

Social Activities

God has created us as social beings, needing to relate communally. Large churches present challenges for parishioners to get to know one another. Some people belong to a parish for years without getting to know others. Newcomers may never get noticed and welcomed. Bible study offers an opportunity for spiritual nourishment as well as inclusion and hospitality.

Occasional social activities are offered in this book. These socials are simple, fun, and non-threatening. In planning your social activities, be a good sport and try to attend and share.

- Agree on a time when most of the group can meet. This could be right before or after Bible study or on a different day of the week, perhaps even Saturday morning.

- Invite people to come to your home for the social time. Jesus was comfortable visiting in the homes of the rich and the poor. So whether you live in a small apartment or a big home, as a Christian you can offer hospitality to those God sends along your way.

"Do not neglect to show hospitality to strangers, for thereby some have entertained angels unawares" (HEBREWS 13:2).

- Keep it simple! Just a beverage and cookies works well. Simplicity blesses others. People can squeeze together on a sofa or stand around the kitchen. The important thing is to offer hospitality and love one another as Jesus did. Don't fuss!

- Help out the group leader. If Bible study meets in someone else's home, invite the group to come to your place for the social time. Don't make the group leader do it all. Jump right in and offer. Be a blessing to others.

- If your Bible study meets in church, do not fall into the convenience of staying at the church for socials. You might have to drive a distance to someone's home, but it may be the first time anyone from the parish has taken the trouble to come out to their home to visit. Trust God. It's worth it. God will bless your efforts at offering hospitality to your Bible study group and also your efforts in accepting the hospitality of others.

Consider the following times for your socials

9:30 a.m.–10:30 a.m.	Saturday coffee	11:30 a.m.–12:30 p.m.	Luncheon
3:00 p.m.–4:00 p.m.	Afternoon tea	8:00 p.m.–9:00 p.m.	Dessert

---

Modify times to meet your specific needs. If the parish has Saturday morning Mass at 8:00 a.m., adjust the time of your social to accommodate those members of your group who would like to attend Mass and need some travel time to get to the social. If lunch after Bible study makes too long of a day for mothers with children, plan the social for another day. A mothers' group might meet after school when high school students are available to baby-sit.

Practical Schedule

Take responsibility for being a good steward of time. If Bible study becomes loose, busy people may drop out. Late starts encourage tardiness and punish the prompt. Be a good steward of time. Begin and end each Bible study with prayer at the agreed upon time. If many people consistently arrive late, investigate whether you have chosen the best time and pray for God's wisdom to determine the best time for most members. If people leave early, check if you have a conflict with the kindergarten or bus schedule. Perhaps beginning a few minutes earlier or later could serve those who need to pick up children.

Suggested Bible Study Class Schedules

Morning Class

~ 9:30 a.m. Welcome, song, prayer
~ 9:50 a.m. Small group discussion
~ 10:30 a.m. Wrap-up lecture
~ 11:00 a.m. Closing prayer

Evening Class

~ 7:30 p.m. Welcome, song, prayer
~ 7:50 p.m. Small group discussion
~ 8:30 p.m. Wrap-up lecture
~ 9:00 p.m. Closing prayer

Afternoon Class

~ 1:00 p.m. Welcome, song, prayer
~ 1:20 p.m. Small group discussion
~ 2:00 p.m. Wrap-up lecture
~ 2:30 p.m. Closing prayer

Wrap-Up Lecture

1) A closing, wrap-up lecture may be presented for your group.

2) Or simply share on the home study questions and close with prayer.

When using a closing lecture, the teacher spends extra time in prayer and study over the passages of Scripture studied and consults several Bible study commentaries. Several members of the Bible study leaders' group could serve in taking turns to prepare the wrap-up lectures. Invite priests, deacons, and religious sisters to give an occasional lecture.

The lecturer's responsibilities include the following:

† Be a faithful, practicing Catholic. Seek out spiritual direction.
† Receive the Sacrament of Reconciliation frequently.
† Obtain the approval and blessing of your parish priest to teach.
† Use several different lecturers, whenever possible.
† Pray for all the leaders and members of the study daily.
† Outline the Bible chapters to be discussed
† Identify the main idea of the Bible passages studied.
† Find a personal application, suggesting what one can do to respond to God's Word.
† Plan a wrap-up lecture with a beginning, a middle, and an end.
† Use index card or notes to keep you focused. Don't read your lecture!
† Proclaim, teach, and reiterate the teachings of the Catholic Church.
† Learn what the Catholic Church teaches and proclaim the fullness of truth.
† Illustrate the main idea presented in the passage by using true stories from the lives of contemporary Christians or from lives of the saints.
† Use visuals—a flip chart or overhead transparencies if possible.
† Plan a skit, act out a Bible story, and interact with the group.
† Provide a question box. Find answers to difficult questions, or ask a parish priest to come and discuss some questions from the question box.
† When difficult or complex personal problems arise or are shared in the group, seek out the counsel of a priest.
† Begin and end on time.
† When you get to the end of your talk, stop and pray.

Begin with Prayer.
End with Prayer.

Challenges

Any group can attract people with problems and difficulties. Don't try to be all things for all people. When problems arise, consult a priest. Try to be faithful in this one thing, Bible study.

Saint Paul encourages us to, "[Speak] the truth in love … be kind to one another, tenderhearted, forgiving one another, as God in Christ forgave you (Ephesians 4:15, 32).

"All scripture is inspired by God and profitable for teaching, for reproof, for correction, and for training in righteousness, that the man of God may be complete, equipped for every good work" (2 Timothy 3:16–17).

We have learned the plan of our salvation from none other than those through whom the Gospel came down to us. They first preached the Gospel, and afterwards, by the will of God, they handed it down to us in the Scriptures, to be the foundation and pillar of our faith.

They went forth to the ends of the earth, spreading the good news of the good things which God has sent to us, and announcing the peace of heaven to men, who indeed are all equally and individually sharers in the Gospel of God. Matthew also issued among the Hebrews a written Gospel in their own language, while Peter and Paul were evangelizing in Rome and laying the foundation of the Church. After their departure, Mark, the disciple and interpreter of Peter, also handed down to us in writing what had been preached by Peter. Luke also, the companion of Paul, set down in a book the Gospel preached by him. Afterwards, John, the disciple of the Lord who reclined at His bosom, also published a Gospel, while he was residing at Ephesus in Asia.

Just as there are four regions of the world in which we live, and four universal winds, and since the Church is disseminated over all the earth, and the pillar and mainstay of the Church is the Gospel, the breath of life, it is fitting that she have four pillars, breathing immortality on every side and enkindling life in men anew. From this it is evident that the Word, the Artificer of all, who sits upon the Cherubim and embraces all things, and who was manifested to man, has given us a four-fold gospel embracing one spirit.

Saint Irenaeus, Bishop (140–202 AD), *Against Heresies,* III.I.1 and III.XI.8

Begin this "Come and See" Catholic Bible Study ~ *The Synoptics* with expectant faith, hope, charity, and prayer.

A Prayer to the Holy Spirit

Come Holy Spirit; open my mind and heart. Show me the Father's will. Enlighten me, Lord Jesus; apply Your Word to my life and use it to transform me. Make me a good listener. Draw me closer to You, Holy God.

CHAPTER 1

Preparation for the Coming of Messiah
Luke 1

Hail, full of grace, the Lord is with thee:
blessed art thou among women. (Luke 1:28 Douay-Rheims)

Blessed are you among women, and blessed is the fruit of your womb! (Luke 1:42)

he Whole World Waits for a Savior ~ The entire human race dwelt for millennia in the darkness of sin and death, separated and deprived of intimacy with God. Meanwhile, God sent prophets to the Jewish people to give them hope and prepare them to identify the Redeemer when He arrived. The Gospels are the story of the Messiah's coming. Those who knew Jesus Christ, the Savior of the world, best on earth wanted to share the wondrous truth with all the rest of the people on earth.

For twenty years or so after the Resurrection, those who wished to hear about Christ could sit at the feet of the apostles and listen to them. The martyrdom of James in 44 AD sent a shock wave through the early church. Christians had to face the fact that they would not always be able to hear the Gospel directly from the apostles' lips. A scribe, Mark interviewed Peter and wrote a transcript, arguably becoming the first Evangelist. His account starts when Jesus is nearly thirty years old and ready to begin his public ministry—about the time when Peter first met Jesus.

Soon, the apostle Matthew began to write his own account. Having once been a tax collector, he had the skills of a scribe. Since Peter and Matthew shared many experiences, the Gospels of Mark and Matthew have a great deal in common. Matthew recorded not only the adult life of Jesus, which he knew first hand, but also the life of young Jesus, which he knew only second hand. Only because of Matthew do we have knowledge of the angel appearing to Joseph, the visit of three magi, the massacre of the Holy Innocents, and the flight of the Holy Family into Egypt.

Meanwhile, persecution intensified and the apostles were martyred, one after another. In the year 69 AD, the martyrdom of Peter dealt a great blow. The early Christians had to decide how best to continue Peter's ministry of teaching and governance. Inspired by the Holy Spirit, they elected a successor, second in the line of popes, which continues to the present day. They realized even more the importance of the written Gospel for future generations. Another scribe, the physician Luke, took up his pen, and wrote a long two-part work, both a Gospel and the Acts of the Apostles. His Gospel begins even earlier than Matthew's, with the annunciation of the conception of John the Baptist. Luke begins his Gospel by paying tribute to the earlier evangelists and acknowledging their contributions.

Luke covers much of the same material as Mark and Matthew. In fact, these three Gospels have so much in common that they can be read side-by-side, or "synoptically." The different details contribute marvelously to a well-rounded picture of the life and message of Jesus. They are like three facets of a single jewel. The subsequent chapters of this study follow the sequence of material in these three Synoptic Gospels: Matthew, Mark, and Luke. Occasionally material from the fourth evangelist, John, who produced a work very different in scope from the other three, will be considered as well.

Chapter One of Luke ~ We rely upon chapter one of Luke alone for our knowledge of three events that take place before the birth of Jesus, over a period of nine months, in three distinct locations:

- ❧ The archangel Gabriel announces the birth of John the Baptist to his father Zechariah, in the temple sanctuary in Jerusalem (Luke 1:5–21).
- ❧ Six months later the same archangel visits the Virgin Mary at her home in Nazareth and invites her to become the mother of the Messiah (Luke 1:26–38).
- ❧ Mary travels to the village of Ain Karem, west of Jerusalem and remains there three months to visit and help her cousin Elizabeth, Zechariah's wife (Luke 1:39–54).

Gabriel Announces the Birth of John the Baptist (Luke 1:5-15) ~ The archangel Gabriel first appears in the pages of Scripture when he delivers a couple of chapter-long messages to the prophet Daniel. He now makes two appearances in Luke 1, one to Zechariah and one to Mary. Gabriel must have appeared in dazzling splendor, because he repeatedly says, "Do not fear" to Daniel and Zechariah and Mary.

The divine revelation given to Zechariah, announcing the birth of John the Baptist, occurs in a very privileged place, the temple mount in Jerusalem. The priest Zechariah was chosen to offer incense inside the temple, in the room *hekel*, which housed the lamp stand and showbread in the tabernacle. A veil separated the innermost holy sanctuary, called *debir*, the "Holy of Holies." Since there were about twenty thousand priests in the country at the time of Zechariah, divided into groups of roughly one thousand priests each, Zechariah enjoyed a rare privilege in offering the incense that burned in the temple twice a day. People saw the smoke from the outside while they prayed, and that smoke drifting toward heaven symbolized their prayers ascending to God's throne. Today the temple in Jerusalem where the angel appeared to Zechariah is gone, destroyed by Titus in 70 AD.

Thirty-one Zechariahs are mentioned in Sacred Scripture. The two most important are Zechariah the prophet, who wrote the book of fourteen chapters found in the Old Testament, and Zechariah the priest, the father of John the Baptist.

Zechariah in Hebrew means, "the Lord remembers." God remembers Zechariah in his old age and gives him a son. This is the last sign before the coming of Christ and concludes God's revelation in the Old Testament. The angel's announcement to Zechariah ends in silence, when Zechariah is struck mute. Zechariah's problem in believing the angel's message parallels our own struggles. When we fail to trust and truly listen to what God tells us through others, our pleas to God will lack power.

Prayer is a dialogue which presupposes trust. Despite Zechariah's lack of trust, God answers his long-standing prayer for a child. The Lord opens the barren womb of Elizabeth as He had previously done in the history of Israel for Sarah, Rebekah, Rachel, and Hannah. A barren woman given a child by God proves God's loving care for those who trust Him.

The Annunciation of Gabriel to the Virgin Mary ~ Nazareth is a Galilean hill town, the hometown of the Blessed Virgin Mary. Here, she conceived the Word of God, and here the Holy Family made their home. Here, Jesus Christ spent the decades of His childhood and adolescence, His so-called "hidden life." In the synagogue of this town, Jesus read from Isaiah and proclaimed the fulfillment of prophecy.

The Franciscan archeologist Bellarmino Bagatti discovered on a grotto wall in Nazareth an ancient inscription from the second century AD: *"Chaire Maria"* (Hail Mary). This archeological treasure helped to authenticate this holy place as the home of Mary. The modest dwelling was situated at the end of the village, where the poorest people lived. Excavations reveal about 20 dwellings which housed approximately 150 inhabitants of Nazareth at that time. This archeologist's findings confirms how the ways of God often contradict the expectations of man, as God chose to come into a poor family in a very small and simple town. The nearby church, finished in 1914, and dedicated to Saint Joseph, houses a water cistern in the crypt of the church and an adjunct grotto believed to be the workshop of Saint Joseph. Experts conclude that the early Christian community celebrated the Sacrament of Baptism here.

Nazareth today holds the largest Christian community in Israel. Pilgrims visit the Basilica of the Annunciation and Saint Joseph Church. Nazareth, never mentioned in the Old Testament, symbolizes for the Christian a new direction, reflecting the contrast between the disobedience of Eve and the perfect submission of the Virgin Mary. Pope John Paul II visited the modern basilica in 2000.

> May Nazareth serve as a model of what the family should be. May it show us the family's holy and enduring character and exemplify its basic function in society: a community of love and sharing, beautiful for the problems it poses and the rewards it brings; in sum, [the family is] the perfect setting for rearing children and for this there is no substitute.
>
> Pope Paul VI, homily at Nazareth (January 5, 1964)

The same archangel who was so tough with Zechariah now appears to the Virgin Mary in Nazareth, but with a different tone. Although Gabriel is God's servant first, He is also Mary's servant. He addresses Mary with the unique description *kecharitomene,* a "woman perfected in grace." No one else in all the pages of Scripture receives this kind of a greeting! Saint Jerome translated this as *"gratia plena,"* and the best English translation is the traditional "full of grace" (Douay-Rheims and RSVCE). Such renditions as "so highly favored " (Jerusalem Bible) or "highly favored daughter" (New American Bible) fail to convey the full depth of meaning.

Nowhere else in the pages of Scripture does an angel (who always speaks infallibly for God) address a human being this way. Angels themselves are full of grace, and Gabriel speaks to Mary as to one like himself. Now, before Christ's death on the cross there was no way for a human being to become emptied of sin. Therefore, the only way Mary could be full of grace is if, like the angel, she always had been. Gabriel reveals that the Virgin Mary was free from sin and full of grace.

> "Full of grace" refers to the doctrine of the Church known as "The Immaculate Conception of Mary." Pope Pius IX proclaimed on December 8, 1854: "The most Blessed Virgin Mary was, from the first moment of her conception, by a singular grace and privilege of almighty God and by virtue of the merits of Jesus Christ, Savior of the human race, preserved immune from all stain of original sin."

This biblical truth has been upheld since the early Church and reiterated throughout the centuries. Mary reaffirmed this truth when in 1858 she appeared to a simple, uneducated young girl, Saint Bernadette Soubirous, in a grotto at Massabielle near Lourdes and declared, "I am the Immaculate Conception." Many healings and miracles in Lourdes prove the truth of God's goodness and underscore Mary's role in salvation history and her power as an intercessor.

Gabriel's demeanor and the tenor of his words defer to Mary not as someone beneath him, as in the meeting with Zachariah, or even on the same level. He appears before his own queen, the future Queen of Heaven who will reign forever as Queen of the angels and saints. God too has confidence in Mary's goodness and respects her freedom. He does not command her to become the mother of the Redeemer, for this would treat her in a way that no woman should ever be treated. Instead, He asks and He invites. Thus, the whole of salvation history hinges on this one woman's "Yes" to God.

> On your word depends comfort for the wretched, ransom for the captive, freedom for the condemned, indeed, salvation for all the sons of Adam, the whole of your race. Answer quickly, O Virgin. Reply in haste to the angel, or rather through the angel to the Lord. Answer with a word, receive the Word of God. Speak your own word, conceive the Divine Word. Breathe a passing word, embrace the Eternal Word.
>
> Saint Bernard of Clairvaux, *In Praise of the Virgin Mother*, 4. 8–9.

The new era of salvation begins with the conception of Jesus in the womb of Mary. Saint Bede compares the first mother of mankind, Eve, with the new mother, Mary. Where Eve once contained in her womb all humanity, which was doomed to sin, now Mary contains in her womb the new Adam, Jesus Christ, who will father a new humanity by His grace.

The angel Gabriel greets Mary as the most beautiful of women. Beauty is more than physical attractiveness. It is interior virtue that has eternal value. This internal beauty occasionally reveals itself to the outside world. The combination of the greeting, "Hail, full of grace," with the assurance, "The Lord is with you," shows that God chose Mary in an exclusive way.

Often the Jewish people failed to follow God faithfully. Yet, despite their unfaithfulness, God was faithful. He protected them and fought for them against their enemies. At times the Chosen People felt abandoned, but they clung to the hope that "Emmanuel" (Isaiah 7:14) would one day come to save them from their sins. This promise was fulfilled in the birth of Jesus, Son of God and Son of Mary.

The Visitation and Magnificat (Luke 1:39-54) ~ Humility and the desire to serve her elder cousin motivate Mary to journey to the hill country of Judea. The Visitation is a very great mystery, with deep levels of meaning. Visibly, two women meet, but invisibly, there are two additional participants in the drama, the last of the prophets, John, along with the very Messiah Himself. Mary knows of Elizabeth's pregnancy because of the message of the angel; Elizabeth knows of Mary's pregnancy because of the Holy Spirit. Both pregnancies are miraculous, like those of Sarah and Hannah in the Old Testament, but here the two mysteries come into each other's presence. Selflessly, Elizabeth acknowledges Mary's miracle as greater than her own.

Saint Elizabeth of Hungary wrote that in Mary's time all Jewish women yearned to meet the mother of the Messiah. Elizabeth experiences the fulfillment of these hopes, and inspired by the Holy Spirit coauthors the Hail Mary. So a biblical Jewish woman helped to write this Catholic prayer, while a future prophet leapt for joy in her womb. John recognized the real presence of Christ even before his mother did. Origen says that the unborn Christ blesses the unborn John. Luke clearly teaches that the unborn are true persons and even capable of religious experience. When a pregnant woman receives Holy Communion, what a blessing for her unborn child!

The Magnificat, Mary's Prayer of Humility (Luke 1:46-55) ~ Another woman, Hannah, was inspired to sing a song of praise to the Lord for the favor of becoming the mother of the prophet Samuel (1 Samuel 2:1–10). Mary speaks in similar words.

My heart exults in the Lord; my strength is exalted in the Lord. My mouth derides my enemies, because I rejoice in thy salvation. —Hannah in 1 Samuel 2:1	My soul magnifies the Lord, and my spirit rejoices in God my Savior, for he has regarded the low estate of his handmaiden. For behold, henceforth all generations will call me blessed. —Mary in Luke 1:46–48

As similar as these two songs seem to be in many details, the underlying attitude could not be more different. Hannah exults over her enemies, but Mary expresses the consummate virtue of humility. Mary does not say, "I have done great things for God," but rather, "He who is mighty has done great things for me" (Luke 1:49). In fact, she was doing a great thing for God and for all of us, but she acknowledges that the "great thing" was only possible because of divine grace.

The Virgin Mary exemplifies the virtue of humility. The word *humilitas* in Latin comes from the root word *humus* (topsoil). *Humus* provides nutrients for plants and helps the ground retain water. Mary did not go out into the world to perform public deeds. She was "down to earth"—truly humble. And in this virtue she surpasses all other saints, apostles, bishops, martyrs, confessors, and Doctors of the church. Humility is the most godlike virtue. "The Lord is great" (Psalm 135:5), but He bends down to care for our smallest needs. Jesus never exalted Himself, but humbled Himself, taking the form of a slave. In her Magnificat, Mary humbly opened a place in her soul for the action of God. *The whole course of civilization changed because one woman was willing to make one Child the center of her life!* The praying church—pope, bishops, priests, monks, nuns, and laity—conclude evening prayer every day of the year by reciting Mary's Magnificat together. In so doing, we honor Mary's great witness of humble service which she has transmitted to us.

The Birth of John the Baptist (Luke 1:57–66) ~ In the biblical world, the birth of a boy caused great joy. When the birth was announced, musicians broke into song causing rejoicing and congratulations. Eight days after birth, a Jewish boy receives circumcision and the conferral of a name. At this moment, the Jewish male receives the promises and privileges reserved for the Chosen People. The blood spilled in circumcision was called "the blood of the Covenant." The outward circumcision was to represent an inner circumcision of the heart.

The gift of life is the result of God's grace. Zechariah and Elizabeth name their child "John" which means "the grace of God." Life reverses the image of death represented by Zechariah's impediment of speech. According to Saint Maximus of Turin (380–465 AD), the power of John's name frees the tongue of Zechariah, which had been bound, so that the old priest might praise God and prophesy John's role in salvation history. This extraordinary miracle causes the gathered people to fear God. The fear or "reverence" of God will later draw people to John the Baptist, who will call them to repent in preparation for receiving God's sacramental mysteries.

Pilgrims visit the sanctuaries of the churches of the Visitation and of Saint John the Baptist in the village of Ain Karem, one of the most picturesque of all biblical sites. The sanctuary of the Visitation, mentioned in early written sources, corresponds to the house outside the village where Mary helped her cousin Elizabeth during the final months of her pregnancy. The isolation of the place preserves the atmosphere of silent prayer and meditation which joined the two holy women together. A pool for ritual purification, discovered in the crypt of the church where Mary pronounced her Magnificat, underlines the religious environment described in Luke 1:39–56.

The sanctuary of the church of Saint John the Baptist resembles a fortress which was built by the Crusaders. The crypt of the church encompasses the grotto which was part of Zechariah's house. No other remnants of the ancient home remain. This grotto, visited by Christians from ancient times, is venerated as the birthplace of John, the precursor of Jesus. The grotto, called "very luminous" by the early Christians, symbolizes the enlightenment of the human heart that responds to God's call.

The Benedictus (Luke 1:67–79) ~ Elizabeth is the first person to hear two great canticles of praise—her cousin Mary's Magnificat, and her husband Zechariah's Benedictus. He is inspired to invoke the mercy of God, which will come when a new kind of day shall dawn, not from the horizon upwards but from the zenith downwards: "When the day shall dawn upon us from on high to give light to those who sit in darkness and in the shadow of death, to guide our feet into the way of peace" (Luke 1:78–79). Because of this mention of the beginning of the Christian era, Zachariah's song is used to conclude Lauds in the Liturgy of the Hours. It thus stands in the same relation to morning prayer as the Magnificat does to evening prayer.

Zechariah emphasizes in the Benedictus that God is faithful in keeping His promises in the history of salvation. God's visitation to His people invites each person to restore the relationship, which was broken with the Lord, through the forgiveness proclaimed by Jesus Christ. God forgives our sins and frees us from both corporeal and spiritual enemies. We no longer "sit in darkness and the shadow of death" (Luke 1:79) as those who were awaiting the Messiah did. Now, because of Jesus Christ, we can "serve [God] without fear in holiness and righteousness" (Luke 1:74–75), walking in the way of peace (Luke 1:79).

The first chapter of Luke shows us much about God and how we are to respond to Him. For instance, the Magnificat expresses the gratitude of the Virgin Mary for God's design of salvation in her. God's intervention into human history enables each person to accept the mercy of God and receive the forgiveness proclaimed and brought about by Jesus Christ. Each of us receives an invitation from God to receive His mercy and to come to know Him in a deeper and more personal way. At the beginning of this study, ponder Mary's "Yes" to God. God is inviting you to go deeper with Him and to draw closer to Him. Will you say "Yes" to God? May God draw you deeper into the great mystery of His divine love for you as you study His Word.

1. What can you learn about Zechariah and Elizabeth in Luke 1:1–10, 18?

angel appear To Zechariah. To say is was going to Father

2. Explain the prophecy about the son to be born to Zechariah and Elizabeth. Luke 1:11–17

3. Who is the messenger of God appearing in Daniel 9:20–25, Luke 1:11–20, and Luke 1:26–38?

4. Compare the following verses.

Malachi 3:1–3	
Malachi 3:23, NAB (Malachi 4:5, RSVCE)	
Sirach 48:10–12	
Luke 1:17	

5. Describe the role and job of St. John the Baptist. CCC 523

To prepare Jesus his was

6. Write down at least five things that the angel Gabriel said to Mary. Luke 1:26–36

be not afraid you found favor with God you have con...

7. How does the angel respond to Mary's question in Luke 1:34? Luke 1:35, 37

8. Describe God's plan from all eternity from CCC 488.

9. Write down Mary's response in Luke 1:38.

—What enables Mary to respond to the angel in the way she does? CCC 148

Behold the Handmaid of Lord

10. How was Mary able to accept the role of the mother of the Savior? CCC 490

angel Gabriel annunciation full of grace

—Was Mary ever hampered by personal or original sin? CCC 494

God caped mary virgen even after birth to her son

11. Discuss Mary's virginal motherhood in God's plan. Choose one. CCC 502–507

12. Compare the following verses.

Isaiah 7:14	
Luke 1:27–31	

13. What does the name "Jesus" mean in Hebrew? CCC 430

14. Following the visit from the angel Gabriel, what did Mary do? Luke 1:39–40

—What does Mary's visit to Elizabeth become? CCC 717

—How does Elizabeth greet Mary? Luke 1:42

15. Compare the following passages.

1 Samuel 2:1–10	Luke 1: 46–55

16. Explain the situation in Luke 1:57–64.

17. How did the people react to this drama? Luke 1:65–66

18. Compare the following verses.

Psalm 72:18	Luke 1:68
Psalm 18:3	Luke 1:69
Psalm 106:10	Luke 1:71
Malachi 3:10	Luke 1:73
Malachi 4:2	Luke 1:78

19. Describe the promise of Luke 1:79.

20. Have you ever faced an impossible situation? What hope does Luke 1:37 give?

** Write down a prayer request on a sheet of scrap paper and share it with someone in your small group. Commit to praying every day for someone else in your group's need or request.

CHAPTER 2

Jesus' Birth and Childhood
Matthew 1–2, Luke 2

Joseph, son of David, do not fear to take Mary your wife, for that which is conceived in her is of the Holy Spirit; she will bear a son, and you shall call his name Jesus, for he will save his people from their sins. (Matthew 1:20–21)

And she gave birth to her first-born son and wrapped him in swaddling clothes, and laid him in a manger, because there was no place for them in the inn. (Luke 2:7)

Two Gospels tell the story of Jesus' birth and infancy. Luke tells the story from the viewpoint of Mary the Mother. In his account the archangel Gabriel appears to Mary. Matthew writes from the point of view of Joseph, the foster-father of Jesus. In his account, an angel appears to Joseph in a dream on four occasions: (1) first, the angel addresses Joseph as "Son of David" (in the line of succession for the throne of Israel!) and gives him the important task of bestowing the holy name upon Jesus; (2) next, an angel warns Joseph of the danger from Herod and tells him to take Jesus and Mary to safety in Egypt; (3) the third angel tells Joseph that Herod is dead, the danger has passed, and the Holy Family can return to the Holy Land, and (4) the fourth angel alerts Joseph to the danger of living in Judea, which is ruled by Herod's son, and so Joseph settles the Holy Family in Galilee instead. Perhaps this was Joseph's guardian angel or several different angels.

The one true God of the universe took on the form of weak and fallen humanity and came to dwell among us. Christians all over the world celebrate the birth of our Lord at Christmas. Even though the exact day of His birth cannot be historically proven, the reality of Jesus' birth changes world history forever. Catholics meditate on this truth in the third joyful mystery of the Rosary.

Pilgrims visiting Bethlehem today often head directly to the Basilica of the Nativity, but may miss some other holy sites to be enjoyed in an atmosphere of prayer and contemplation. Milk Grotto and Shepherds' Field are two nearby sites. Bethlehem today houses the largest Christian community in the west bank of the Jordan. The largest groups are Greek Catholics, Greek Orthodox, and Roman Catholics, called "Latins."

The Emperor Justinian built the Basilica of the Nativity, the oldest church in the Holy Land and one of the oldest in the whole world, in the sixth century on the foundation of an older church built in 325 AD by Saint Helen, the mother of Constantine. Her architect destroyed the Roman shrine to Adonis, which was purposely built in 135 AD over the spot where Jesus was born in an attempt to humiliate Judeo-Christians who were expelled from the area. The invading Persians in the seventh century destroyed all the churches in the Holy Land, except the Nativity, because of the three magi portrayed in Persian robes on the facade. Today, a small grotto in the crypt reminds the pilgrim of the stable where Jesus came into this world. Pilgrims usually kiss the silver star with the Latin inscription: "Here was born Jesus Christ from the Virgin Mary." The fourteen points of the star signify the number of generations in the genealogy in Matthew 1:1–17 and point ahead to the fourteen stations in the Way of the Cross.

A small niche in the grotto belongs to the Latin Church, and is cared for by the Franciscan Fathers. Tradition holds that the crib of Jesus was here. Crusaders took the crib to Rome, and some wood from the crib is preserved under the main altar of the basilica of Saint Mary Major. The striking poverty of Bethlehem leads one to ponder the relationship between the grotto of the Nativity and Calvary. Jesus comes into this world from the back door through the manger because there is no room in the inn and leaves this world from the back door as a criminal crucified in the old quarry.

Next to the Nativity Basilica stands the Latin church of Saint Catherine of Alexandria, built at the end of the 19th century after difficulties erupted between the Orthodox and Catholics over the control of the Basilica. Here, the Latin Patriarch offers the Catholic midnight Mass each Christmas. Subterranean grottoes within the church are dedicated to Saint Joseph and the innocent babies martyred by King Herod. Saint Jerome, who translated the Bible from its Hebrew and Greek origins into Latin, the Vulgate, lived nearby in a cave. He and his disciple, Eusebius of Cremona, were also buried here. So, near the place where God became a human being in Jesus, God's Word was rendered understandable for the Roman Empire, which in the 4th century used Latin as their common language.

Milk Grotto ~ One of the quiet holy places in Bethlehem is Milk Grotto. After the birth of our Lord, Joseph probably moved his family from the stable to more suitable housing. Milk Grotto, similar to Mary's house in Nazareth, was situated on the outskirts of the settlement, indicating the Holy Family's poverty. Saint Justin the Martyr (100–165 AD), one of the first Christian writers and a native of the Holy Land, says that Jesus was born on the edge of the city. Matthew 2:11 relates that the magi went "into the house" to see the child with Mary, His mother.

The reference in Matthew 2:16 about Herod killing all the baby boys, two years and under, suggests that the Holy Family may have stayed in Bethlehem a considerable time before they escaped to Egypt. In addition, a sanctuary built by Saint Paula, a disciple of Saint Jerome, and the later monastery of Saint Nicholas, built after the Crusades, underscores the importance of the location where the Holy Family lived in Bethlehem.

Byzantine tradition refers to Milk Grotto as the place where the Virgin nursed her baby, and legend tells us that, when the Holy Family fled to Egypt, a few drops of Mary's milk fell on the ground and the rock of the cave became white. For centuries, pious women have come to Milk Grotto to pray for a pregnancy. Barren women would scrape powder from the rock, mix it with water to drink, and pray the third joyful mystery of the Rosary until a baby is born. Even today, sterile couples come to Milk Grotto to ask the Virgin Mary to bless them with a child. More than 200 miracles, documented by letters and pictures, attest to the birth of hoped for babies, as well as to miracles of healing which bear witness to the nature of this grotto.

Shepherds' Field ~ Two sites, which are linked to the angel's revelation of the birth of Jesus to the shepherds, are situated east of Bethlehem in the suburb of Bet Sahour. The more authentic site seems to be the Orthodox Church where a mosaic floor in a chapel, built by Saint Helen, is still visible today. Nearby is a second site, which contains the ruins of a Byzantine monastery and which belonged to the Franciscans. Two caves nearby witness to early Christian worship at this site, where angels brought the good news of the birth of the Savior to the shepherds. One cave nearby lies within the Franciscan property and another cave is in the Orthodox monastery. These sites encourage modern-day Christians to reflect on how and where God revealed the spectacular mystery of the Incarnation.

The Narrative of Jesus' Birth in the Gospels ~ Both Matthew and Luke record the birth of Jesus. These Gospel writers each include a genealogy of Jesus (Matthew 1:2–17 and Luke 3:23–28), with Matthew emphasizing Jesus' Jewish lineage and Luke going back to Adam, linking Jesus with all of humanity. Both evangelists identify the place of Jesus' birth as Bethlehem. Matthew presents the account of the wise men from the east (Matthew 2:1–12), while Luke presents the shepherds (Luke 2:8–20). Only Matthew recounts the flight into Egypt and the return (Matthew 2:13–21). Luke provides the only source of information on the circumcision and presentation of Jesus in the temple (Luke 2:21–30), the reference to the childhood of Jesus in Nazareth, and the pilgrimage of the Holy Family to the temple in Jerusalem (Luke 2:41–52).

The Birth of Jesus ~ At the time of Jesus there were three steps in Jewish marriage. (1) The engagement was arranged through parents or a professional matchmaker. (2) The betrothal ratified the engagement and lasted one year. It was absolutely binding and was usually accompanied by the groom's payment of part of the bride price. The betrothal could only be terminated by the divorce of the couple. The bride and groom were officially pledged to each other, but had not yet consummated the marriage. (3) The marriage came at the end of the betrothal year, when, in the full sense of the law, the wife went to live in the house of her husband, and they began to live together as husband and wife.

While in the midst of their betrothal, Mary's pregnancy became evident. "She was found to be with child of the Holy Spirit" (Matthew 1:18). Joseph knew Mary as a holy woman and did not doubt her virginity. However, since the conception had occurred without his involvement, perhaps Joseph thought that God did not intend him to remain in her life. Like a true gentleman, Joseph wanted to divorce her quietly and withdraw from her life. Public divorce would have exposed Mary to public humiliation. Joseph, however, was a "just man" (Matthew 1:19), which is the highest praise given to any man in the pages of Scripture. The Wisdom literature of the Hebrew Bible goes to great length to describe the virtues of a "just man." Does Joseph fear intruding on this sacred scene in which he feels he has no part to play at all? The angel clarifies Joseph's role to him. First the angel confirms Mary's account of the pregnancy and then the angel announces to Joseph that Mary's Son will be the Messiah, "for He will save His people from their sins" (Matthew 1:21).

In order for Jesus to be the universal Savior, He must be the Jewish savior first. In order for Him to be King of all nations, He must be king of Israel first. Hence, He must come of the house and lineage of David (Luke 2:4). Joseph contributes his historical patrimony to the Messiah. The kingship passes from father to son in Israel, according to Nathan's prophecy to David (2 Samuel 7). Only a woman, Mary, can bring God into the world, but only a man, Joseph, can bestow upon Him the kingship of Israel. All twelve tribes of Israel yearned for Messiah, but it was the tribe of Judah that would provide the Messiah. Mary yearned to receive the Messiah and she did receive Him. Joseph yearned, like all the men of the tribe of Judah, to give the Messiah to Israel, and he did. While Jesus is not physically descended from Joseph, He received his legal identity and rights from Joseph as a citizen of Israel. All throughout His life, the legal name of the Son of God on earth was "son of Joseph."

At Calvary, Mary stands at the foot of the cross, while Joseph is absent, presumably dead by then. But, Joseph's contribution in salvation history appears in the sign "king of the Jews." Jesus is the King of the Universe because of God the Father, but He is King of the Jews because of Joseph. Joseph is not merely the man who happened to be there to help Mary and Jesus; he is the one destined from all eternity to give the Incarnate Word a human identity. Joseph's reward is being named first after Mary in the mystery of redemption through the Incarnation, the supreme act of God's mercy. Joseph also receives the honor belonging to the father of naming the child Jesus-Savior.

The conception in Mary fulfills the Isaiah 7:14 prophecy. Mary becomes the New Eve in the re-creation of humanity through the action of the Holy Spirit. And there is an obvious contrast between her behavior and Israel's. The representatives of the religious establishment saw themselves as the righteous ones, despite the fact that the Jewish people were often unfaithful to the Covenant. Mary, on the other hand, a faithful daughter of Israel, obedient to God, and faithful to His plan for her life, appears to be unfaithful to her espoused husband, Joseph.

Matthew 1:24–25 reveals that Joseph took Mary as his wife, but knew her not until she had born a son, called Jesus. The word "until" becomes problematic when people incorrectly interpret this verse by wrongly assuming that Joseph only guarded Mary's virginity until the birth of Jesus. If we look at the Old Testament story of Michal, the daughter of Saul who disdained her husband David's dancing before the Lord and was punished by having no child *until* the day of her death, we wouldn't then assume that she had children after her death. The Catholic and Orthodox Churches have always believed in the perpetual virginity of Mary. Saint Joseph guarded Mary's purity before marriage and protected her virginity throughout their marriage.

It helps us to understand the terms first-born and only-begotten when the Evangelist tells us that Mary remained a virgin "until she brought forth her first-born son." For Mary, who is to be honored and praised above all others…never became the Mother of anyone else, but even after childbirth she remained always and forever an immaculate virgin.

Didymus the Blind (313–398 AD), *The Trinity*, 3.4.

The people of Nazareth, where Jesus grew up, call Jesus *the* son of Mary (Mark 6:3), not *a* son of Mary. When Joseph and Mary return to the temple to find Jesus (Luke 2:41–51), they hunt alone. Any family who has ever lost a child in a crowd knows that if there are other family members, everyone looks for the lost child! Clearly in Luke, Joseph and Mary are searching for Jesus alone, because the three alone—Jesus, Mary, and Joseph—comprise the Holy Family.

In Luke's Gospel, following Mary's viewpoint, the early Church Fathers find many allegories. Saint Bede (673–735 AD) notes the birth of Jesus occurred during peacetime in the reign of Augustus to show that He will lead us to heavenly peace. Jesus, our peace, makes both Jews and Gentiles one through the cross (Ephesians 2:14–16). Peace comes to us through the Eucharist.

Ancient Oriental icons depict the baby Jesus as a loaf of bread, and Bethlehem means "the house of bread." Saint Cyril of Alexandria regards the baby in the manger as no longer the feed for animals but the bread from heaven, the bread of life.

The swaddling clothes demonstrate the humility of Jesus. John the Monk (520–616 AD) sees the swaddling clothes loosing the bands of sin beginning from Adam and Eve and extending to all. Saint Jerome (347–419 AD) considers the dung of the stable as our sins. Jesus, born on a dunghill, lifts up those who come from it (Psalm 113:7). The paradox of "no place in the inn" reflects the human heart unwilling to accept Jesus as its guide. Being without shelter, Jesus goes to prepare many mansions (John 14:2) in the house of His heavenly Father for us.

Shepherds and wise men, the extremes of the humble and lofty, come to worship Jesus. In biblical imagery, the shepherd is an image of God (Psalm 23, Ezekiel 34). The monotonous work of guarding the flocks points out the moral imperative to care for the defenseless and protect the vulnerable. The Babe in the manger calls us to defend the rights of the poor and innocent in our midst. Mary keeps "all these things in her heart" (Luke 2:19) demonstrating that every activity, even the most noble or humble, must be balanced with prayer and contemplation.

Parthians, wise men from the East, disturbed King Herod who had used the Romans to gain power from the legitimate rulers of Palestine, the Hasmoneans. When Herod was troubled, the whole nation suffered with him. However, the magi showed humility by diligently following the star which guides them to worship and adore Jesus. Saint Peter Chrysologus (405–450 AD) sees the wise men as those who respond to God's call and recognize Jesus as Savior. The Magi's gifts refer to the price which the follower of Christ must pay to fight attachments to this world. Gold symbolizes wisdom, frankincense the fragrant pursuit of holy speech, and myrrh the mortification of the flesh. At the moment the Magi encountered the Infant, they became apostles and returned to their own country filled with joy and the zeal of missionaries.

> Let us rejoice in the Epiphany with trembling, that at Septuagesima we may go into the vineyard with the laborers with cheerfulness, and may sorrow in Lent with thankfulness; let us rejoice now, not as if we have attained, but in hope of attaining. Let us take our present happiness, not as our true rest, but as what the land of Canaan was to the Israelites—a type of shadow of it. If we now enjoy God's ordinances, let us not cease to pray that they may prepare us for His presence hereafter. If we enjoy the presence of friends, let them remind us of the communion of saints before His throne. Let us trust in nothing here, yet draw hope from everything—that at length the Lord may be our everlasting light, and the days of our mourning may be ended.
>
> John Henry Newman (1811–1860), *Sermon: "The Season of Epiphany"*

The Circumcision and Presentation in the Temple (Luke 2:21–38) ~ The circumcision of a Jewish boy on the eighth day corresponds with naming him. Jesus, in Hebrew "Joshua," means savior—the name given to Mary by the angel (Luke 1:39). Just as after the death of Moses, Joshua led the Jewish people from slavery to the Promised Land, Jesus will defeat Satan and the slavery of sin, leading the believer to new life.

Luke next describes the Presentation. The first fruits, including the first fruits of the womb, were to be presented to God in recognition of God's gracious power in giving life. Mosaic law required paying five shekels (Numbers 18:16) to the priest to buy back the male child from God.

The next scene, which Luke describes, involves the purification of Mary after childbirth. A mother was ritually unclean for 40 days after the birth of a boy and 80 days after the birth of a girl. If a family was poor, the law mitigated the offering of a lamb and one young pigeon to only two pigeons (Leviticus 12:2–8). Joseph and Mary brought forth two pigeons, the offering of the poor. The Presentation is the fourth joyful mystery of the Rosary.

Joseph couldn't afford a lamb, but he did bring one for Jesus Himself was the Lamb. When the infant Jesus is carried into the temple, the temple becomes the house of God in a new and perfect way. Already it was the site on earth inhabited by the Almighty. Now the Word of God comes into the temple.

For Origen (185–253 AD), this humble state, in which the Holy Family could only offer the sacrifice of the poor, represents the virtues of poverty and chastity. Saint Bede sees the Eucharist, the sacrament of Jesus' body and blood, prefigured here as Joseph and Mary bring the child Jesus for His circumcision and Presentation in the temple.

Simeon, meeting the Holy Family in the temple, recognizes Jesus as the salvation of the gentiles and the glory of Israel. He proclaims that Jesus will be a sign of contradiction (Luke 2:34). And, tells Mary, "A sword will pierce through your own soul" (Luke 2:35) pointing to Mary's sorrow at the crucifixion. Saint Ambrose and Saint Basil the Great see the "sword" as God's revelation in Jesus' words and deeds throughout His ministry (Hebrews 4:12). That "sword" heals the person who accepts the miraculous power of God's Word and condemns him who rejects it.

The widowed Anna, a prophetess, personifies both the Church and those who live faithfully by her precepts. Anna waits, patiently and prayerfully, longing to see the face of God. The Church awaits the beatific vision and the union of the Church Militant with the Church Triumphant. Modern interpretation allows us to see in Anna those who follow her example of praying and waiting, while growing in virtue and devotion in imitation of Christ.

The Flight into Egypt and Return (Matthew 2:13–23) ~ The Holy Family hardly had time to settle in Bethlehem, when Joseph's faith was again tested. After hastily moving to his birth town under the stress of almost immediate delivery, Joseph now leaves his new home for the safety of the Child. Icons depict Joseph walking next to the donkey which carries Mary and Jesus. Apocryphal writings from the second to fourth centuries suggest that Joseph, an orthodox Jew, intended to remain in the Holy Land under any circumstances. However, like Abraham, Joseph put his unconditional faith in God, which became his justification. Jesus, the new Moses, liberates those who will accept Him, not from the political shackles of slavery, but from the bondage of sin. The plight of the Holy Family fleeing into Egypt shows Jesus' solidarity with all the immigrants of the world, especially the immigrant children who are the most vulnerable.

As our Lord Jesus Christ, accepting death on the cross, associated Himself with those unjustly condemned to die and with criminals, so also in the flight from Bethlehem He identifies Himself with children who are the object of persecution imposed by the choices and decisions of others.

No reliable source gives the exact number of babies killed by King Herod in Bethlehem and surrounding areas. These children were the first martyrs of Christ's coming, according to Chromatius. Whatever the number of the Holy Innocents might be; it pales in comparison with those innocent babies killed today before they have the chance even to see the light of day. The slaughter of the Innocents parallels the shame of abortion in our day. The miracles of children born to sterile couples after prayer at the Milk Grotto, where Mary nursed Jesus, demonstrate God's providence in stark contrast to the culture of death.

The Holy Family stayed in Egypt for two years according to Armenian sources, or three years according to the Coptics. Today there are several holy places in Egypt which claim to be the stops of the Holy Family in search of protection for their divine Baby, who was unwanted by the powerful of his world. Saints Sergius and Bacchus Byzantine Church in Old Cairo retains a crypt where Jesus, Mary, and Joseph lived. Not long after Joseph establishes his family in the land of the Pharaohs, an angel comes to Joseph in a dream, and he once again abandons his earthly security to obey. Being warned by an angel suggests Joseph's profound trust in the Lord supported by his righteousness, enabling him to discern God's perfect will without pride. Joseph, upon returning, doesn't seek refuge with family members, but instead moves to Nazareth.

Jesus Childhood in Nazareth and Pilgrimage to the Temple (Luke 2:39–51) ~ The life of every Jewish boy passes a milestone in the thirteenth year, when he becomes a legal adult and full member of the community of the faithful of Israel, marked by the family's joyous celebration of Bar-Mitzvah. The Lucan narrative describes Jesus' pilgrimage to the temple at the age of transition to adulthood. Travel to the holy sanctuary for Passover was an exciting occasion accompanied by dancing and singing (Psalm 42:4). This Gospel presentation parallels the last pilgrimage of Jesus to Jerusalem for the Passover feast which ended with His Passion, death and Resurrection. The colorful, adventurous story of Luke 2:41–52 presents a lad who acts independently of His parents. Saint Ambrose sees the three days of His disappearance as the anticipation of the Resurrection in three days. The puzzlement of Jesus' curious behavior becomes more difficult with His statement to the anxious parents: "Did you not know that I must be in my Father's house?" (Luke 2:49).

Mary realized that Jesus did not belong entirely to her. She would prepare to share Him with us. Jesus uses His transition to adulthood to identify God as His Father. The basic truth of God's relationship to human beings in the Gospel reveals that God is our Father and we are his children. "And because you are sons, God sent the Spirit of his Son into our hearts, crying, 'Abba! Father!'" (Galatians 4:6). Even though we acknowledge this relationship, we cannot live it without constant prayer and reflection. Mary offers the best example (Luke 2:51) of how one discovers the presence of God the Father in all the blessings of life. The Holy Spirit enables this relationship to mature in virtue with our ascetical efforts. The sacraments of Christian initiation, Baptism, Confirmation, and Eucharist, help us to enter into the presence of God.

Jesus increased in wisdom and favor with God and man. Spiritual growth supported by the obedience of faith increases through concrete deeds of kindness and charity. The constant but very beautiful challenge for all those who dare to call God their Father is to abandon themselves completely to Jesus the Savior and trust Him to draw them deeper into the Father's love.

1. Jesus' royal descent begins in Matthew 1:2 with whom?

   —includes which King in Matthew 1:6?

   —and ends with a family of what three people in Matthew 1:16?

2. What can you learn about the following women in the genealogy of Jesus?

Tamar	Genesis 38	*became pregnant through deceiving her father-in-law*
Rahab	Joshua 2:1–15	
Uriah's wife	2 Samuel 11	
Ruth	Ruth 1:3–4	

3. Compare the following verses.

Isaiah 7:14	
Matthew 1:23	
Luke 1:27, 34–35	

4. Describe in your own words the drama in Matthew 1:18–25.

5. What does God promise in Jeremiah 23:5–6?

6. Identify the significance of the following passages.

Micah 5:2	
Matthew 2:1–7	
Luke 2:1–16	

7. From the Incarnation, the Word Incarnate is _____. CCC 333

8. What sin is presumed in Matthew 1:18 and what is its punishment? Deuteronomy 22:23–24

   —Why did God call Joseph to take Mary as his wife? CCC 437

9. Can a rational mind understand the virginal conception of a child? CCC 497

10. What name does Joseph give the child and what does it mean? Matthew 1:25, CCC 452

    —Who originally picked out the name? Luke 2:21

    —What can you do with this information? CCC 2666

11. Why did Matthew and Luke write these accounts? CCC 515

12. Describe the scenario in Matthew 2:1–12. What does it mean? CCC 528

13. Read the passage in Luke 2:1–20 aloud now, and also with your small group. What is the purpose of the action in Luke 2:21? CCC 527

14. Describe the events in Luke 2:22–38.

    —What do the events in Luke 2:22–38 signify? CCC 529

15. Compare the following verses.

Hosea 11:1	
Matthew 2:15	

16. What happened in Matthew 2:16–18?

17. Why does Joseph move again and where does he go? Matthew 2:19–23

—What do the flight into Egypt and the massacre of the innocents reveal? CCC 530

18. What happened to Jesus in Nazareth? Luke 2:40, 52

—How did Jesus spend the majority of His life? Luke 2:51–52, CCC 531

19. What did Jesus relationship with His parents demonstrate? Luke 2:51, CCC 532

20. Identify three things that you can learn from the hidden life of Jesus. CCC 533

** Choose something that you have learned from the example of Jesus, Mary or Joseph in this lesson and practice that virtue in your daily life this week. Share the results with your group.

CHAPTER 3

The Baptism of Jesus

Matthew 3, Mark 1, Luke 3

In those days Jesus came from Nazareth of Galilee and was baptized by John in the Jordan. And when he came up out of the water, immediately he saw the heavens opened and the Spirit descending upon him like a dove; and a voice came from heaven, "Thou art my beloved Son' with thee I am well pleased." (Mark 1:9–11)

Catholics meditate on Jesus' baptism in the Jordan River in the first Luminous Mystery of the Rosary. All of the Gospel writers, at the beginning of their Gospels, present the baptism of our Lord. They show the presence of the Holy Spirit and God the Father revealing the identity of Jesus as the Son of God. In this one passage, all three members of the Holy Trinity, Father, Son, and Holy Spirit, are evident. The Old Testament prophecies come to an end with the mission of John the Baptist, and a new chapter in the history of salvation opens with the beginning of Jesus' public life and ministry.

The Place of Jesus' Baptism ~ Called El-Maghtas in Arabic, the place of Jesus' baptism is located a few miles east of Jericho, northeast of Qumran. This same location is linked to the Israelites' passage across the Jordan under the guidance of Joshua (Joshua 3) and the sanctuary in Gilgal dedicated to the twelve tribes of Israel (Joshua 4:19–5:9). This is also the site where Elijah went up to heaven (2 Kings 2:11–12).

Pilgrims visit the Jordan River, which separates Israel and Jordan. On the west bank, near a Greek orthodox monastery dedicated to Saint John the Baptist, are five small chapels, belonging to different Orthodox communities. On the east side of the river, called Bethany beyond the Jordan by Saint John (John 1:28), is the church of Anastasis and chapel dedicated to Saint Mary of Egypt. The name "Beth Oniah" (the house of the boat) distinguishes this sight from the Bethany in John 11 where Jesus raised Lazarus from the dead. An ancient sixth century AD Madaba map shows the cave called "Bethabara" (house of crossing) on Jordan's east bank, which is associated with Saint John the Baptist. Ancient pilgrims would purify themselves at this place. Egeria, a prominent pilgrim to the Holy Land in the fourth century speaks of Wadi Karkar, which links the baptismal site of Jesus with Mount Nebo where Moses died.

Today, pilgrims visit the Jordan River at Jardenit, close to the mouth of the Jordan at the lake of Galilee, to renew their baptismal vows. The symbolism of the Jordan River abounds. The Jordan, considered a dead river, has more water at its source than at its end, losing water as it approaches its estuary, the Dead Sea. An even more powerful contrast regards the separation of the Holy Land on the right bank from the polluted land of the Gentiles on the left. In the biblical viewpoint, the right side is always positive. The river, as a symbol of separation, reminded the Jews in Jesus' time of the crossing accomplished by Joshua after the death of Moses. The decision of the Israelites to obey God enabled them to enter the promised land given by Yahweh (Joshua 3). John reminded those baptized in the Jordan to repent and prepare themselves inwardly for the solution of history provided by the soon expected Messiah. Leaving their past on the left bank of the river, they were to avoid sin and meditate on the hope of eternal life.

The geography of the river, relative to sea level, offers more symbolism. The descent of the Holy Spirit at the baptism of our Lord occurred at the lowest spot on the face of the earth. Jesus descended to the depths of human misery, taking our sins on His shoulders and carrying them to the cross in Jerusalem. Curiously enough, shortly before His Passion, Jesus came to the same place at the Jordan where John baptized Him at the beginning of His ministry (Matthew 19:1).

> Then Jesus came from Galilee to the Jordan to John, to be baptized by him. John would have prevented him, saying, "I need to be baptized by you, and do you come to me?" But Jesus answered him, "Let it be so now, for thus it is fitting for us to fulfill all righteousness." Then he consented (Matthew 3:13–15).

Matthew's Account of the Baptism of Jesus ~ One peculiar feature mentioned only by Matthew concerns the attitude of John the Baptist, who tries to dissuade Jesus from being baptized (Matthew 3:14). Here, John the Baptist, along with Peter (Matthew 16:22–23), represents confused humanity failing to understand the mystery of the Cross. From the Jordan River, Jesus starts His journey to Calvary. The Holy Spirit dwells in Him and will be surrendered on the Cross for the forgiveness of sins (Matthew 27:50). The Virgin Mary's position differs from the general attitude of others, when at Cana in Galilee (John 2:3–5); she encourages Jesus to commit Himself to that crucial hour. Only Mary, and in the climax of the Gospel in the Garden of Gethsemane, God the Father, encourage Jesus to take up His cross (Matthew 26:30–46).

Certainly Jesus committed no sin and therefore had no need of a baptism of repentance. Theodore of Mopsuestia (d. 428 AD) argues that Jesus submits to baptism in order to symbolically transfer the faithful from this present life to the one which is to come. Saint John Chrysostom (344–407 AD) explains God's righteousness, which links Jesus' baptism to His act of redemption from the penalty of sin. This commentary flows from the Gospel of John where John the Baptist identifies Jesus as "the Lamb of God, who takes away the sin of the world" (John 1:29). The righteousness of God is, therefore, the unconditional and sacrificial love which doesn't spare the divine Son in order to procure happiness for fallen humanity (Romans 8:32). The Son of God became the curse and sin (Galatians 3:13, 2 Corinthians 5:21) so that we may renounce our sin and take part in the blessings of His life.

Mark's Perspective of the Baptism of Our Lord (Mark 1:9–11) ~ Despite the brevity of the description of Jesus' baptism in Mark, the shortest of all the Gospels, the evangelist doesn't lose the essential perspective—the revelation of Jesus' identity as the "Son of God." Mark proclaims this identity at the beginning of his Gospel (Mark 1:1) and again at the end (Mark 14:62; 15:39). The baptism of Jesus is the seed which grows until it becomes the tree of the Cross.

The baptism of Jesus shows the divine identity of Jesus, the nucleus from which the rest of the revelation of His divinity develops. In His baptism, Jesus is revealed to be the Son of God, and also reveals God as His Father and ours. Mark, along with the other Synoptics, faithfully presents the baptism of our Lord as the revealing of the vocation of Jesus. He receives the name of the Son from His Father, which also identifies His mission. The humanity of Jesus enables Him to become our brother. Despite our sin and weakness, we are invited to immerse ourselves in the waters of Baptism and reestablish our broken communion with the Lord.

This miracle of redemption is only possible by the intervention of the Holy Spirit. Jews associate the presence of the Holy Spirit with the work of creation, when out of chaos the world was created (Genesis 1:2). The Spirit, the Creator and Giver of life, also provides a constant flow of life in maintaining the order of creation by re-creative power. Recall the Old Testament account of the valley of dry bones in Ezekiel 37. The full sense of the prophecy can't be limited to the return of the chosen people from exile, but also includes the Spirit of the Lord which resurrects humanity to new life at this crucial moment in salvation history. Jesus Christ, empowered with the Holy Spirit at His baptism, can re-create life in the soul which was dead in its sin.

All the evangelists report the dove descending upon Jesus at His baptism. The dove represents God's love which ends the flood (Genesis 8:8–12) and also refers to the eagles which brought the people to freedom when crossing the Red Sea (Exodus 19:4). Dove in Hebrew is "Jonah," which recalls the prophet who spent three nights in the belly of a fish in order to appreciate the grace and mercy of the Lord in fulfilling His mission to Nineveh (Jonah 2:10). Christian Baptism, corresponding to the flood, the crossing the Red Sea, or the belly of the fish, submerges the negative past way of life. The dove, in contrast, represents the positive meaning of Baptism. According to Origen (185–253 AD) wherever there is reconciliation with God there is a dove, as in the case of Noah's ark, announcing God's mercy to the world and at the same time making clear that what is spiritual should be meek and without wickedness, simple and without guile.

Luke's Baptism of Jesus (Luke 3:21–22) ~ The Lucan narrative uniquely presents the prayer of Jesus (Luke 3:21). The third Gospel emphasizes Jesus' prayer life. Jesus often retires and prays in solitude (Luke 5:16). Jesus prays before calling the twelve apostles (Luke 6:12), prays before foretelling His Passion in Jerusalem (Luke 9:18), and prays at the Transfiguration (Luke 9:28). His disciples ask Him to teach them to pray (Luke 11:1). Jesus prays intensely and sincerely at His agony in the garden of Gethsemane (Luke 22:41–45). No wonder Jesus asks His followers to pray for those who mistreat them (Luke 6:28), insisting that they should always pray and never give up (Luke 18:1), in order not to fall into temptation (Luke 22:40).

Luke links prayer with the Holy Spirit, who resonates through Zechariah (Luke 1:67) and Simeon (Luke 2:25–27). Jesus instructs His disciples to pray for the Holy Spirit to be sent from the Father (Luke 11:13). This emphasis on prayer and the Holy Spirit continues through the Gospel of Luke into his Acts of the Apostles. Jesus' apostles and Mary devote themselves to prayer in the Cenacle before the descent of the Holy Spirit (Acts 1:14). The apostles ask for the gift of the Holy Spirit when praying for the first deacons of the Church (Acts 6:1–6). Peter and John pray that the Samaritans might receive the Holy Spirit (Acts 8:15). Ananias, laying his hands on Saul, is immersed in prayer that Paul's sight may be restored and that he be filled with the Holy Spirit (Acts 9:11–17). Peter prays for Cornelius, the first Gentile convert, who receives the gift of the Holy Spirit (Acts 10:4–47). Paul warns the elders from Ephesus to protect themselves and their flock guarded by the Holy Spirit (Acts 20:28).

Another feature of the Lucan narrative is his concern for numbers. For example, Luke reports that Jesus was baptized along with a multitude of people. Also, Luke presents Jesus in the list of the genealogy of seventy-six representatives of humanity starting with Adam. Jesus is seventy-seventh, the biblical number of fullness. In the baptism of Jesus mankind is saved and baptized. Jesus becomes the *new* Adam. So, in effect, Luke inverts the chronology, putting Jesus on the top of the list to emphasize His origin from God in the history of salvation (Saint Ambrose of Milan 333–397 AD). The Lucan presentation of Jesus' baptism, with the inclusion of the genealogy of His ancestors, reveals the teaching of the Church on the forgiveness of original sin through Baptism. Before Jesus, all the generations of the genealogy are lost in chaos and darkness through their sin. After Adam's rebellion intimacy with God was broken. People no longer considered themselves children of God, but were alienated and estranged from God.

Because of Adam's sin, man "hid" himself from the Father. In Jesus, man is found and brought back into fellowship with God. Jesus links all the pieces of the broken chain of humanity and gives it back to God so that people might once again become what they were intended to be from the very beginning of creation—the sons and daughters of God the Father in heaven.

God the Father proclaimed to Jesus: "Thou are my beloved Son; with Thee I am well pleased" (Luke 3:22). Jesus, the beloved Son, is the new Adam who makes it possible for all the sons of the original Adam to enter into a new relationship of sonship with the heavenly Father. For this reason, Paul calls Jesus Christ "the first fruit of creation" (1 Corinthians 15:20–23).

The relationship between Adam and Jesus affects every human being on earth. Jesus Christ ransoms the life of every son of Adam and daughter of Eve in His death on the cross, identifying Himself with sinful humanity. Jesus involves every Christian starting with Baptism and culminating with the final resurrection. Paul explains the role of Christ who offers the solution to the fallen humanity: "For as by a man came death, by a man has come also the resurrection of the dead. For as in Adam all die, so also in Christ shall all be made alive. But each in his own order: Christ the first fruits, then at His coming those who belong to Christ" (1 Corinthians 15:22–23).

Christ is bathed in light; let us also be bathed in light. Christ is baptized; let us go down with Him and rise with Him. John is baptizing when Jesus draws near. Perhaps He comes to sanctify His baptizer; certainly He comes to bury sinful humanity in the waters. He comes to sanctify the Jordan for our sake and in readiness for us, He who is spirit and flesh comes to begin a new creation through the Spirit and water … Jesus rises from the waters; the world rises with Him. The heavens like Paradise with its flaming sword, closed by Adam for himself and his descendants, are rent open.

Let us do honor to Christ's baptism and celebrate this feast in holiness. Be cleansed entirely and continue to be cleansed. Nothing gives such pleasure to God as the conversion and salvation of men, for whom His every word and every revelation exists. He wants you to become a living force for all mankind, lights shining in the world. You are to be radiant lights as you stand beside Christ, the great light, bathed in the glory of Him who is the light of heaven. You are to enjoy more and more the pure and dazzling light of the Trinity, as now you have received—though not in its fullness—a ray of its splendor, proceeding from the one God, in Christ Jesus our Lord.

Saint Gregory Nazianzus, Bishop (330–389 AD), *Oratio 39, "Sancta Lumina,"* 14–16, 20.

---

1. Read the following passages aloud and meditate on them.

Matthew 3:13–17	Mark 1:9–11	Luke 3:21–22	John 1:29–34

2. Explain the evidence offered in John 1:34.

3. What can you learn from comparing the following verses?

Matthew 3:11

Matthew 3:13–14

Matthew 16:21–23

4. Choose one or two of the accounts of the Baptism of Jesus and identify the three persons of the Blessed Trinity. Please write down the verses.

God the Father		
Jesus Christ		
The Holy Spirit		

5. How would you respond to someone who says the "Trinity" is not in the Bible?

6. What is the attitude of God the Father toward Jesus? Matthew 3:17, Mark 1:11, Luke 3:22

7. List the following eyewitnesses and what they profess about Jesus in these verses.

John 1:34	*John the Baptist*	
Matthew 16:16		
Mark 15:39		

8. What can you learn from the *Catechism* about the baptism of Jesus? CCC 536

9. What does Jesus' baptism begin or inaugurate? CCC 535

10. What happens for the Christian in the sacrament of Baptism? CCC 537

11. Who is involved in these passages and what do they do?

Matthew 28:18	
Acts 2:38	
Acts 8:12–13	
Acts 10:47–48	
Acts 16:14–15	
Acts 18:8	

12. What does Saint Paul explain in Galatians 6:3–4?

13. How does Saint Gregory of Nazianzus describe Baptism? CCC 1216

14. Compare the following verses.

1 Corinthians 12:13	
Galatians 3:27	
Romans 6:3–4	
Colossians 2:12–13	

15. What does the sacrament of Baptism do for you? CCC 1213

16. What is necessary for Baptism? CCC 1253

17. What does Baptism make you into or enable you to be?

2 Corinthians 5:17	
Romans 8:16–17	
1 Corinthians 6:19	

18. Ephesians 4:25 suggests that Baptism makes us related to one another. Explain this.

19. Give two terms for this incorporation. CCC 1267

20. From what you've learned in this lesson, is your birthday or your baptismal day more important for you? Find out what your baptismal day is and celebrate it next year.

CHAPTER 4

Temptation in the Desert

Matthew 4, Mark 1, Luke 4

**And he was in the wilderness forty days, tempted by Satan;
and he was with the wild beasts; and the angels ministered to him.** (Mark 1:13)

Three evangelists tell of Christ's temptation in the desert. The briefest account is Mark's single verse. The temptation in a nutshell: located in the wilderness, the time frame of forty days, the testing by Satan, companionship provided by wild beasts, and the ministry of the good angels.

The desert is never far from the settled areas in the Middle East. The great rivers of the Nile, Jordan, Tigris, and Euphrates all pass through desert country. Going out into the desert is often less than an hour's walk. Jerusalem and Bethlehem are near to the great mountainous desert of the Negev to the south and to the low-lying desert of the Dead Sea plain. In these unsettled deserts the first monastics, the Desert Fathers, withdrew to focus on a life of prayer.

Midbar, the Hebrew word translated "wilderness" or "desert" designates a dry, deserted area without water as opposed to good land blessed by God. The root of this word is *dabar* meaning "word." The desert is the theater of the human struggle of searching for God and His "word" in times of trial. We all have our desert experiences of struggle. Nonetheless, the wilderness becomes the privileged place of the covenant with God (Exodus 19–21). On Mount Sinai God gives Moses the Decalogue—the Ten Commandments. In the desert, God's people become aware of their true identity as God's "own possession ... a kingdom of priests, a holy nation" (Exodus 19:5–6). For the prophets, the wilderness is the place of purification: "I will allure her, and bring her into the wilderness, and speak tenderly to her ... and there she shall answer as in the days of her youth, as at the time when she came out of the land of Egypt" (Hosea 2:14–15). Responsibility and awareness, key components of discipleship, are nurtured in the desert.

The time frame of Jesus' desert experience is forty days. Forty designates a long period of human life or endurance. A man reaching age forty is mature. Eighty means ripe old age (Psalm 90:10) and three times forty was the maximum span of life (Genesis 6:3). Proof of divine favor is shown in David's and Solomon's forty years reign (2 Samuel 5:4; 1 Kings 2:11, 11:42). However, the forty years of Saul's rule are seen in a negative light (Acts 13:21–22), as are the forty years that the Israelites wandered in the desert before entering the promised land (Numbers 14:3, Psalm 90:10). Forty days also recalls the length of the flood (Genesis 7:4), the days of embalming Jacob (Genesis 50:3), the stay of Moses on Mt. Sinai (Exodus 24:18), the spies exploring the promised land (Numbers 13:25), the prayer of Moses (Deuteronomy 9:25–29), the arrogance of Goliath (1 Samuel 17:16), the fasting of Elijah (1 Kings 19:2–8), the probation of Nineveh (Jonah 3:4), and Christ's ministry after His Resurrection (Acts 1:3).

The testing by Satan here is similar to that in the Book of Job. God gave Satan permission to try Job in order to shake his resolve (Job 1: 11–12). Although Satan is motivated only by hatred of humanity, God uses him to test and strengthen the resolve of the saints. The greater the saint, the stronger are the temptations. In contrast to Adam and Eve, who fail in their test and die in their sin, Jesus overcomes the devil and by this victory opens the passage to the Kingdom of God. Temptation fundamentally involves the alternatives man may choose. Christ always chooses the service of others in obedience to the Father rather than choosing a selfish option. In this Jesus reminds the Christian that the possibility—the choice—of repentance and conversion always exists, despite grave sin and human mistakes. When we choose with Jesus to offer our lives for the sake of others we choose life and love. The opposite choice leads to violence and death.

Temptation is an attack, an attempt to violate our integrity by separating our wills from our consciences. Even if someone is strong with an immoveable will, that person still experiences temptation as a form of suffering. Christ's temptation in the desert parallels His agony in the garden. In the desert, Jesus turns aside a cup that the Father did not will. In the garden, Jesus accepts the cup that the Father did will. Perhaps He sweated drops of blood in the desert as in the garden. Both were part of His Passion, the spiritual and the physical aspects of His suffering.

Wild beasts were Jesus' companions. Animals were with Adam in the Garden of Eden, and wild beasts were with Jesus in the desert of temptation. Isaiah prophesied the taming of wild beasts in the great Messianic vision (Isaiah 11:6–7). God's creatures also suffer as a result of original sin. "All creation yearns and groans" for the coming of the Son of Man (Romans 8:22).

Mark and Matthew tell us that angels ministered to Jesus. Angels helped God's chosen as they wandered in the desert (Exodus 14:19; 23:20–23) and helped Elijah to flee into the desert during his persecution (1 Kings 19:5–7). After Jesus successfully repels temptation, the desert becomes like heaven on earth. Just as angels gather around the heavenly throne, so they gather around Jesus in the desert. The term "desert" means a deserted place, but the wilderness of Judea quickly becomes populated during the temptation of Christ with Jesus, Satan, wild beasts, and good angels all milling about. If we could look with spiritual eyes into our churches, we would see the same thing—the Divine Presence, ministering angels, saints, and even devils lurking about.

And he fasted forty days and forty nights, and afterward he was hungry. And the tempter came and said to him, "If you are the Son of God, command these stones to become loaves of bread." But he answered, "It is written, 'Man shall not live by bread alone, but by every word that proceeds from the mouth of God.'" (Matthew 4:2–4)	And he ate nothing in those days; and when they were ended, he was hungry. The devil said to him, "If you are the Son of God, command this stone to become bread." And Jesus answered him, "It is written, 'Man shall not live by bread alone.'" (Luke 4:2b–4)

The Greek verb for tempt, *peirazo*, means to seek to seduce, or to make proof or trial of a person. Temptations may be experiences in which you either "prove yourself" or perish. Satan deceives, trying to make Jesus "perish," in the same way he seduced Adam and Eve with the temptation to indulge the belly. Instead of succumbing to vainglory, the cause of Adam's sin, Jesus challenges the devil. "It is written, 'Man shall not live by bread alone, but by every word that proceeds from the mouth of God'" (Matthew 4:4). Maximus of Turin (380–465 AD) sees in Jesus' response a solution to the sin of human pride. The Christian who feeds on the Bread of Life can resist the food of this world. The Savior Himself is the bread from heaven (John

6:41). Not opting for economic Messianism, Jesus quotes the passage from Deuteronomy 8:3, which recalls the first temptation of Israel in the desert when they grumbled due to their hunger for bread. The manna provided in the desert prefigures the gift of God's Word and the Eucharist (John 6:32–29). Knowledge of Scripture provides a source of life for critical situations when the Christian, in his daily struggle for material goods, is tempted to disregard his spiritual life.

Then the devil took him to the holy city, and set him on the pinnacle of the temple, and said to him, "If you are the Son of God, throw yourself down; for it is written, 'He will give his angels charge of you.' and 'on their hands they will bear you up, lest you strike your foot against a stone.'" Jesus said to him, "Again it is written, "You shall not tempt the Lord your God." (Matthew 4:5–7)	And he took him to Jerusalem, and set him on the pinnacle of the temple, and said to him, "If you are the Son of God, throw yourself down from here; for it is written, 'He will give his angels charge of you, to guard you,' and 'on their hands they will bear you up, lest you strike your foot against a stone.'" And Jesus answered him, "It is said, 'You shall not tempt the Lord your God.'" (Luke 4:9–12)

Matthew's second temptation is Luke's third. Luke concludes at the temple, nearer to the center stage in his Gospel. For instance, Luke's Gospel begins inside the holy of holies of the temple, where the archangel Gabriel appears to Zechariah. Not surprisingly, Luke narrates the temptation at the pinnacle of the temple in the climactic third position in his account. The temple is also an integral element in the climax of Jesus' mission when, at His death, the curtain of the temple is torn as Jesus becomes the spiritual temple of reconciliation and forgiveness (Luke 23:45).

After having rejected economic Messianism, obsession with the material world, Jesus is then tempted by religious Messianism. Temptations emerge when the search for God is not founded on faith in divine providence but rather in desires that lead to idolatry. Excessive curiosity can lead to perversion of faith, if one seeks the gifts of God rather than the Giver.

Satan tempts Jesus to become the ultimate and all-powerful religious leader. His power would enable Him to control and dominate the crowds. Jesus refuses to yield to the temptation to dominate and to compromise His mission of serving mankind as a brother. Jesus again answers the devil by quoting Scripture in its context. Trust in God requires listening to Him and loving Him without seeking compensation. Living faith never puts God to the test (Deuteronomy 6:16). Saint John Chrysostom (344–407 AD) explains that the devil is overcome not by miracles but by Jesus' forbearance and long-suffering which are the virtues of obedient faith.

The devil took him to a very high mountain, and showed him all the kingdoms of the world and the glory of them; and he said to him, "All these will I give you, if you will fall down and worship me." Then Jesus said, "Begone, Satan! For it is written, 'You shall worship the Lord your God and him only shall you serve.'" (Matthew 4:8–10)	The devil took him up, and showed him all the kingdoms of the world in a moment of time, and said to him, "To you I will give all authority and their glory, for it has been delivered to me, and I give it to whom I will. If you then will worship me, it shall all be yours." Jesus answered "It is written, 'You shall worship the Lord your God, and him only shall you serve.'" (Luke 4:5–8)

Tradition locates this temptation west of Jericho on the cliff of the mountain Jebel Qarantal, where Simon Maccabeus built his fortress named "Dok" and where he and two of his sons were treacherously killed (1 Maccabees 16:15–17). The Hasmoneans began, and Herod the Great continued, to build a series of mountaintop castles beginning from Masada, Hyrkania, Kypros, Dok, and Alexandreion. The fortress of Dok was set on this high point in order to control the area of Jericho and the lower Jordan Valley far below. This is also the site for the parable of the Good Samaritan, who helped a man who had been robbed and beaten on the lonely road from Jerusalem to Jericho.

The Christian history of this site begins with Saint Chariton (d. 350 AD), who retired here from Ain Phara, near Anatot, the birthplace of the prophet Jeremiah. His disciple Elpidius built a primitive monastery around 340 AD on the site of Jesus' temptations. Grottos inhabited by hermits still adorn the south side of the cliff today. On top of the mountain the ruins of a Byzantine chapel witness to early Christian worship. Both men and women pilgrims can visit the present Greek Orthodox Monastery of Temptation, built in 1874. This church with more than 100 icons is found just past some water cisterns. A flight of steps leads from the church to a small chapel where there is a stone linked to the first temptation of Jesus. Pilgrims in the midst of the desert contrast Moses and the Israelites falling into sin with the perfect example of Jesus' heroic obedience of faith in resisting sin and Satan's lures. The monastery affords a panoramic view of the ancient city of Jericho and the Jordan valley.

The last Messianic temptation is to political power. The splendor and glory of this world are products of ambitious human pride with its desire to rule. Jesus' glory of the Cross stands in stark contrast. The poor, the oppressed, and the unhappy are drawn by this display of infinite love that liberates from evil. Jesus, in obedience to the plan of His Father, refuses political power, the golden calf of this world. Jesus faced this temptation repeatedly. Peter was called Satan because he wanted Jesus to avoid the Cross (Matthew 16:23). The crowd also demanded that Jesus come down from the cross (Matthew 27:42). Jesus, by His command of Sacred Scripture, rebukes Satan and states His intention to serve exclusively for God's purpose (Deuteronomy 6:13). Jesus' obedience reveals Him as the suffering Servant (Isaiah 42–53), the King reigning from the Cross and the instrument of God's love for us, which defeats Satan forever.

Jesus, the Son of God, chooses to show His solidarity with sinful humanity. Instead of choosing power, riches, and fame, Jesus embraces the way of salvation. Theodore of Mopsuestia (d. 428 AD) reflecting on the redemption of mankind argues that the Spirit led Christ into the wilderness in order to enfeeble the devil's force by Someone of far greater strength. According to Hilary of Poitiers (315–168 AD), the devil envied God's presence in Adam before the fall and thus enticed him to sin. For this same reason, the devil attacked Jesus immediately after His baptism. Satan's temptations indicate his sinister attempts against those who have been sanctified and how eagerly he desires victory over the saints. Jesus suppresses His hunger for food with His thirst for the salvation of souls. The devil is defeated by the same Flesh that he tormented.

Origen (185–253 AD) recalls that the Patriarch Abraham twice had to deal with the temptation to reject God's plan. The first temptation occurred when Abraham was asked to abandon his homeland (Genesis 12:1) and the second when God demanded the sacrifice of his son, Isaac (Genesis 22:2). Abraham's obedience foreshadows the obedience of Christ.

The rabbis stress that by overcoming temptation Abraham proved control of *Yetzer tob* (the good impulse) over *Yetzer rah* (the evil impulse). Jewish theology stresses subjecting temptations to common sense. Christian theology relies more heavily on the decisive role of God's grace in the struggle against temptations. Without grace, man is unable to resist the action of evil. Luke sees temptation as part of everyday life. We live in this world, but we are not of this world (John 17:14). Once we receive the sacrament of Baptism, we belong to Christ. Christians expect temptations on the way to the heavenly Jerusalem but know the sufficiency of grace.

Jesus did not take any shortcuts from the cross. Neither should we. Blessings and strength await those who face temptations and fight them in obedience to God's Word and with the help of His grace. The world, the flesh, and the devil tempt us to be bad, but the Holy Spirit "tempts" us to be good. Let us fall into the temptation of being good every day of our lives!

---

1. Why did Jesus go out into the desert?

Matthew 4:1–2	Mark 1:12	Luke 4:1–2

2. Jesus fasted forty days. What does this recall?

Genesis 7:4	
Exodus 24:18	
Deuteronomy 9:25–29	
1 Kings 19:2–8	
Jonah 3:4–10	

3. What liturgical season does the Catholic Church offer to invite us to enter into Jesus' experience in the desert? CCC 540

4. What good can prayer and fasting do? CCC 1434

5. How did Jesus instruct the disciples when their prayers weren't working? Mark 9:14–29

6. What is the fourth precept of the Catholic Church? CCC 2043

7. Have you ever tried fasting and almsgiving along with prayer?

8. Define "temptation." Use a dictionary or the *Catechism*.

9. Compare the three temptations of Christ from Matthew 4 and Luke 4.

Matthew 4:3	Luke 4:3
Matthew 4:5–6	Luke 4:5–7
Matthew 4:8–9	Luke 4:9–11

10. How did Jesus respond to Satan's temptations?

Deuteronomy 8:3	Matthew 4:4
Deuteronomy 6:16	Matthew 4:7
Deuteronomy 5:6–7	Matthew 4:10
Deuteronomy 6:13	

11. What does Jesus' mastery over Satan's temptation teach us? Hebrews 4:14–16

12. Compare the following verses.

13. Star (*) your favorite verse and commit it to memory this week.

Matthew 6:13	
Luke 22:40	
1 Corinthians 10:13	
James 1:12	
1 Peter 1:6–7	
Revelation 3:10	

14. What would you say to someone who thought God was tempting him? James 1:13

15. What are some sources of temptation? James 1:14–15

James 4:4	*the world*
James 1:14–15	
1 Thessalonians 3:5	

16. How did the disciples avoid falling into temptation?

CCC 2612	
Luke 22:40, 46	

17. Satan tempted Jesus when he was hungry and weak. How can you stay strong?

Psalm 25:1–5	
Proverbs 3:5–6	
Proverbs 4:23	
Matthew 7:7–11	
John 8:31–32	
John 15:3–7	

18. Explain the difference between "temptation" and "sin." CCC 1858–1859

19. Should a Christian expect to be bothered by the devil? 1 Peter 5:8–10

20. Share some effective ways to deal with the tempter and temptations. James 4:6–8

Monthly Social Activity

This month your small group will meet for coffee, tea, or a simple breakfast, lunch, or dessert in someone's home. Please remember to "keep it simple!"

Pray for this social event and for the host or hostess. Try, if at all possible, to attend. Offer hospitality so that one of the socials is held at your home.

Activity

Take a sheet of scrap paper and write down three things about yourself.

Two things should be true. One should be false.

Don't write your name on the paper.

When you get to the social, put the scraps of paper into a basket.

Each person should read one aloud and guess whom it describes.

Then determine which item is false.

Examples

1. I wanted to enter a religious order.
2. I am in a bowling league.
3. I was a lifeguard.

1. I'm a Dodgers' fan.
2. I tinker with cars.
3. I took Dad's watch apart at age 5.

1. I do volunteer work in a nursing home.
2. I like scary movies.
3. I never learned to ride a bike.

CHAPTER 5

The Announcement of the Kingdom of God

Matthew 4:13–17, Mark 1:14–15

The time is fulfilled, and the kingdom of God is at hand; repent, and believe in the Gospel.
(Mark 1:15)

The announcement of the kingdom of God and the Invitation to Conversion provide meditation for the third Luminous Mystery of the Rosary. Luke presents a programmatic homily regarding the coming of God's kingdom in Luke 4:14–30. This passage doesn't mention the term "kingdom of God" specifically, but rather identifies it by quoting Isaiah 61:1–2 and 58:6. Since Luke presents the social and political aspects of the kingdom rather than naming it theologically, this commentary will focus primarily on presenting the texts from Matthew 4 and Mark 1:14–15.

Capernaum is the main site of Jesus' mission in Galilee. Pilgrims entering the archeological site of Capernaum are welcomed with the sign: "Capernaum—the City of Jesus." Since Jesus lived and worked in the house of Peter in Capernaum for His three years of public ministry, we could consider this the very first parish, mission, or even the first Vatican of the Church. The Gospels record twelve miracles of Jesus in Capernaum, more than anywhere else in the Holy Land.

Capernaum lies at the northwest shore of the Sea of Galilee just two miles west of the river Jordan's estuary to the lake. At the time of Jesus, the Roman road, Via Maris, passed through the town providing revenue for this fishing and agricultural community. The closest town to Capernaum on the way to Damascus was Bethsaida, the hometown of Peter, Andrew, and Philip. Bethsaida was probably more cosmopolitan than Capernaum. Archeologists unearthed the house of Peter, where Jesus lived as a guest, and found a poor home, characteristic of Jesus' simplicity and humility. Jesus adapted Himself to the rural living conditions of Palestine. The floor of large basalt stones posed dangers for children and the elderly in the dark houses. There was no drainage, no running water, no windows, and only a few openings in the wall to let fresh air come into the narrow, rectangular room. The climate at the lake for most of the year, except winter, is oppressively hot and humid. Even today in Capernaum, snakes, lizards, scorpions, and above all mosquitoes, which are never mentioned in the Gospels, abound.

People lived together in large extended family units or clans in Jesus' time. Social life centered on the central courtyard which was surrounded by simple primitive houses built of black volcanic stone with roofs covered by straw. People retired to their homes for private activity or to spend the night. Similar structures remain in the third world today, but are now rarely found in Palestine. In the third century, the house of Peter was transformed into a house synagogue. The architect left the central room, divided by an arch, virtually intact. Jewish Christians, banned from worshiping with other Jews, came to worship here. Inscriptions with the names "Jesus" and "Peter" were found on the plaster walls along with hooks for votive lamps. When Christianity became the official religion of the Roman Empire in the fifth century, a small church was built on this site. This simple octagonal building with elevated mosaic floor reserved the inside for worshipers and provided an outside corridor for catechumens.

During the seventh century, the city was abandoned. Franciscan archeologists, Orfalli, Corbo, and Loffreda, rediscovered this treasure in the past century. Jewish visitors find the synagogue of the fourth century, oriented toward Jerusalem, to be the most important building in Capernaum. This synagogue was built on the foundations of the original synagogue of the first century, which is mentioned in the Gospels (Luke 7:5 and John 6:59). Huge white limestone blocks and columns were imported at considerable cost. Julian the Apostate may have built this structure shortly after 360 AD with imperial funds as a sign of his opposition to Christianity. Roman art on the architraves supports this theory. Also, the incorporation of Greek and Roman art was no longer regarded as offensive to Judaism in the fourth century AD. This synagogue, one of the largest and most beautiful in Palestine, has a main hall, a balcony, a separate entrance for women, a ritual pool, and an adjacent room for keeping the scrolls.

The Kingdom of God in Matthew ~ Matthew quotes Isaiah 9:1–2 to show the theological importance of Jesus' identity as the one fulfilling the Messianic prophecies of the Old Testament. Matthew 4:13 makes striking connections between Capernaum and the sea. The Greek adjective, *parathalasios,* employed in Matthew in the accusative is translated into English using the phrase "by the sea." This unique term, called *hapax legomenon,* is used only in this one place in the entire New Testament and suggests a meaning deeper than merely geography. Capernaum by the sea refers to the bottom of the spiritual chasm created by the sin of Adam as opposed to the mountain heights where God draws the privileged closer to Himself. Jesus begins His ministry at the point of spiritual poverty, abandonment, and rejection caused by human arrogance. Jesus' baptism at the entrance of the Jordan River into the Dead Sea, the lowest point on the surface of earth, shows Jesus' desire to identify with the tragedy of the lowly sinner. Indeed, divine mercy reaches down to human misery, and the heavens are opened (Matthew 3:16).

Matthew's use of the noun "sea" in reference to the lake of Galilee differs from Luke's more exact usage of the term "lake" (Luke 5:1–2). For the nomadic tribes of the Middle East the "sea," whether lake or ocean, represents enemies dangerous to human life. The Jews of Jesus' time understood the passage through the Red Sea as more than liberation from political and social oppression. Religious tradition recognized the sense of liberation from the slavery of sin, as well.

The territory of eastern Galilee was originally allotted to the tribes of Zebulun and Napthali. The tenth son of Jacob and sixth son of Leah (Genesis 30:19–20), Zebulun, from the Hebrew root *zbl* meaning "exalt," shows a topographical reference since his tribe inhabited the mountainous (exalted) region of lower Galilee. This tribe, considered one of the bravest in Israel (Judges 4:6–10), failed to drive out the Canaanites from their territory (Judges 1:30). Napthali, the sixth son of Jacob and the second of Bilhah, Rachel's handmaiden, did not have the status of a full descendant. Despite military skills and leadership, Napthali drew even closer to the Gentiles and intermingled with the Canaanite population (Judges 1:33). Naphtali's region extended from the west shore of the lake of Galilee to the north along the commercial route to Syria.

Matthew suggests that Jesus' motive in moving from Nazareth to Capernaum was more than simply to get away from the intense opposition in His hometown. According to St. Cyril of Alexandria (d. 444 AD), Jesus moves from the conservative Nazareth to Capernaum in order that His preaching of the Gospel may gain momentum and impact a greater number of people, Jews as well as Gentiles. A similar movement is detected in the Matthean Gospel when Joseph decides to move to Nazareth in order to fulfill the Old Testament prophecies rather than moving back to Judea with Mary and Jesus (Matthew 2:22–23).

Now in Capernaum Jesus proclaims His message, "Repent, for the kingdom of God is at hand" (Matthew 4:17). John's Gospel portrays Jesus as the "light." Jesus, the light promised to Israel, and through her to all people, brings about the dawn of the Church. Jesus provides our personal passage from night/death to the day/life of God. Jesus fulfills the spiritual proclamation of the Old Testament prophets with the preaching of hope and the universal promise of the kingdom of heaven through repentance. The Hebrew word for repentance is *teshuvah*; the root, *shuv*, means to turn or to change. Prophets of the Old Covenant exhorted people to change their lives and turn from sinful ways to righteousness. Sin deviates from the ideal way of life. Repentance means to return to original righteousness. Jewish theology presupposes that human beings are capable of changing their behavior, repenting of their mistakes, and returning to a decent way of life.

Christian theology emphasizes the vital role of God's grace in repentance. There is no concept of original sin in Judaism and, therefore, no understanding of the original fallen nature that every person in the world is born into and which separates every person from a relationship with God. Rabbis agree that simple contrition is insufficient for reconciliation. Confession of sin in the process of repentance is essential so that the same sin is not easily repeated. Trespassing against another person requires that the offender express contrition and the offended person offer forgiveness for the completion of *teshuvah*. This situation is implicit in Jesus' teaching: "So if you are offering your gift at the altar, and there remember that your brother has something against you, leave your gift there before the altar and go; first be reconciled to your brother, and then come and offer your gift" (Matthew 5:23).

Sins committed against God can only be forgiven by God. The word *teshuvah* also means to "answer." All sin is ultimately an offense against the perfect, pure, and all-holy God. The Good News is that God loves sinful human beings. Despite the fact that we can never deserve God's love or mercy, Jesus offers us the love and mercy of God. God's free offering demands a response—an answer. Jesus pays the price for all the sins of mankind and then invites each individual to accept the salvation that He has bought and paid for with His precious blood shed on the cross. Jesus demands an answer from individuals when He presents His offer of the kingdom of God. The Christian has nothing to offer to God apart from what God has already given. The only sensible response for the sinner is to repent and accept redemption from Jesus. Have you repented and accepted God's gift of salvation?

The Kingdom of God ~ What is the meaning of "heavenly kingdom?" This expression, without a doubt, is original to Jesus. The Synoptic Gospels use this term 104 times, 51 times in Matthew, 14 times in Mark, 39 times in Luke. Since Matthew used this term 51 times, it is clear that he had a special interest in this theme. Matthew modifies the expression "kingdom of God" to "kingdom of heaven," probably for pietistic reasons in making his Gospel acceptable to Judeo-Christian readers, who avoid the use of God's name. The fundamental aspect of the heavenly kingdom is that it belongs to God. It connects the earthly reality to the spiritual domain.

Origin (185–254 AD) sees the "kingdom of heaven" personified in Jesus (*autobasileia*). The kingdom of heaven also symbolizes a spiritual condition identified by the presence of virtue in the human life. When we repent of our sin and accept the gift of redemption offered by Jesus, then Jesus comes to us and remains within us in the virtues of wisdom, justice, and truth. For St. Paul, the kingdom of God is "righteousness, peace and joy in the Holy Spirit" (Romans 14:17). The Christian may proclaim with Paul: "It is no longer I who live, but Christ who lives in me" (Galatians 2:20). Repentance allows Christ to fill the empty void of our souls so that with Mary we can proclaim the opening lines of her Magnificat: "My soul magnifies the Lord" (Luke 1:46).

The gift of the heavenly kingdom can always be trusted. If the Christian is not good, Christ always is. If a Christian is not holy, Christ is perfectly holy. If the Christian is not wise, Christ is the font of wisdom. If the Christian is not acceptable, Christ is. Paul Claudel says "Christ is more with me than myself." Repentance is more than an individual decision; it is the gift of God. This divine treasure of the kingdom of God, alive in us, is revealed through the mission of Jesus, in His teaching, healing, death, and Resurrection (Acts 10:38–40). That grace of God, a true treasure, remains alive in the Church through the sacraments of Baptism, Reconciliation, and Eucharist (Matthew 26:28, Mark 1:4, Acts 2:38).

The Kingdom of God in Mark 1:14–15 ~ For Mark, the need to achieve the goal of God's kingdom is the theme of Jesus' preaching, which is called gospel. The use of the word "gospel" (*evangelion*) by Mark in the beginning of his writing (Mark 1:1, 14) and at the end (Mark 16:15) indicates its crucial importance to him. For Mark the thrust of the Gospel is the message of the kingdom of God.

> Mark articulates the importance of the theme of the kingdom of God in four ways:
> 1) The fulfillment of time
> 2) The kingdom of God is at hand
> 3) Repentance
> 4) Faith in the Gospel

Three different terms in the New Testament indicate the notion of time.

1) Ordinary time, *chronos*, corresponds to the philosophical definition of movement. This time measures the events of history. It presupposes the creation of the world and doesn't include time before or after this present world. The human being has no control over such movement. *Chronos* reminds the human of his limits and inability to control history. Only God is beyond this category and He is the Creator of *chronos*.

2) *Aion*, the "eternal" life to come, is another word for time. It is developed from Jewish apocalyptic speculation and concerns the distinction between the present, sinful world and the everlasting reality to come. The oppression of *chronos* will be eliminated in aion, and the relationship between God and man will be totally different.

3) The time with the deepest theological significance is *kairos*, the right, proper, or critical time. Jesus stresses the importance of *kairos*, in which the crucial moments of salvation history unfold as He inaugurates the kingdom of God and moves forward in the Father's perfect timing toward His Passion, death, Resurrection and parousia. These crucial events in salvation history challenge each person to make a personal decision and respond to the call from the Lord to

personal discipleship. Jesus speaks to every man, woman, and child when He says "Follow me" (Matthew 4:19). The fishermen immediately left their nets to follow Jesus. They did not miss the moment—*kairos*—of His visitation. Have you recognized the importance of God calling you to follow Him? Could this be a *kairos* moment for you to hear God's call and respond totally?

The coming of Jesus, the central event of salvation history, joins the time before creation, the time of history, and the future, which will never end. Jesus transcends all time. He is the Alpha and the Omega who exists in all eternity. He both stands outside of time and is also present in every moment of time. Critical to our personal call is the present, not the past or the future. The person of Jesus, always present and crucial in every moment of your personal history, becomes your *kairos*. The reality of God's kingdom in the present overcomes the tyranny of the past and allows us to enter into the potential of sharing eternity with our Creator.

The moment of your personal call begins at baptism through which your life becomes consecrated for the Lord. Baptism initiates your *kairos* in belonging exclusively to the Lord. This moment and this decision constitute the most important event in your personal history. The message of God's kingdom presents a dynamic program for each individual, which begins in Baptism and continues throughout eternity. The kingdom of God enables the human being to become completely transformed into the image of God. Our hope is for the new man in a new world. God's kingdom is the goal and the movement of history. It is not of this world, but belongs to this world in order to transform it.

For Mark, the employment of "the kingdom of God is at hand" (Mark 1:15) indicates that the reigning presence of God is at the door, almost here, but not yet fully present. This simple statement of Jesus summons forth a response, indeed commands a response from the human soul.

Faith and repentance constitute opportune responses to the challenge of beginning anew in the presence of God's kingdom. John the Baptist heralds the call to repentance, and Jesus Christ walks onto the stage of human events to provide Someone true enough to believe in, Someone great enough to live for, and Someone good enough to die for. Indeed, He will live and die for us, so that we may live.

The reign of God is discovered in the person and teaching of Jesus, in the word of the Good News (Mark 1:1,15). Luke, perhaps the most emphatic, brings forth the meaning of His presence: "Today this scripture has been fulfilled in your hearing" (Luke 4:21). People long for the interior and spiritual realities of God's kingdom while still embracing the reality of the material world. Repentance turns away from sin and looks radically to the mercy offered in the person of Jesus. The Christian looks forward with faith to the future coming promised by Jesus-His parousia.

The follower of Christ does not act alone in the process of conversion. The Greek word most commonly used for repentance is *metanoia*. It is often translated "change of mind" but may also be translated "interior change." Repentance and faith are more than mere intellectual activities. Repentance and faith involve breaking pride and the life of sin, and totally embracing the Gospel of Jesus. The Holy Spirit bestows the power to turn from sin and follow the example of Jesus. The rest of the Gospel offers the fulfillment of God's kingdom in the words and deeds of Jesus, which evoke the reaction of others, especially the disciples.

1. Compare the following Old Testament verses.

Exodus 15:1, 18	
Psalm 47	
Psalm 93:1–2	
Psalm 97	
Psalm 103:19	
Psalm 145:11–13	
Daniel 4:3 RSV Daniel 4:31 NAB	
Obadiah 21	

2. Now compare these verses from the Gospels.

Matthew 4:17	
Matthew 25:34	
Mark 1:15	
Mark 4:11	
Luke 4:43	
Luke 16:16	
John 3:3	
John 18:36	

3. Why did Jesus inaugurate the kingdom of heaven on earth? CCC 541

4. How does St. Paul explain the kingdom of God? Romans 14:17

5. Use the *Catechism* to define "the kingdom of God." CCC 542

6. Who does Jesus invite to enter His kingdom?

	CCC 543
	CCC 544
	CCC 545

7. What does Saint Peter say you must do to come into the kingdom of God? Acts 2:38

8. What instruction does Jesus give to enter the kingdom of God? Mark 1:15

9. The kingdom of God is a matter of what three things?

John 3:17	*salvation*
John 10:10	
Mark 1:17	

10. In your own words describe the following scenes.

Matthew 4:18–22	Mark 1:16–20

11. What are Jesus' words of invitation in the following verses?

Matthew 4:19	Mark 1:17

12. How do the fishermen respond to Jesus? Give the verse.

13. Imagine that Jesus asks you to follow Him. How would you respond?

14. What is the relationship between Jesus and His disciples?

CCC 787	
John 15:15	

15. When do Catholics renew their Baptismal promises? CCC 1254

16. What does Jesus offer in Matthew 11:28–30?

17. Describe what a disciple of Jesus must do. Luke 14:27

18. When will the fulfillment of the kingdom occur? Luke 22:28–30, Revelation 12:9–10

19. What does St. Peter suggest and promise in 2 Peter 1:10–11?

20. Have you ever made a commitment to follow Jesus during your adult life? If so, when? If not, please ponder for a while and see if you can pray the following prayer.

**Jesus, I repent of my sins. Please forgive me and make me Your disciple.
I believe that You are the Messiah sent from God.
Thank you for dying for my sins.
Jesus, please reveal Yourself to me more and more.
Take my life. Show me the Father's will for me every day. Lead me and guide.
Amen.**

CHAPTER 6

Jesus Calls the Apostles

Matthew 4:18–22, Mark 1:16–20, Luke 5:1–11

Follow me, and I will make you fishers of men. (Matthew 4:19)

Jesus Calls His Apostles. The Location of the Call ~ The Lake of Galilee, of volcanic origin is more than 600 feet below sea level, 13 miles long from north to south, and seven miles wide. It is one of the most picturesque sites in the Holy Land. Because of its oval shape, the original biblical name in Arabic and Hebrew was *Kinneret*, which means "the harp." The Lake of Galilee is also called Gennesaret, a name derived from the fertile plain of Ginnosar on the northwest shore of the lake, or Tiberias (John 6:1, 21:1), which was the capital of Galilee during the public life of Jesus. Since the Hebrew language is relatively poor in variety of expressions, only Greek-speaking Luke uses the term "lake." Matthew and Mark employ the term "sea."

> Jewish people pose a riddle to their children. "Why is the lake of Galilee full of fish and drinkable water, while the Dead Sea has no fish or fresh water?" The lake receives water from the Jordan River and then gives it away, while the Dead Sea only receives water from the Jordan but gives nothing away. Similarly, the person who receives and gives to others is full of life like the Sea of Galilee. But, he who only takes and never gives becomes as sterile as the Dead Sea.

At the time of our Lord the country on the east bank of the lake was called by its administrative name, Decapolis, with its two cities, Hippos and Gadara alongside the lake. The east bank of the Lake of Galilee is the Golan. The Golan Heights provides a border between Israel, Lebanon, and Syria. Mt. Hermon (2814 meters), the highest peak visible from the Lake of Galilee, is shared today by Lebanon, Syria, and Israel. After the Six Day War in 1967, Israel gained control of this area and pushed the border 15 miles to the east. International conflicts have plagued this peaceful area of the Lake of Galilee.

The perimeter of the lake is 30 miles. Numerous streams create wadis on the east side of the lake during the rainy season. The depression of the lake along with the open valley from the north enables strong winds to create treacherous storms during the winter. The Gospels recount the storm on the "sea" (Matthew 8:23–27, Mark 4:35–41, Luke 8:22–25), which is no exaggeration. The lake, about 135 feet deep, teems with numerous types of fish, including sardines and Saint Peter's fish, mushot.

The Lake of Galilee in modern Israel provides the largest reservoir of potable water in this area of the Middle East, an indispensable treasure for local agriculture in this arid land. Pumping this water may cause serious long-term ecological problems. Hence, no hotels or tourist establishments are allowed to be built near the lake, and commercial fishing is strictly monitored. Attempts to designate part of the northwest shore as a national park linked to the public life of Jesus would contribute to the preservation of this countryside, which is a precious Christian landmark.

As he walked by the sea of Galilee, he saw two brothers, Simon who is called Peter and Andrew his brother, casting a net into the sea; for they were fishermen. And he said to them, "Follow me, and I will make you fishers of men." Immediately they left their nets and followed him. And going on from there he saw two other brothers, James the son of Zebedee and John his brother, in the boat with Zebedee their father, mending their nets, and he called them. Immediately they left the boat and their father, and followed him. (Matthew 4:18–22)	And passing along by the sea of Galilee, he saw Simon and Andrew the brother of Simon casting a net in the sea; for they were fishermen. And Jesus said to them, "Follow me and I will make you fishers of men." And immediately they left their nets and followed him. And going on a little farther, he saw James the son of Zebedee and John his brother, who were in the boat mending the nets. And immediately he called them; and they left their father Zebedee in the boat with the hired servants, and followed him. (Mark 1:16–20)

Matthew and Mark provide almost identical passages on the call of the disciples. Both evangelists link the call to discipleship with the message of the kingdom of God and the need to repent. Matthew stresses the movement of Jesus along the lake—"walking"—in contrast to Mark's "passing." Matthew informs us that Simon was called "Peter," a fact not given in Mark's account. Matthew points out that James and John were in the boat together with their father Zebedee and his hired servants, whom Mark mentions when the sons leave their father to follow Jesus.

Jesus arriving at the Sea of Galilee, the territory of the Gentiles, brings "great light" to this people who sit in darkness and the shadow of death (Matthew 4:16). This often-turbulent sea also connotes the uncertain world and volatile history of people. Simon and Andrew, dependent on the sea to make their living, "cast their nets into the sea." Their personal lives are immersed in the sea of their work. Here, in their everyday activities, Jesus meets these common people. He doesn't threaten or manipulate them. The apostles are not, at this particular moment, involved in religious ritual, prayer, or reading the sacred texts regarding Israel's promised Messiah. But when Jesus touches their hearts, they decide to radically abandon all to follow Him.

> **The Gospels use three different terms to describe net.**
> *Diktyon* refers to fishing net in general.
> *Amfiblesteron* used here is a circular net used by one person casting into shallow water.
> *Sagene* (Greek) is a dragnet pulled between two boats.

The net symbolically represents the proclamation of the Gospel by the Church. Two pairs of men, possibly already disciples of John the Baptist (John 1:37), are called by Jesus to the task of "casting into the sea," that is to preach God's word. The net is the plan to capture souls for Christ. The net of God's word catches people from this frenetic and dangerous world and brings them into the safety of the Church. The Holy Spirit prepares souls to respond to evangelism.

The prospective disciples face a radical decision to abandon everything to follow God's call. According to Tertullian (155–240 AD) all worldly resources must be left behind in response to the coming of the reign of God. Fishermen were not the poorest segment of society in Palestine.

However, fishermen would have to make up for losses if the catch was meager and they needed to transport the fish, fresh, dried, or pickled throughout the country. Fishermen, then as today, would not be considered among the wealthiest stratum in society. Their decision to follow Jesus would involve great personal risk for themselves and their families.

The evangelists first focus on Christ's radical call to Peter and Andrew and then turn to James and John, who appear to be wealthier. Their decision to abandon everything required even more courage. Jesus calls people in their daily activities, both rich and poor. Peter and Andrew partnered with the larger fishing family of Zebedee, who also had hired workers (Mark 1:20). An inscription found on a Capernaum synagogue column from the fourth century testifies to the importance of this family in the city. All the fishermen approached by Jesus left everything, including their family ties, in response to Christ's promise to make them fishers of men.

Jesus' invitation, "Follow me and I will make you fishers of men" provides rich symbolism. For the Hebrew, water is the symbol of life, but also a symbol of death and destruction (Exodus 14:21–29). The parting of the Red Sea provided life for the Israelites, but death for Egyptians.

Fish in the deep, dark sea refer to the spiritually ignorant prior to hearing God's word. The apostle, the fisher of men, helps the listener comprehend the truth of God's message. The proclamation and reception of God's Word transfers the human soul from the darkness of sin into the light of grace. The unsaved "fish" are caught by the Gospel and brought to the Lord to be consecrated to Him in baptism, dying to the old life in order to take on new life in Christ. The four men in the Gospel, Peter, Andrew, James, and John, represent all who accept God's Word, repent, and put their faith in the Gospel of the Lord. Both Matthew and Mark recount their "immediate," hopeful, and joyful response. The call to follow Jesus, to choose His way of life, continues throughout the public life of our Lord. The apostles respond and follow Jesus all the way to Calvary and beyond. We too are invited to follow Jesus continually in our everyday life.

> While the people pressed upon him to hear the word of God, he was standing by the Lake of Gennesaret. And he saw two boats by the lake; but the fishermen had gone out of them and were washing their nets. Getting into one of the boats, which was Simon's, he asked him to put out a little farther from the land. And he sat down and taught the people from the boat. And when he had finished speaking, he said to Simon, "Put out into the deep and let down your nets for a catch." And Simon answered, "Master, we toiled all night and took nothing! But at your word I will let down the nets." And when they had done this, they enclosed a great shoal of fish; and as their nets were breaking, they beckoned to their partners in the other boat to come and help them. And they came and filled both the boats, so that they began to sink. But when Peter saw it, he fell down at Jesus' knees, saying, "Depart from me, for I am a sinful man, O Lord." For he was astonished, and all that were with him, at the catch of fish which they had taken; and so also were James and John, the sons of Zebedee, who were partners with Simon. And Jesus said to Simon, "Do not be afraid; henceforth you will be catching men." And when they had brought their boats to land, they left everything and followed him. (Luke 5:1–11)

The Call to Discipleship in Luke 5:1–11 ~ Luke addresses his Gospel to Theophilus, or to every person who is "eager to listen." While Mark puts the call in the beginning of his Gospel (Mark 1:16–20), demonstrating this basic principle of the Christian life, Luke later in his gospel discusses the motives in answering the call, pointing out the ecclesiastical elements. For Luke, Jesus calls the whole community to obedience to His word. Luke presents the crowd pressing on Jesus, not due to personal, selfish reasons but to hear His word that is filled with authority. The gathering of the crowd precedes the call of the disciples. The response of the multitude is analogous to the response of the Virgin Mary who conceives in her obedience to God's Word (Luke 1:38). Jesus, the Good Shepherd, gathers His people who had been standing at the sea of death and prepares them to embark with Him on the Exodus experience to find new life.

The next scene presents two boats left by the disciples after fishing unsuccessfully during the previous night. Washing the nets was necessary for religious as well as practical reasons to prepare them for the next day's fishing. Matthew 13:47–50 shows the fishermen separating the good Kosher fish from the bad ones without scales, which were not to be eaten due to the prohibition in the Jewish law. Fishermen washing their nets recalls the six stone jars for the Jewish rites of purification (John 2:6). Similarly, purification is a necessary action before responding to God's Word.

Jesus chooses Peter's boat as His pulpit to announce the Good News to those on the shore who are being blessed by the obedience of faith. Peter's boat represents the Church, from which we receive the instruction of Jesus, the Divine Word. The Church applies the teaching by first accepting it and then putting it into practice by the grace of God's Word.

After dismissing the crowd, Jesus turns His focus to Peter. He coaches Peter and presents him with a challenge. Risk will be involved in serving God's kingdom. Peter must put out into the deep. Peter, who is both in charge and yet collaborates with the others, lets down the nets for the catch. Skillful and experienced fishermen know that nighttime, when it is dark, is the best time for fishing. Here, in daylight, it is Peter who is in darkness—ignorant of the power of the Lord. Casting the nets during the day shows the dawning of faith in Peter's soul and his humble obedience. The call into the deep recalls the re-creation of humanity through Noah (cf. Maximus of Turin). Trust in the Lord must be unconditional. The apostolic mission begins in total obedience to the Word of God. Peter is blessed through obedience as was Mary (Luke 1:38), the servants in Cana (John 2:9), and the disciples at the miraculous catch of fish after Jesus' Resurrection (John 21:6). The key to success for the Christian is total trust and obedience to God's Word despite, at times, contrary experience or "expert" advice.

Discipleship requires knowledge of God and His law, as well as complete relinquishment, abandoning everything to follow God's will rather than one's own. Jesus' call to Peter involves repentance and obedience. In this scene, Peter recognizes who Jesus is and reacts appropriately. A turning point in Peter's life is realized when Peter falls on his knees and says, "Depart from me, for I am a sinful man, O Lord" (Luke 5:8). The first among the disciples falls on his knees, just as the Master does in the Garden of Gethsemane, where Jesus offers Himself totally to the will of God (Luke 22:41).

The centurion at the foot of the cross will recognize the Lordship of Jesus in a way similar to Peter when he says, "Truly this man was the Son of God" (Mark 15:39). The crucifixion shows that discipleship cannot be taken lightly. Casting the net into the deep requires all the energy of those who decide to follow Jesus. Shallow enthusiasm or a half-hearted decision fails to provide sufficient response to the call. All the apostles of Jesus, except for Saint John, will answer the call of Jesus by sacrificing their lives in persecution and martyrdom.

The disciples react to the miraculous draught of fish with amazement and fear. The disciples form a unique body, a community generated by obedience to the Divine Word. They must not fear. Peter recognizes that he is a sinner with absolutely nothing to offer God, but himself. Peter receives his vocation when he repents and acknowledges Jesus as Lord. The mission of preaching God's Word does not diminish when a disciple realizes that he is still a sinner. On the contrary, the message of salvation proclaims that Jesus came to redeem all people from their sins. Peter's weakness is obvious throughout the Gospels. He would have never become a rock of the Church without the saving presence of the Lord. Jesus says "Simon, Simon, behold Satan demanded to have you, that he might sift you like wheat, but I have prayed for you that your faith may not fail, and when you have turned again, strengthen your brethren" (Luke 22:31–32).

Peter and his companions on the boat of the Church were called for Jesus' plan of bringing salvation to all mankind, which had been lost since Adam's fall. Conquered by Christ, they were destined to catch men. The literal translation from the Greek is "you will be taking men alive." This nuance brought forth by Luke is even more powerful than Matthew and Mark's "fishers of men." The Greek Bible (Septuagint, LXX) uses this verb to indicate those who are saved from death in battle and remain alive (Numbers 31:15, Deuteronomy 20:16, Joshua 2:13). Jesus calls His disciples to carry the gift of eternal life, contained in the Gospel, to all corners of the world (Matthew 28:16–20).

As Jesus passed on from there, he saw a man called Matthew sitting at the tax office; and he said to him, "Follow me." And he rose and followed him. (Matthew 9:9)	And as he passed on, he saw Levi the son of Alphaeus sitting at the tax office, and he said to him, "Follow me." And he rose and followed him. (Mark 2:14)	After this he went out, and saw a tax collector, named Levi, sitting at the tax office; and he said to him, "Follow me." And he left everything, and rose and followed him. (Luke 5:27–28)

One third of the way through his Gospel, Matthew tells the story of his own call—well after that of Peter, Andrew, James, and John. In the parallel accounts of Mark and Luke, the same story is told with additional details. It is only from them that we learn that Matthew is also called Levi. Only from Mark do we learn that the name of Matthew's father is Alphaeus. Matthew never tells us his father's name, but he does tell us that there are two apostles with the name James—one is called the son of Zebedee, and the other the son of Alphaeus. Wait! Doesn't that sound familiar? Yes, just as two apostles are sons of John (Peter and Andrew) and two are sons of Zebedee (James and John), so two are sons of Alphaeus. It is quite possible that Matthew and James are brothers. If so, then fully half the apostles are pairs of brothers.

All three Synoptics describe how Jesus dined at Matthew's house that evening. Matthew leaves his fine house and everything else to observe and serve Jesus—observations that he will later incorporate into his Gospel. What a calling he received—to be not only an apostle, but also an evangelist! Just as He called His first disciples, Jesus calls us to follow Him and to share in His mission to bring the Gospel to a hurting world. People need the Lord. Some people don't even know that they are sinners, desperately in need of God's mercy. Will you share the Good News?

> The mission of Christ the Redeemer, which is entrusted to the Church, is still very far from completion. As the second millennium after Christ's coming draws to an end, an overall view of the human race shows that this mission is still only beginning and that we must commit ourselves wholeheartedly to its service. It is the Spirit who impels us to proclaim the great works of God.
>
> Pope John Paul II, *Redemptoris Missio* (March 25, 1987), 1.1.

1. Who was called in the following verses? What was their response? Matthew 4:18–20

Apostle	Invitation	Response

2. Describe the situation in John 1:40–42.

3. Who does Jesus call in these verses? What is their response? Mark 1:19–20

Apostle	Son of...	Response

4. Tell as much as you can about Jesus' call of two more apostles in John 1:43–51.

Apostle	Invitation	Response

5. Describe what you can about the sons of Alphaeus. Matthew 10:3, Mark 2:14, and Acts 1:13

6. Find as much as you can about these apostles. Matthew 10:3–4

Philip	
Bartholomew	
Thomas	
Matthew	
James	
Thaddaeus	
Simon	
Judas Iscariot	

7. Cite any biblical evidence to suggest that Levi and Matthew could be the same person.

8. What did Jesus establish with Peter? CCC 880

9. Describe the Petrine office. CCC 881

10. Who is Peter's successor? CCC 882

11. By what other name is Thaddaeus called? Luke 6:16, Acts 1:13

12. How did the apostles replace Judas Iscariot? Who replaced Judas? Acts 1:20–26

13. Write some of Peter's words recorded in the Sacred Scripture.
14. Put an asterisk in front of your favorite verse and memorize it.

Luke 5:8	
Luke 9:20	
Matthew 16:16	
Matthew 18:21	
Matthew 19:27	
Matthew 26:33	
Matthew 26:72	
Mark 9:5	
John 13:6–9	
John 13:37	
John 21:17	

15. Find as many pairs of brothers as you can among the apostles. List the verses.

16. Describe one more call from the Lord, the response, and the result. Mark 10:21–22

17. What did Jesus relate to the rich young man? Mark 10:21

18. Did Jesus intend to call you personally, or just some people? Matthew 11:28

19. What commission and promise did Jesus leave? Matthew 28:19–20

** Pray. Brainstorm as many ways of evangelizing as you can. Then, try some and share.

The Beatitudes

Matthew 5:1–12, Luke 6:20–26

Blessed are the poor in spirit, for theirs is the kingdom of God. (Matthew 5:3)

Blessed are you poor, for yours is the kingdom of God.
But woe to you that are rich, for you have received your consolation. (Luke 6:20b, 24)

Today the Church of the Beatitudes can be found on a small hill north of Tabgha, the place of the multiplication of the loaves and fishes on the northwest shore of the Sea of Galilee. Built shortly before World War II, the famous Italian architect Antonio Barluzzi designed this octagonal church with each side corresponding to one of the eight beatitudes. On the mosaic pavement you see the three theological virtues: faith, hope, and charity, and the four cardinal virtues: wisdom, justice, chastity, and fortitude. A portico surrounding the church offers a breathtaking view of the lake and its surroundings, which are so closely associated with the public ministry of Jesus. The magnificent, almost spiritual, panorama and the splendid garden with flowers and birds enhance the reflective atmosphere enabling pilgrims to meditate on the Sermon on the Mount.

An earlier Church of the Beatitudes, built by the Byzantines, is much closer to the shore along the ancient road, Via Maris. Natural springs near the intersection of roads provided a place of refreshment for travelers. Christian tradition associates three important events in Jesus' life at this place. Next to the Sermon on the Mount is the place of the multiplication of the loaves and fishes and the site where the Risen Lord appeared to the disciples and provided the miraculous draught of fish. Today pilgrims find a particular pilgrim church dedicated to each event.

Beatitudes in Matthew 5:1–12 ~ The text of the beatitudes in Matthew, in comparison to its parallel in Luke, is more coherent in its presentation. Matthew offers eight interrelated beatitudes. Luke presents four beatitudes and four contrasting woes. Matthew's solemn introduction distinguishes between the crowds, who are noticed by Jesus, and the disciples approaching Jesus. Discipleship requires drawing near to Jesus and abandoning everything else to follow Christ. Here the disciples approach Jesus to hear His teaching—the Good News. Matthew's Gospel ends with Jesus approaching the disciples and entrusting them with the great commission to spread the Good News (Matthew 28:18).

The mountain, on which the Beatitudes are proclaimed, symbolically shows that Jesus intends to communicate something of great importance. The mountains in the Gospel of Matthew highlight the most important crossroads in the life of our Lord. Jesus appears on the mountain seven times in Matthew: the mount of temptation (Matthew 4:1–11), the Beatitudes (Matthew 5:1–12), the multiplication of loaves and fishes (Matthew 15:29–39), the mount of the Transfiguration (Matthew 17:1–9), the Mount of Olives (Matthew 21:1–17; 26:36–46), the mount of Golgotha (Matthew 27:32–44) and the mount in Galilee of Jesus' farewell (Matthew 28:16–20).

Matthew emphasizes that Jesus sits and speaks with authority, *ex Cathedra*: "He opened His mouth and taught them" (Matthew 5:2). *Torah*, the Hebrew word for the first five books of the Old Testament, in Hebrew means teaching—letting God instruct the heart. Jesus is the new Moses who completes the revelation of the Old Testament (Matthew 5:17). The term "blessed," in Hebrew *"ashreh,"* is very common in the Old Testament. Psalm 1:1 begins "Blessed is the man who walks not in the counsel of the wicked nor stands in the way of sinners." In other scripture verses, people are called blessed who take refuge in God and long for peace. They care for the poor, strive for justice, and fear the Lord during their earthly existence.

The New Testament Greek *makarios* describes a joy which is undefiled, free, and unchangeable. Such joy is greater than human happiness, which may be fleeting and dependent on circumstances. Jesus' beatitudes describe a joy which transcends the suffering and sorrows of this world. Eternal joy is found in the person of Jesus and His message of the kingdom of God.

Blessed are the poor in spirit, for theirs is the kingdom of God. (Matthew 5:3)	Blessed are you poor, for yours is the kingdom of God. But woe to you that are rich, for you have received your consolation. (Luke 20b)

The first beatitude calls the poor in spirit blessed. According to two early Church Fathers, Saint Hilary and Jerome, the poor in spirit are the humble who have surrendered completely to God. One who is poor in spirit is meek and humble of heart, in contrast to the proud and arrogant. He who humbles himself is able to repent and embrace the wealth of God's kingdom. Matthew uses the Greek word *ptochos* which describes "extreme poverty" to emphasize the necessity of humility in allowing the Holy Spirit to transform the human spirit. The more the Christian renounces selfishness and materialism, the freer and richer he can become in Christ.

Jesus' radical message calls for revolutionary change. In secular terms the poor are considered unfortunate and unhappy, while the rich are seen as successful and content. Jesus offers a joy, which transcends conventional worldly wisdom. Saint Paul explains that spiritual freedom can be found in the service of others. "Jesus … did not count equality with God a thing to be grasped, but emptied himself, taking the form of a servant, being born in the likeness of men" (Philippians 2:6–7). Saint Paul also reminds us that "our Lord Jesus Christ, … though he was rich, yet for your sake he became poor, so that by his poverty you might become rich" (2 Corinthians 8:9).

The poverty in Matthew 5:3 refers not only to the sociological sense, but also encompasses a religious dimension. Depriving another of an honest wage or the means to survive is in itself a social sin. But poverty in a spiritual sense recognizes our complete dependence upon God for everything. He who is poor in spirit detaches himself from material things for the sake of spiritual gain, becoming completely attached to God and thus inheriting His kingdom.

Blessed are those who mourn, for they shall be comforted. (Matthew 5:4)	Blessed are you that weep now, for you shall laugh. Woe to you that laugh now, for you shall mourn and weep. (Luke 6:21b, 25b)

Jesus promises divine joy to mourners in this beatitude. God is near to the brokenhearted and will comfort those who mourn (Isaiah 61:1–30). In the theological sense, mourners are those who recognize their personal sins and humbly beg God's mercy. This mourning also involves an encounter with others, grieving over sin and showing empathy for the suffering of others. The Messianic reality confronts sin and offers forgiveness through Jesus' victory over Satan by His death on the cross. The Holy Spirit convicts of sin, gives comfort, and blesses those who repent. The Holy Spirit also blesses those who care for the sufferings of others.

Blessed are the meek, for they shall inherit the earth. (Matthew 5:5)	The meek shall possess the land, and delight themselves in abundant prosperity. (Psalm 37:11)	Beware of practicing your piety before men... you will have no reward from your Father in heaven (Matthew 6:1)

In Greek, the attribute *praus* (meekness) describes the self-controlled person. Meekness, the virtue that contrasts with human pride, depends on God's mercy for spiritual growth. Rabbis claim that Abraham in his later years had complete mastery over evil impulses. Numbers 12:3 states that Moses was more humble than anyone on earth. Certainly Moses had a temper, but was able to control his temper until the right time. In inviting us to come to Him with our burdens, Jesus describes His nature: "I am gentle and lowly in heart, and you will find rest for your souls" (Matthew 11:29b). The humility of Jesus attracts the hearts of others. The purpose of the Christian life is to grow in wisdom and favor with God and men (cf. Luke 2:52). To inherit the earth (Psalm 37:11) means to receive the Holy Spirit. The poor in spirit obtain meekness, attracting others to Christ. If the meek are truly blessed, they will inherit not this sinful earth, but the new heavens and new earth in the kingdom of God.

Blessed are those who hunger and thirst for righteousness, for they shall be satisfied. (Matthew 5:6)	Blessed are you that hunger now, for you shall be satisfied. Woe to you that are full, for you shall hunger. (Luke 6:21a, 25a)

The psalmist expressed religious yearning in terms of hunger and thirst: "My soul thirsts for God. ... When shall I come and behold the face of God?" (Psalm 42:2). The prophets invited people to come and find nourishment in God: "Every one who thirsts come to the waters; and he who has no money, come buy and eat" (Isaiah 55:1). Jesus says that those who feel this yearning are blessed. Hunger and thirst are impulses to preserve life. Struggling for righteousness requires more than pious desire. "Hunger and thirst for justice" not only looks to a future reality, but demands that people work for justice now. The Messianic prophecies call Yahweh our righteousness and justice (Jeremiah 23:6, Isaiah 11:1–4). Fulfilling God's will, therefore, requires finding His love despite social or political oppression. Lasting joy on earth comes to those who use their means to quench the thirst and hunger of others and strive to find the love of our Father who is in heaven. The righteous share the love and mercy of God with others. Luke seems to emphasize material deprivation. Hence, Matthew blesses a yearning soul, but Luke blesses an empty stomach. God feeds the hungry soul, but He also feeds the hungry body (Psalm 37:19, Isaiah 49:9–10).

Blessed are the merciful, for they shall obtain mercy. (Matthew 5:7)	Give to him who begs from you, and do not refuse him who would borrow from you. (Matthew 5:42)

Matthew presents a central teaching of Jesus in the fifth beatitude. Mercy is named twice as God's blessing for those who search for Him. The faithful will find in the future what they possess right now. *Mercy is the distinct quality of divine righteousness.* God's love and mercy, which will last throughout eternity, are beyond human comprehension. The Incarnation of our Lord is perhaps the most vivid illustration of God's mercy. Jesus took upon Himself our human condition—blood, sweat, and tears. Saint Irenaeus tells us that in Jesus, God gave us everything, for He gave us Himself. In Latin *"miseri-cordia"* means giving one's heart to someone poor, sad, or in misery. The Christian, in this call for divine joy, is asked to model God's behavior and show mercy to the poor. The Lord's Prayer demands that we forgive others in order to be forgiven. To be compassionate to others, even to enemies, will bring blessings because God is compassionate to us.

Blessed are the pure in heart, for they shall see God. (Matthew 5:8)	For where your treasure is, there your heart will be also. (Matthew 6:21)

Purity in common usage refers to clean clothes or unspoiled or unaltered food. Matthean spirituality here refers to Psalm 24:3–4 "Who shall ascend the hill of the Lord? And who shall stand in His holy place? He who has clean hands and a pure heart, who does not lift up his soul to what is false and does not swear deceitfully." The pure heart describes the forthright person without hidden desires and plans. Those who see their neighbors through God's eyes, rather than through their own prejudices, will be blessed. These transparent people see God in all things (1 Corinthians 15:28). Jesus praises such an attitude when He says that the children's angels always behold the face of My Father who is in heaven (Matthew 18:10). To see God requires faith achieved through abandoning one's own perspective and biases. Jesus, our example, displays purity of heart in reconciling sinful man to His Father.

Blessed are the peacemakers, for they shall be called sons of God. (Matthew 5:9)	Leave your gift there before the altar and go; first be reconciled to your brother, and then come and offer your gift. (Matthew 5:24)

Peacemakers will be called sons of God according to the seventh beatitude. Even in the revelation of the Old Testament, peace is the great gift of God to His people. *Shalom*, frequently on the lips of many people in Middle East today, originates in an intensive verb designating personal involvement and risk to bring about peace. Paul's theology identifies God as a God of peace (Romans 15:33). Jesus shed His own blood on the Cross—becoming our Prince of Peace. He brings peace, but not the romantic dream of political superiority that some people had expected. Jesus cautions, "in me you may have peace. In the world you have tribulation; but be of good cheer, I have overcome the world" (John 16:33). Jesus brings peace within oneself and peace among others in interpersonal relationships, in families, and communities.

Saint Augustine describes steadfast peace as the struggle to keep desire from conquering the mind. God blesses those who strive to create harmony with others and to achieve peace within themselves. Peace begins in baptism when we become children of God and brothers and sisters of others because we share the one Father, through Jesus Christ, our brother and Lord.

Blessed are those who are persecuted for righteousness sake, for theirs is the kingdom of heaven. Blessed are you when men revile you and persecute you and utter all kinds of evil against you on my account. Rejoice and be glad, for your reward is great in heaven. (Matthew 5:10–12)	Blessed are you when men hate you, and when they exclude you and revile you, and cast out your name as evil, on account of the Son of man! Rejoice on that day, and leap for joy, for behold, your reward is great in heaven; for so their fathers did to the prophets. … Woe to you when men speak well of you. (Luke 6:22–23, 26)

Matthew's last beatitude praises those who are persecuted for righteousness sake. God is righteous and expects His children to be righteous as well. Jesus warns His disciples that they will pay a high price in spreading the righteousness of God. Hunger for God's love and righteousness doesn't fit into the plans of the powerful of this world. So the blood of the martyrs will accompany the history of the Church until Jesus comes again in glory. However, the kingdom of God in the history of the world will survive under the sign of the Cross. Those who love God will consider it a joy to be counted worthy to suffer dishonor for the name of Jesus (Acts 5:41). The example of the first Christians proves that we must enter the kingdom of God through many tribulations (Acts 14:22).

The Beatitudes in Luke 6:20–26 ~ Luke's structure differs from that of Matthew. The first striking difference is the symbolic position of Jesus in imparting the "Magna Carta" of His teaching. Matthew presents Jesus on the mountain, while Luke places Jesus on the level place, in an inferior position, lifting up His eyes to see His disciples (Luke 6:20). Luke seems to use this device to show Jesus' solidarity with sinful mankind rather than His divine authority. Another difference concerns the beatitudes themselves. Luke presents only four beatitudes addressed to the poor, the hungry, the afflicted, and the persecuted and contrasts them with four woes. Matthew directs the beatitudes exclusively to the disciples, while the Lucan woes warn the disciples and the gathered crowd.

In the Old Testament, God gave the Ten Commandments, or Decalogue, to Moses to teach the moral code of behavior to the chosen people. In contrast, the Beatitudes provide a statement about the greatness of God's love for His people. Here, the emphasis is on what God does, not on the action of man, who fails to obey the law. The beatitudes do not require the individual to act upon a command or prohibition, but rather to adjust his own standards to those of God who is speaking to the human heart. The beatitudes are only understandable to the disciples who belong to the community of those who have left everything to follow Jesus. The apostles found their vocation in discovering the treasure of the Father's love present in His Son.

For Luke, the first beatitude and first woe speak in the present. The poor are needy in every sense of the word and deprived of their human dignity. Poverty is not intended by God as the ideal status in society. Rather, the prophets of the Old Testament see poverty as a scandal and a curse (Ezekiel 16:49, Amos 2:7). The New Testament reverses the plight of the destitute. Jesus blesses the poor, because, in spite of their destitution, God loves them. God loves the poor, not on the basis of their merit, but because of their real need. The lack of human dignity through poverty can predispose the poor to place all hope and trust in God. In contrast, the rich, in self-sufficiency and pride, may place trust in material security or self-confidence. The rich person may rely on himself rather than depend upon God. Perhaps it is easier for a poor person to turn to God for mercy and love than for a rich person, who doesn't even recognize his need for a Savior. God loves the rich and the poor alike. Jesus was comfortable in the homes of the rich and the poor and He died for all. The wise rich person will generously put his resources at the disposal of God, from whom all riches and blessings come.

The Woes of Jesus Reflect His Sorrow ~ Jesus warns the hard-hearted rich to consider the plight of the needy. That Jesus became poor for the sake of the poor should motivate us to fight the exploitation of the weak. In the synagogue of Nazareth, Jesus announces the Good News to the poor and exhorts His disciples to invite the poor to a banquet (Luke 4:18, 7:18–22, 14:21).

Recall several parables: the rich man planning to store more crops unaware that God will require his soul that night and poor Lazarus who ends up in Paradise, while the rich man lands in hell (Luke 12:15–21, 16:19–31). Jesus warns us not to trust in riches. He does not condemn those who have resources without being possessed by them. Jesus was accused of "eating with sinners" and some of those sinners were wealthy. Some disciples were rich—Joseph of Arimathea, Nicodemus, and Matthew the tax collector. Some, rich and poor, have done insufficient planning for eternal life. Jesus praises the generosity of the rich Zacchaeus as well as the poor widow.

Those who hunger now lack basic nutrition. In the Old Testament God feeds the hungry (Psalm 37:19, Isaiah 49:9–10). Jesus also feeds the hungry in the multiplication of the loaves and fishes (Luke 9:10–17). Mary's Magnificat praises God who fills the hungry with good things and sends the rich away empty (Luke 1:53). Those in this second woe (Luke 6:25), full of self and not striving for righteousness, are self-satisfied and have no concern for the needs of others. Their tragedy is that they fail to understand the greatness of God's love and never become the instruments of His providential care for the poor and needy. Self-absorption deprives them of experiencing the immense blessings of God.

The third beatitude focuses on those who are weeping now. Luke describes the widow of Naim weeping over her dead son and the family of Jairus' daughter weeping (Luke 7:13, 8:52). Jesus weeps over the city of Jerusalem (Luke 19:41–44) for missing its time of visitation. The women of Jerusalem weep over Jesus on the way to His crucifixion (Luke 23:28). Peter wept bitterly after his betrayal of Jesus (Luke 22:62). Perhaps the best example of weeping that displayed sorrow for sin is the woman who washes the feet of Jesus with her tears and wipes them with her hair (Luke 7:36–50). In the "Hail Holy Queen" prayer, Catholics say they are "mourning and weeping in this vale of tears." While we "weep" because of sin, Christian virtue and a good conscience produce the spiritual fruit of joy so that we can "Rejoice in the Lord."

Those who laugh now may be foolish (Sirach 27:13), superior over others, and self-confident. Laughter here is seen in the sense of irony. Superficial persons lacking in faith make fun of the things of God and religion. The warning to them is that they will find their assumptions to be dead wrong. Remember the newspaper headline "Even God Can't Sink the Titanic!"

Luke's fourth beatitude, longer than the others, shows people persecuted by hate, insult, and defamation. Hate will test the faith of Jesus' disciples, but they will be compensated in the kingdom of God. The disciple models his life on the Master and counts it joy to suffer for the sake of the kingdom. May we bear hardships with courage for the sake of God. May we humble ourselves and rely entirely on Divine Providence for all of our needs.

> Here Jesus pointed to the hillside sloping downwards toward the seashore and said:
> "Consider the lilies of the field, how they grow; they neither toil nor spin;
> yet I tell you, even Solomon in all his glory was not arrayed like one of these.
> But if God so clothes the grass of the field,
> which today is alive and tomorrow is thrown into the oven,
> will he not much more clothe you?
> (Matthew 6:28b–30a)

1. Read Matthew chapter 5 and write down your favorite verse.

2. Read Luke chapter 6 and write down your favorite verse.

3. Where was Jesus in the following passages?

Matthew 5:1	
Luke 6:17–20	

4. What are the Beatitudes? CCC 1716

5. What do the Beatitudes do? CCC 1717

6. Fill in the Beatitudes below.

Blessed are the poor in spirit,	for theirs is the kingdom of heaven	Matthew 5:3
Blessed are the meek for their will		Matthew 5:4
		Matthew 5:5
		Matthew 5:6
		Matthew 5:7
		Matthew 5:8
		Matthew 5:9
		Matthew 5:10

7. What can you learn from these Old Testament passages?

Psalm 2:11(12)	
Psalm 41:1–2	
Psalm 84:4–6	as the sparow a nest to settle her young
Psalm106:3	
Psalm 112:1	
Psalm 128:1	

8. Find some biblical examples of mourning for sin.

2 Samuel 12:13–17	
Luke 7:36-50	
Luke 22:60–62	

9. What is earthly peace and where can you find it? CCC 2305

10. Define meekness, using the passages below.

Psalm 37:11	
Matthew 5:5	
Matthew 11:29	

11. Compare the following verses on hunger and thirst.

Isaiah 55:1–2	
Matthew 5:6	
John 4:14	
John 6:48–51	

12. Share what you know about mercy.

Exodus 34:6–7	
Matthew 5:7	
Matthew 18:23–35	
James 2:13	

13. Explain what it means to be pure of heart from the passages below.

Psalm 24:3–6	
Psalm 73:1	
Matthew 5:8	
CCC 2518	

14. What did Jesus offer in John 14:27?

15. How should a Christian respond to trials, tribulations, and persecution? James 1:2–4

16. Compare the following blessings and woes. Luke 6:20–26. Write the verses.

Blessed are you poor, for yours is the kingdom of God. (Luke 6:20)	Woe to you rich, for you have received your consolation. (Luke 6:24)

17. According to the *Catechism*, who are the poor and lowly? CCC 544

18. Find a model and example for living the Beatitudes. CCC 520, Philippians 2:5–11

19. Why did God make you? What does Beatitude make us? CCC 1721, 2 Peter 1:4

20. If you are an American, you are richer than most of the rest of the world. What can you do practically this week to be "poor in spirit" and avoid the woes of the rich and full? Be specific.

CHAPTER 8

The Lord's Prayer
Matthew 6:9–13, Luke 11:2–4

In praying do not heap up empty phrases as the Gentiles do; for they think that they will be heard for their many words. Do not be like them, for your Father knows what you need before you ask him. (Matthew 6:7–8)

He was praying in a certain place, and when he ceased, one of his disciples said to him, "Lord, teach us to pray, as John taught his disciples. (Luke 11:1)

The most comprehensive prayer of Jesus in the Gospels is the "Our Father," also known as "The Lord's Prayer." Two evangelists, Saint Matthew and Saint Luke, recount Christ's offering of this prayer to His disciples. In Matthew, the prayer stands at the exact midpoint of the Sermon on the Mount (Matthew 6:9–13) and is part of a larger discourse on the nature of prayer. Matthew also provides the longer, more complete version of the prayer. In Luke 11:2–4, Saint Luke presents the more concise version of the "Our Father" given during Jesus' journey to Jerusalem.

Matthew depicts Jesus giving the Lord's Prayer on the mount of Beatitudes. The sanctuary of our Father on the Mount of Olives is dedicated to Jesus' prayer. Around 325 AD, when the emperor Constantine permitted Christians to freely practice their religion in the Roman Empire, his mother, Saint Helen, built three churches in the Holy Land. The basilica of Anastasis is dedicated to the Resurrection of our Lord. The basilica of the Nativity reverences the site of Jesus' birth in Bethlehem. And a third church, named Eleona, after Helen was built on the top of the Mount of Olives.

The pilgrim Egeria relates that the early Church prayed at this place following Jesus' example. Originally a grotto was at the site. Now a few remnants of Saint Helen's church, as well as additions made at the time of the Crusades remain. In the eighteenth century, Countess Aurelia de Bossi built a Carmelite monastery, where today eighty panels of the Lord's Prayer in various languages and dialects adorn the sanctuary and courtyard. Aramaic, the native tongue of Jesus, shows the language in which He bestowed this great treasure to His Church. Today the Maronite and Antiochene Christians of the Middle East and India still recite the Lord's Prayer in Aramaic, the Lord's own language.

"Pray then like this: Our Father who art in heaven, Hallowed be thy name. Thy kingdom come. Thy will be done, on earth as it is in heaven." (Matthew 6:9–10)	And he said to them, "When you pray, say: Father, hallowed be thy name. Thy kingdom come." (Luke 11:2)

Recall the beautiful words of the Psalmist: "Our God is in the heavens; he does whatever he pleases" (Psalm 115:3). One of the titles of God in the Old Testament is "God of Heaven" as in Psalm 136: "O give thanks to the God of heaven, for his steadfast love endures for ever" (v. 26). In the theological language of the day, sometimes the Jews avoided the use of the name of God by substituting the word "heaven" for "God." Hence, the "kingdom of Heaven" in the parables of Matthew is really the "kingdom of God" in the corresponding parables of Luke.

Claiming God as His Father was characteristic of Jesus' prayer and preaching. However, He did not invent this language. In the Old Testament, the Psalmist compares God to a human father: "As a father pities his children, so the Lord pities those who fear him" (Psalm 103:13). God confirms the comparison when He says, "For I am a father to Israel" (Jeremiah 31:9). Tobit's prayer of thanksgiving says, "Exalt him he is our Lord and God, he is our Father forever"(Tobit 13:4). Clearly, the prayer vocabulary of Jesus has deep roots in the Hebrew tradition.

In His own Aramaic tongue, Jesus called out to God the Father: "Abba!" This original vocabulary has survived at three places in the New Testament (Mark 14:36, Romans 8:15 and Galatians 4:6). Greek and Latin have the same word *Pater* for Father, as in Pater Noster. Only Mark preserves Jesus' own words in the agony in the garden:

And he said, "Abba, Father, all things are possible to thee; remove this cup from me; yet not what I will, but what thou wilt." (Mark 14:36)	And going a little farther he fell on his face and prayed, "My Father, if it be possible, let this cup pass from me; nevertheless, not as I will, but as thou wilt." (Matthew 26:39)	Father, if thou art willing, remove this cup from me; nevertheless not my will, but thine be done. (Luke 22:42)

See how Luke, writing for a Greek readership, retains only the Greek word for father. Mark, on the other hand, is closer to the Semitic original and gives both the Aramaic word Abba and the Greek word Father side-by-side. Mark's bilingualism was a courtesy to two sets of readers, and it is a precious window for us into the original wording of Jesus' prayer.

The New Testament develops the idea of the fatherhood of God. "See what love the Father has given us, that we should be called children of God" (1 John 3:1). Paul invites us all, male and female, to participate in the sonship of Jesus through adoption: "God has sent the Spirit of his Son into our hearts, crying 'Abba! Father!' So through God you are no longer a slave but a son, and if a son then an heir" (Galatians 4:6–7). The generation that exists within the blessed Trinity is not the way that human fathers beget children. Similarly, God is not a human king; He is the King above all kings. So also, God is not a human father; He is the Father above all fathers.

Our Father Who Art in Heaven ~ Matthew addresses the first of the seven petitions of the Lord's Prayer to God as "Our Father." Luke simply says, "Father." Addressing God by this name occurs rarely in Judaism (2 Samuel 7:14, Psalm 89:26, Isaiah 63:16, 64:8). Jesus instructs believers to call God "Father" through His example in prayer and His explicit instruction, "Pray then like this: Our Father" (Matthew 6:9). Only Jesus can provide this relationship with God the Father by becoming a human being in the Incarnation and then taking the sins of all of humanity upon Himself on our behalf. When Jesus becomes a man, He becomes our brother. By His Passion and death, He enables us to become adopted sons of our Father.

If God is our Father then we are all His sons and daughters. There is no room for selfishness or going it alone. We don't pray "my" Father, but "our" Father, indicating our mutual responsibility to one another. God knows us and loves us deeply. God loves everyone. The all-holy God desires to have a personal relationship with each of us. God also desires that His children will love one another as He loves. Jesus loved us enough to suffer and die for us. Jesus commands us to love one another in the same way, and in so doing to give glory to our Father.

"Heaven" is that sphere of bliss beyond human comprehension. God is eternal, omniscient, and omnipresent. Our knowledge of God through biblical revelation and Church Tradition is only the tip of the iceberg. God is so huge and we are so small. We don't know everything about God. But, all eternity awaits to explore the grandeur and majesty of God. "Our Father who art in heaven" indicates that God is holy and transcendent. But, He is also very personal and immanent.

Jesus warns His disciples not to babble like pagans. The Our Father shows full trust in the Providence of God. Ritual and incantations requiring the repetition of formulas to achieve some favor have no place in the community of the followers of Jesus. Superstitious faith, characterized by shallow repetition of words, does not reflect a personal relationship with the Lord.

The basic truth underlying the Lord's Prayer is acceptance of God's will. God is supreme and the Christian submits his will to the will of the Father. God loves you. He wants to give you the best and He knows what is best for you in the long run. The first part of the Lord's Prayer acknowledges God's nature and supreme goodness. The second part addresses the needs of human beings: food, forgiveness, help in temptation, and deliverance from the Evil One. This prayer brings God into the life of each Christian, and each life into the presence of God.

Hallowed Be Thy Name ~ The Christian praises God in every circumstance—an enormous privilege. Honoring God's name respects His unique character. Even people of the Old Testament understood that, despite the transcendent nature of God, He still desires to reveal Himself personally and by name to those who will trust in Him (Psalm 9:10, 20:7). God's name commands reverence. The Holy Trinity works in the Christian life, and this activity is apparent in the Our Father. God the Father, the Creator of everything, gives us our sustenance. Jesus Christ, our Savior and Redeemer, forgives our sins. The Holy Spirit strengthens us against temptations and empowers us to fight off the devil's work in our lives. The whole of your life, past, present, and future, belongs to God. Jesus teaches us to pray to our Father in love and trust.

The Lord's Prayer consists of seven petitions. The first three petitions deal with the glory of God. The next four petitions present human needs. Only after praising God, should the Christian turn to God with his own needs. This structure parallels the pattern of the Decalogue. The Ten Commandments first present three statutes about the supremacy of God, (His Person, His Name, and His Day), followed by the seven commandments for ensuring right human relationships.

Thy Kingdom Come, Thy Will Be Done ~ The kingdom is an important theme in both the preaching of John the Baptist and Jesus. Both proclaim the message: "Repent, for the kingdom of heaven is at hand!" (Matthew 3:2, 4:17). Jesus went through Galilee preaching the Gospel of the kingdom. The Sermon on the Mount has seven references to the kingdom, including the beautiful verse: "But seek first his kingdom and his righteousness, and all these things shall be yours as well" (Matthew 6:33). Jesus rejects Satan's offer of "all the kingdoms of the world" (Matthew 4:8), and instead promotes the kingdom of God. He tells Pilate "My kingship is not of this world" (John 18:36). On the last day, "the King will say to those at his right hand, 'Come, O blessed of my Father, inherit the kingdom prepared for you'" (Matthew 25:34).

The coming of God's kingdom requires obedience to God's will. The kingdom embraces heavenly and earthly realities. Since it comes in the person of Jesus, the kingdom is not only spiritual but also social and historical. We pray that the present reality reflects God's will as perfectly here as in heaven. Implementing the social justice and political ideals of God's kingdom would make life here resemble paradise. Social justice begins with individual justice. Therefore, we also pray that the kingdom of God be established and reign first in us. God's kingdom calls for total submission of the heart and will to God's will.

> Personal conversion brings about God's kingdom. Personal holiness reveals the dynamism of the kingdom of God. Mother Teresa's shining example, pouring out her life for the poor, inspired many to imitate her example and gave a glimpse of the kingdom of God to the whole world—to believers and unbelievers alike. Each Christian pushes back evil and brings about the kingdom of God by embracing the will of God and clinging to Jesus for the grace to do the Father's will.

At this point, the prayer shifts now from praise to petition. There are four kinds of prayer—adoration, intercession, contrition, and thanksgiving. Thanksgiving is a special kind of adoration, and contrition is a special kind of intercession. Hence, the four kinds of prayer boil down to two. The Lord's Prayer begins with adoration/thanksgiving and continues with intercession/contrition.

Give Us This Day Our Daily Bread ~ Bread is the basic component of human sustenance. God fed His people in the wilderness with manna (Exodus 16:15–26). When tempted, Jesus tells Satan, "man shall not live by bread alone, but by every word that proceeds from the mouth of God" (Matthew 4:4). Now Jesus prepares His disciples for an even more remarkable gift. What kind of God would feed the body but allow the soul to starve? Our deepest need is nourishment for the soul. Christians need daily food for physical survival, and the bread of God's Word and the Body of Christ for spiritual survival. So the most sublime answer that God gives to this petition in the Lord's Prayer is the gift of the Eucharist: "This is the bread which comes down from heaven, that a man may eat of it and not die" (John 6:50).

Children of the one Father in heaven praise His name and help build His kingdom on earth by sharing their bread with the hungry. Old Testament wisdom teaches us to be happy and enjoy life as long as we live (Ecclesiastes 3:12). Sharing bread with others brings joy (Acts 2:46). We pray "give us this day our daily bread." The plural demands that we share the physical and spiritual bread, God's Word and Eucharist, with the believers who are all loved by God. The Greek *epiousion*, translated as "daily," is found only here in the New Testament and emphasizes the necessity to live our lives in the present—not selfishly, but offering our lives for others.

Our Father knows what we need before we ask. Matthew stresses this truth. People do not need to tell God their needs. God already knows. We pray to confirm our trust and obedience to the Father who takes care of everything. Prayer that focuses exclusively on our needs sabotages the full dimension of faith. Christians approach God not as One who is badgered into meeting demands, but as a Father who is eager to provide everything we need. The purpose of prayer is to approach God with the desires of our hearts, and then wait to see the Father's will accomplished.

And Forgive Us Our Trespasses As We Forgive Those Who Trespass Against Us ~ The prayer now becomes probing and introspective. The Christian must recognize his own sin, which is difficult in today's culture. The biblical notion of sin includes sins of commission and omission. We do wicked things, and we fail to do the good that God calls us to do. We fail to fully become what God intends us to be. The Jews missed the mark when they rejected Jesus, preventing Israel from becoming a sign for the nations, God's plan for them throughout salvation history. The Holy Spirit empowers every single believer to become perfect—the call that God gives us. Failure to be docile to the Holy Spirit in one's interior life is called "sin."

The Greek word, *ofeilema*, means "debt." Failure to pay what is due includes neglecting to do good for others. Sins of omission may be part of the debt that those who have been given much owe to the needy. If we are forgiven by God, we owe a debt to model God in forgiving others. Jesus ben Sirach prefigures the teaching of Jesus ben Joseph. "He that takes vengeance will suffer vengeance from the Lord, and he will firmly establish his sins. Forgive your neighbor the wrong he has done, and then your sins will be pardoned when you pray. Does a man harbor anger against another, and yet seek for healing from the Lord? Does he have no mercy toward a man like himself, and yet pray for his own sins? If he himself, being flesh, maintains wrath, who will make expiation for his sins?" (Sirach 28:1–5).

Jesus takes this one step further, and there is terrifying logic when we ponder this. *The Lord's Prayer gives God permission not to forgive us unless we have forgiven others.* That billions of people pray this prayer asking *not* to be forgiven unless they have forgiven others is amazing. We all take this vow to forgive, and yet families and neighbors refuse to speak!

Compared with an all-perfect, all-holy God, every person falls short of the mark and is a sinner. The mercy of reconciliation depends upon the acknowledgment of personal sin and willingness to forgive others. God's mercy tastes sweet and it must be shared with others. Human efforts at forgiveness cannot match the graciousness of God's forgiveness in Christ. When an offense seems almost impossible to forgive (the rape or murder of a child, for example), only God's grace can enable one to forgive. The human will submits to God and trusts grace.

Jesus in Hebrew means "Savior," expressing His character in terms of mercy. Praying the Our Father fulfills God's will on earth when forgiveness is extended to others for their wrongdoing. Forgiving others is the best remedy to heal the wounded soul. The healing process of God's grace works when we forgive and heal human relationships. Forgiving others and being reconciled with God is the goal of human life. It is essential that each believer learns to forgive.

And Lead Us Not Into Temptation ~ The Greek word *peirasmos*, translated "temptation," doesn't translate easily. In this case, temptation does not mean the seduction to do evil, but rather the "testing of faith." God tested the faith of Abraham to prove his loyalty. Jesus uniquely demonstrates perfect obedience when He resists the devil in the desert and later accepts the humiliation of the Cross. Jesus accepts the test and fulfills the Father's perfect will. "God cannot be tempted with evil and He himself tempts no one" (James 1:13). The Holy Spirit doesn't want anyone to fall into sin. Pray that God will give us the grace to resist the sin of pride and enable forgiveness at all costs, thereby passing the test of faith.

We have been put on earth precisely for the purpose of being tested. Perhaps the best sense of testing comes from the words of the Lord's Prayer. We make a solemn commitment to forgive all our enemies, friends, family members, strangers, and those who have hurt and betrayed us. Then we pray: Please God; don't let me be tempted to fall into unforgiveness. Don't let me hold a grudge. Don't let me keep a record of wrongs to be hurled at another in the next verbal battle. Despite our best intentions, the effects of original sin still scar us. Our blood still boils with the primitive call to conflict and vengeance, and we human beings have no enemy greater than our own violent instincts. Deliver us, O Lord!

But Deliver Us From Evil ~ Evil is the enemy of God. Pray to avoid sin, and also invoke the grace of the Holy Spirit to be protected from the temptations of the devil. In the Old Testament Satan, the adversary, falsely accuses Job and plots evil. In the New Testament, *diabolos*, the devil, tries to thwart God's plans and ruin mankind. The devil attacks in subtle ways and poses dangers to the human soul. However, God will not allow us to be tempted beyond our strength, and He has sufficient grace for us. The Book of Revelation shows us that in the end God has the victory and Satan will be bound forever. In the context of this life, we pray that the Holy Spirit will give us the strength to resist the Evil One with resolution and determination.

The Lord's Prayer has prominence in the liturgical life of the Church. At the end of the Eucharistic Prayer, and before the communion rite, the Our Father is prayed in every Catholic Mass. The most solemn recitation of the prayer comes on Good Friday, after the proclamation of the Passion and veneration of the Cross. The Lord's Prayer also holds importance in the devotional life of the people of God. The five-decade Rosary has six recitations of the Our Father. They are given prominence by standing at the head of each decade. Six times in each Rosary, we give God permission not to forgive us unless we have forgiven one another. The world as we know it could never get enough prayers like that.

Some Christians add an ending to the Lord's Prayer that Jesus did not offer in Matthew or Luke: "For Thine is the kingdom, the power, and the glory forever." While this is a very beautiful and an inspirational addition, it was added after Jesus' Sermon on the Mount. Luke provides the shortest version of "The Lord's Prayer." The longest is in the second century document, the Didache, section 8. But, Matthew's version is the one adopted for usage by the Church.

---

1. Can you find a summary of the whole Gospel? CCC 2761

2. What can you learn from comparing the following Old Testament passages?

2 Samuel 7:14	
Psalm 89:26–27	
Psalm 103:13	
Isaiah 63:16 Isaiah 64:7–8	
Malachi 2:10	

3. What must we do before calling God "Father?" CCC 2779

4. Compare and discuss the following passages.

Matthew 5:44–48	
Matthew 11:25–27	
Mark 11:24–25	
Luke 12:30–32	
John 6:35–40	
John 17:1-6, 11–15	

5. Write and compare the Lord's Prayer from both Gospels.

Matthew 6:9–13	Luke 11:2–4

6. What does Saint Thomas Aquinas believe about the Lord's Prayer? CCC 2763

7. Who should be your model for prayer? CCC 2765

8. What can you learn about prayer from Matthew 6:5–7?

9. How should you pray? John 14:12–17

10. What is prayer? CCC 2558–2561, 2590

11. From whence does prayer come? CCC 2562

12. What is the basis of prayer in the New Covenant? CCC 2565

13. How long did Peter persevere in prayer in the garden? Matthew 26:40–41

14. Do you have a regular time and place for prayer every day? When? Where? How long?

15. Name and describe the types of prayer from the following chapters.

CCC 2626–2628	
CCC 2629–2633	
CCC 2634–2636	
CCC 2637–2638	
CCC 2639–2643	

16. Find a prerequisite of prayer in Matthew 5:23–24 and 18:21–22. *Should you act here?

17. What do these discourses of Jesus encourage you to do?

Matthew 18:23–35	
Matthew 25:31–46	
Luke 12:16–21	
Luke 13:22–30	
Luke 16:19–31	

18. Describe the eschatological dimension of the Lord's Prayer. CCC 2771

19. What can you learn from John 14:13–14, 15:7, and 16:24?

**Ask God to tell you how, where, and when to pray. If you don't have a regular prayer time, start with fifteen minutes a day. Be faithful for a full week. Report back to your group.

Monthly Social Activity

This month your small group will meet for coffee, tea, or a simple breakfast, lunch, or dessert in someone's home. Please remember to "keep it simple!"

Pray for this social event and for the host or hostess. Try, if at all possible, to attend. Offer hospitality so that one of the socials is held at your home.

Activity

Take something out of your wallet or purse.

Share with your group why this item is meaningful to you.

What does this thing tell about you?

CHAPTER 9

The Parables of Jesus

Matthew 13:1–9, 18–23; Mark 4:1–9, 11–15; Luke 8:4–8, 11–15; 15:1–32

As for what was sown on good soil, this is he who hears the word and understands it; he indeed bears fruit, and yields, in one case a hundredfold, in another sixty, and in another thirty. (Matthew 13:23)

Today even Jewish scholars agree that Jesus was the greatest parable teller of all time, leaving more than seventy parables and parabolic sayings recorded in the Bible. A few parables told by the rabbis are recorded in the Talmud, but they pale in comparison with the artistic parables of Jesus in the Gospels. The parable, an ancient Oriental literary genre, presents several comparisons eliciting an important moral conclusion. The parable's mechanism provides a comparative stimulus that triggers a crucial decision. In the parable of the Good Samaritan (Luke 10:30–37), Jesus compares the response of a Levite, a priest, and a Samaritan to a beaten man on the side of the road. Jesus triggers His listeners with the imperative: "Go and do likewise" (Luke 10:37).

The parable of the sower is unique in that, after giving the parable, Jesus provides the interpretation of the parable as well. The realistic imagery in the parable of the sower can be seen in the geography of Palestine, a diverse country with enormous contrasts. All four types of soil in the parable can be found almost everywhere in Palestine, except in the desert regions, which cover about forty percent of the country. Jesus rarely visited the desert, preferring to address His crowds near the lake of Galilee, the most fertile part of the Holy Land. Here archeologists discovered agricultural settlements originating from the Stone Age due to the favorable natural conditions. Galilean soil is extremely fertile, "a land flowing with milk and honey" (Exodus 3:8), and fits the story of seed falling on good soil and bringing an abundant harvest.

Rocks present a permanent challenge in this dry region of the Middle East. "A time to cast away stones, and a time to gather stones together" (Ecclesiastes 3:5) speaks to the work of farmers. Thorns abound, and a common shrub, called *poterum spinosa*, is believed to have been the plant used to make Jesus' crown of thorns. These thorns, which grew everywhere, plague Palestinian peasants. The "wayside" can be found in any country, and the farmer who accidentally scatters good seed on the path or the road will lose his hoped-for harvest.

The Parable of the Sower ~ In the Gospel of Matthew, chapter 13, Jesus addresses the first parable to the crowd, and follows it with three others parables concerning weeds, the mustard seed, and yeast. Jesus then continues with four parables directed specifically to the disciples. They are the parables of the treasure, the pearl of great price, the fishing net, and the new and old treasures of the householder. The parable of the sower is recorded in all three Synoptic Gospels.

While the text of the parable of the sower in Matthean and Marcan versions is longer than in Luke, the gist of the parables are the same in all three Gospels. In the Sermon on the Mount,

Jesus stood before the crowd in a position of authority. In all three Synoptics, Jesus sat in the boat, which symbolizes the Church, showing that the teaching authority of the Church "ex cathedra" comes from Christ. Here, the crowd stands on the security of solid ground at the shore, while Jesus sits in the fragile wood of the boat, tossed about by the waves of the sea. Jesus' boat, the Church, is the new ark of Noah sent by God to save humanity. Jesus speaks from the boat and offers people hope in following Him. Security comes by staying within the safe arms of Holy Mother Church.

The farmer sowing seed represents Jesus preaching the Gospel of the kingdom. The soil, in various conditions, refers to Israel's reception of the message and of the person of Jesus. The parable contrasts those who accept Jesus and those who reject Him. A peasant scattering seed is a familiar sight in any agrarian society. Even the most skillful farmer cannot prevent some seed from falling along the path, or being scattered on rocks, or cast among thorns. The birds and wind present additional hazards. The farmer strives to sow his seed into the good soil, despite the risks described.

Saint Jerome believes the diversity of soil stands for different souls. The seed is a metaphor for God's Word, sown by Him through Moses and the prophets in the Old Testament, and also of Jesus buried in the tomb, but rising on the third day. According to Saint Bede, the role of Jesus, the sower, is renewed with the help of those in the Church who will preach the Word until the final resurrection of the dead, when God will "be everything to everyone" (1 Corinthians 15:28). The listeners bear a serious responsibility, struggling with the most crucial issue of salvation—whether to embrace Jesus or not and whether to choose the victory of life over death or not.

Jesus explains that the birds eating the seed represent Satan and that the path refers to hardness of heart. Saint Albert the Great equates the quality of the soil with the disposition of one's heart. If the heart is disposed toward evil, then the word is devoured by the devil. The subsequent image of rocky ground shows the plant unable to root in the shallow soil, therefore withering when the sun rose. Jesus explains that superficial people will fall away from the Gospel during trouble or persecution.

The seed falling among thorns describes those who hear and initially accept the Word, but are later seduced by the cares of the world and the lure of wealth. These people do not sustain the growth of their faith by the nourishment of God's Word. Rather, they trust in material prosperity, which gradually takes away the hope of a spiritual harvest, and in the end they yield nothing.

Only Luke discusses lack of moisture (Luke 8:6). Isaac of Stella sees this lack of moisture as the absence of the virtues of humility and charity. In Saint Cyril of Alexandria's reflection on this passage, the hearers with hardened minds do not receive the divine seed, but become a well-trodden way for unclean spirits. Saint Bonaventure considers lack of devotion as the cause of their fall from the grace of God's Word.

A positive message emerges. The potential of seed to germinate is incredible. Seeds found by archeologists in Egyptian tombs after thousands of years of stagnation can sprout even today. Just as the earth can receive the seed, so the human heart can prepare to accept Christ. However, not everyone who hears the Good News can accept Jesus' ideal of giving everything to God.

The negative dimension of this parable is evident in the surprising number of people who refuse to embrace Jesus and His invitation to conversion. Many spectators enjoyed the miracles of Jesus, ate the bread and fish, but rejected His teachings. In announcing the kingdom of God, Jesus refused to change His approach to adapt to the mentality of the crowd. Jesus, strengthened through prayer and fasting in the desert, resisted temptation. He offers free and clear choices. With the vigor of the farmer, He casts the seed of His divine Word constantly and without discrimination. Jesus is conscious of the vital force of His message of the kingdom, knowing that death cannot destroy it.

Today, the seed of God's Word continues to be scattered. The third Luminous mystery of the Rosary invites meditation on Jesus' announcement of the kingdom of God and His invitation to conversion. The Word of God is presented at Mass, on television and radio, in books and magazines, and through retreats and renewal movements. A person may accept the invitation of God to come to know Him in a personal way and to grow deeper in Christian commitment. However, it is always a choice. God never forces; He beckons. God gave us free will; so Jesus invites us: "Come to me, all who labor and are heavy laden, and I will give you rest. Take my yoke upon you, and learn from me; for I am gentle and lowly in heart, and you will find rest for your souls" (Matthew 11:28–29).

The seed requires sacrifice, for unless the seed falls on the ground there can be no budding of new life. The Christian life also demands sacrifice. The challenge of freedom proves costly. One must die to self and relinquish self-will to take on Christ's life and accept the will of the Father. Knowing that many will reject Him, Jesus continues to proclaim the kingdom hoping that the miracle of faith will blossom in generous hearts.

Isaac of Stella sees this parable as an allegory of periods of salvation history. God, the sower, first sowed among the angels. The bad angels on the wayside turned from Him in pride. Next, in Paradise Adam proved to be rocky ground, following the serpent's lure rather than clinging to God's promise. Then God sowed through Moses to the Jewish people, whose rigid legalism hindered spiritual understanding. Finally, God sowed through Christ and the apostles to the whole world.

Pray that pride will not choke the truth of God's Word. Where and when did you experience the announcement of the kingdom of God and the invitation to conversion? Can you see yourself in the parable? Where has the seed of faith fallen in your life? Are you nurturing the Word of God in your heart and allowing God to transform you so that you can bear fruit for Him?

Parable of the Prodigal Son - Luke 15 presents three parables that are distinct from the other Synoptics: the parables of a lost sheep, a lost coin, and a lost son. Mark Twain, the American literary genius called the "Parable of the Prodigal Son," the greatest short story ever written. This parable is so familiar that the underlying themes warrant fresh consideration.

Careful reading of Luke 15 shows a dimension of the gracious mercy and tremendous love of God the Father for all of His children. The prodigal son is the sinner who exercises free will in making poor moral choices. Failing to grasp the goodness of his father, he sacrifices his place of privilege in the family to go out seeking adventure—looking for love in all the wrong places. A great famine in the land represents a hunger for God's Word. Sometimes a whole society can appear to be wasting in ignorance of God's plan. The swine represent unclean or evil spirits.

A turning point in the story comes in Luke 15:17 when the young man comes to his senses and recognizes his sin. Not only does he acknowledge his sin, but he returns to his father and confesses his sin. The need for the sacrament of Reconciliation emerges clearly here. The son acknowledges that he has sinned against heaven, *God the Father*, and against man, *his earthly father*, and he confesses rightly. He doesn't beat around the bush, make excuses, or blame his older brother or the society for misleading him. He simply comes home and humbly confesses his wrongdoing. He asks to be treated as a servant, expecting no mercy from his father.

The father shows magnificent generosity and mercy. He waits and watches for his son, longing for him to be reconciled to the family. Note the reference to "killing the fatted calf" (Luke 15:23, 27, 30) stated three times in this passage. The older son is outraged that this prized possession has been sacrificed for a wayward sinner. This foreshadows the sacrifice that God the Father will make in allowing His beloved, only begotten Son to be sacrificed for the sin of humanity. The sacrifice of Christ is hidden in the parable that He tells, foreshadowing His Passion and death. The merrymaking, music, eating, and dancing prefigure heaven, where believers will enjoy perfect harmony with God. The heavenly banquet is also prefigured in the Eucharist.

The older son represents the nation of Israel, rejecting the person of Christ and the unfolding of the kingdom of God. The Jews expected a political leader, a great and glorious king. Jesus is a great and glorious King, who chose to come as a humble servant, sacrificing Himself to redeem sinful human beings and bring them into the family of God. Both the younger and older brothers miss the goodness of their father, but the situation of the older brother is worse. The older son never calls his father *"Father."* He refers to his brother as "that son of yours!" He keeps a record of how hard he has worked for his father and what he feels he is entitled to receive in return.

> Saint Bernard of Clairvaux expands this parable into an allegory. A powerful King made man as his son, who ate of the forbidden tree and wandered far off through the world of sin. Fallen into the devil's power, he was imprisoned in Despair. The Father could not forget his son and sent Fear to bring him back, but Fear could not rouse him. Then the Father sent Hope, which raised him from the filth, and placing the son upon the horse, Longing, led him forth. Prudence and Temperance were sent by the Father to meet them, and the reins of Discretion were placed on Longing. Joined by Fortitude, the party proceeded to the camp of Wisdom, surrounded by the ditch of Humility and the wall of Obedience.
>
> Stephen Wailes, *Medieval Allegories of Jesus' Parables*

Can you see yourself in the parable of the prodigal son? Was there a time when you strayed into a far country and then came to your senses? Have you tasted the mercy of reconciliation with your loved ones and your Father in heaven? Have you been like the older brother, self-righteous, and unforgiving? This parable could be named the "Parable of the Loving Father." Have you ever reflected on God's great mercy? Have you ever been in a situation where you could imitate your merciful Father and show forgiveness to another? If you have been estranged from a family member or friend, ask God for the grace to reach out in mercy and friendship to that person. Great rejoicing in heaven can occur when we reconcile with loved ones and share God's mercy.

1. Explain the parable of the sower and give the verses? Matthew 13:1–9, 18–23

The sower	*Matthew 13:3*	Jesus is tell up a lot
The seed		is just like us. if we don't have good heart
Seed snatched away		anytime come other thorns. I fell apart
Rocky ground	*is*	when we all week.
Thorns		when we don't open all ears.
Good soil		when we strong in the Lord

2. Describe one practical way of preparing good soil for nurturing God's Word in your life.

3. Use the *Catechism of the Catholic Church* to learn more about parables. CCC 546

4. Name the parables found in Matthew 13:44–46 and tell what they mean to you.

5. Compare the parable in the following passages and give the moral of the parable.

Matthew 13:31–32	We lesson to are Lord. We grow as mustard seed.
Mark 4:30–32	its all about growing. and be strong.
Luke 13:18–19	is when we planted in are heard, an grow with it
Moral	that means tha is nobary Can pul you away.

6. What is the moral of the parable found in Matthew 18:22–35?

forgive and as many Times, it needs.

7. State a practical application for your life from the above parable.

to open my ears. and my heart.

8. What is the meaning of the parable of the two sons in Matthew 21:28–30?

that means do to your wrathe wat Jesus does to you

9. What interpretation of the parable does Jesus give in Matthew 21:30–32?

be prepary to forgive. at all Times and dont look back

10. Compare an Old Testament prefigurement of a parable recounted by all Synoptics.

Isaiah 5:1–7	*its when we pray we dont get wat we wont is because we nat zeal*
Matthew 21:33–46	*its all about. turned your eyes to God*
Mark 12:1–12	*we need to a behold your*
Luke 20:9–19	*God and ledon.*

11. Jesus agrees with His listeners' interpretation of the parable and quotes a psalm. What is it?

Psalm 118:22–23	

12. Compare the parables of the wedding in Matthew 22:1–14 and Luke 14:16–24.

Matthew 22:1–14	*when God invit us be aleat on goi*
Luke 14:16–24	*? mor...*

13. What is the meaning of "no wedding garment" in Matthew 22:11? Matthew 25:34–40.

not dressed ?

14. Explain the moral of the parable in Matthew 25:1–13.

about 10 Virgins 5. good 5. foolish

15. Luke records a parable of a rich fool (Luke 12:16–21). Can you make a practical application?

yes when we have a lot we want more we should shair with oders

16. Read the parable of the prodigal son in Luke 15:11–32. Use your imagination to describe the possible attitudes and reactions of the characters in the story.

Father	
Younger son	*realy to me*
Older son	
Servants	
The boys' mother	

17. With which of the three primary characters above can you most closely identify?

18. What restores intimate friendship with the Father? CCC 1468

19. What remarkable sign did Jesus demonstrate to show God's forgiveness? CCC 1443

20. Grace is needed to avoid sin and grow in virtue. What do you do when you sin? CCC 1700

Chapter 10

The Miracles of Jesus

Matthew 8:28–34, Mark 5:1–20, Luke 8:26–39

**Go home to your friends,
and tell them how much the Lord has done for you,
and how he has had mercy on you.** (Mark 5:19)

Jesus heals people. He gives blind people the gift of sight, provides hearing for the deaf and speech for the mute. Jesus cures the crippled and paralyzed. He cures leprosy, the most dreaded disease of the time. Jesus delivers those bound by evil spirits. These amazing events astound the people around Him, who recognize that such powers of healing can only come from God.

In a physical miracle, the laws of physics that govern our universe are suspended by divine intervention. In a moral miracle, the grace of God frees the human soul of constraints to obtain spiritual wellness. Jesus worked physical miracles, such as healing, for the sake of moral miracles, such as forgiveness (Matthew 9:6). Exorcism of demons reveals a moral miracle, wherein supernatural goodness expels the influence of preternatural evil. The battle between good and evil is clear in such an encounter.

The healing of the demoniac provides one of the most intriguing miracles of Jesus and elicits many questions. Was the demoniac mentally ill, as well as possessed by evil spirits? Was it necessary to destroy a herd of two thousand swine to heal one man? Some questions are unanswerable because only God knows, for sure, why He chooses to work a miracle. But there is no question that the healing of the demoniac confirms Jesus' authority as the Son of God, as He overpowers the forces of evil.

The three Synoptic Gospels narrate Jesus expelling a legion of demons after Jesus' miracle of the quieting of the storm. Jesus works one miracle on His way to working another miracle—He stills the sea so that He can cross over to heal a troubled human being on the other side. Mark and Luke continue their narrative with the healing of Jairus' daughter and the woman with the hemorrhage (Mark 5:21–43, Luke 8:40–56). Matthew follows with the healing of the paralytic (Matthew 9:1–8).

Gadara and Gerasa were two of the towns making up the Decapolis (the ten cities). Nine cities lay to the east across the Jordan River. Matthew refers to Gadara, the capital city of the Decapolis, which is located south of the sea of Galilee. Mark and Luke refer to Gergesa, about 35 miles further south on the east side of the Jordan.

Archeologists recently discovered the Byzantine basilica of Kursi, where this miracle took place at the eastern shore of the lake of Galilee in Gentile territory. Here once stood a large monastery surrounded by walls with Greek inscriptions dating to the first century, and a mosaic floor depicting fruits, vegetables, birds, and even oranges and bananas, which were not thought to be

in wide use during this period. It also contained mosaics of swine, which were later obliterated by the iconoclasts. The monastery included a large basilica with atrium, baptistery, well, and oil press. Public buildings, private homes, agricultural and fishing facilities, and guesthouses for pilgrims were all crowded within the enclosure. Probably the monastery functioned as a catechetical center attracting many visitors. When Muslims arrived in the Holy Land in the seventh century, the monastery was abandoned. Until 1967 a Syrian military position stood on this place, where the Talmud reports there once stood a pagan temple of Nebo for star worship. Today, on the cliff above the lake, a chapel has been built in the grotto where the possessed man once lived.

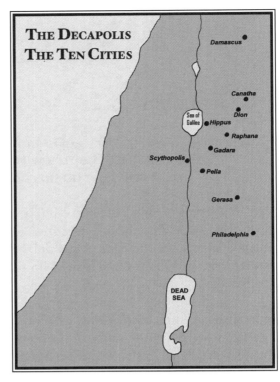

The geography of this miracle augments the theological significance. During the time of Jesus, Greek speaking Gentiles and Hellenistic apostate Jews inhabited the territory of the Decapolis. Observant Jews did not keep swine. So the presence of swine, as in the land to which the prodigal son traveled, signifies ritual uncleanness and unholiness. A good Jew, therefore, might see this as a demonic area.

Prior to the freeing of the demoniac, in the miracle of the storm at sea, Jesus slept in the boat, prefiguring His death and burial. Waking from sleep, as passing from death to life, Jesus took up His role of Savior. Our Lord has control over the powers of light and darkness. When He enters the region of the demons and engages the unfortunate outcast who dwells apart from human beings on the mountains and in the tombs, the chaos and suffering created by sin and evil yields to the power of the divine Word. The demons are subject to Jesus' divine power and the possessed man is freed from the power of darkness and made whole. Thanks to Jesus, the man receives new life, just as every human being who encounters the love of Jesus can be freed from sin and experience new life.

Mark describes the violent nature of the demoniac's behavior and the use of chains as an unsuccessful means to control this man. Luke reveals that he had worn no clothes for a long time. Matthew speaks of two demoniacs (Matthew 8:28); so perhaps there are two similar miracles.

> Though Luke and those who follow him say it was one person, but this evangelist two, that does not exhibit any discrepancy at all. I grant that if they had said, there was only one, and no other, they would appear to disagree with Matthew, but if that spoke of the one, this of the two, the statement comes not of disagreement, but of a different manner of narration. That is, I for my part think, Luke singled out the fiercest one of them for his narrative, wherefore also the more tragic.
>
> Saint John Chrysostom (344–407 AD), *Homilies on the Gospel of Matthew*, 28.

Mark provides theological insight when he reports that, as soon as the demoniac saw Jesus, he "ran and worshiped him." Luke's account indicates that the possessed man cried out and fell down before Jesus. Clearly the local community had tried unsuccessfully to restrain this unfortunate man. Taking the three Gospel accounts together, a picture emerges of a naked, homeless, violent man—a danger to himself and others. This tormented man is exactly the kind of person Jesus came to earth to find and save. Because the demons have control of this man's actions, his true personality is disguised and only becomes evident after the exorcism when he sits clothed and in his right mind. Jesus transforms this man from being tormented by demons to being himself. Only after Jesus heals him, do we see the real man.

In Luke's account, Jesus enters into dialogue with the demoniac. In Mark the demons arrogantly beg Jesus not to send them out of the country, while in Luke they beg Him not to command them to depart into the abyss. All three Synoptics agree that the demons begged to be sent into the swine. Matthew and Mark use the sharp imperative verb *aposteilon*, meaning to "send" (Matthew 8:31, Mark 5:10). Thus the same word that Jesus uses to send the apostles out to preach the good news, the demons use to beg Jesus to send them into the swine.

Mark divulges the number of two thousand swine in the herd, making it a very large and prosperous income potential for the owners. Mark's use of the verb *theoreo* meaning to "view attentively" suggests that the onlookers scrupulously and critically assess this miracle (Mark 5:15, 38). Luke shows the healed man sitting humbly at the feet of Jesus. After this astounding event and the loss of revenue, the people implore Jesus to depart from their neighborhood. The healed man begs Jesus to be allowed to go with Him. But, Jesus refuses and directs the man to go home to his friends and tell them how much mercy God has shown him. Luke adds that all men marveled at this miracle of Jesus.

Jesus interacts with all of the characters in this drama: the possessed man, the demons, the townspeople, and the cleansed man. During this first missionary journey of Jesus, He demonstrates compassion, eagerly bringing the message of new life to people living in spiritual death brought on by Adam's sin. Jesus arrives in a boat, which is the image of the Church. The first person to encounter Jesus, the man possessed by the demons, is the image of spiritual death.

Did this possessed man suffer from a mental illness? The Gospel writers attest to his possession by an unclean spirit and describe his antisocial behavior. Jesus has power over both illness and evil. Without Jesus, every human soul is subject to the forces of darkness. Jesus asks, "What is your name?" and hears, "My name is Legion; for we are many" (Mark 5:9). A Roman legion, about 6,000 soldiers was a common sight in this territory. This vast number shows how the presence of evil can multiply in the human soul. The devil tries to obliterate the image of God in the person who chooses evil, attempting to reduce man to the status of an animal. In spite of interior suffering, people constantly hunger for God, and the devil cannot completely obliterate man's longing for the Author of life. The tortured man spotted Jesus from afar and worshiped Him. The authority of Jesus' word controls the violent impact of evil inside the human being.

Demons recognize Jesus and His unique relationship to God. Their knowledge goes beyond the realm of this world to the spiritual sphere beyond human recognition. Despite certain privileges in understanding the supernatural and their claim for separation from Jesus ("What have you to do with us, O Son of God?" [Matthew 8:29]), it is Jesus who demonstrates complete power

and authority over evil spirits. The mere presence of Jesus demonstrates His victory over evil. Jesus has power not only to cast out the unclean spirits, but also to heal the suffering man. Jesus came to defeat the whole power of sin and evil. Jesus exposes the darkness, and then, makes men whole.

Jesus puts the demons in a humiliating position. The legion, cast into the sea, can no longer torment the inhabitants of the countryside, which Jesus purifies. According to Book of Hebrews, Jesus "partook of our nature, that through death, He might destroy him who has the power of death, that is, the devil, and deliver all those who through fear of death were subject to lifelong bondage" (2:14–15). The image of the swine focuses attention on the issue of cleanliness. The Old Testament classifies the pig as an unclean animal, forbidden to be eaten (Leviticus 11:7–8, Deuteronomy 14:8). The drama of the situation unfolds in that the unclean spirits ask to be sent into unclean animals. The swine drown in the sea. There will be no sea in the heavenly Jerusalem for no evil will dwell there (Revelation 21:1). The accusation that Jesus casts out demons by the prince of demons (Mark 3:22) proves totally illogical.

The image of the swine drowned in the sea may recall the forces of evil represented by pharaoh and his army drowning while in pursuit of Moses and the children of God. The evil spirits of slavery and darkness could not stop the march of the Jewish people to freedom (Exodus 14:21ff). The boat, the image of the Church, safely carries Jesus and the apostles to the opposite shore, where Jesus multiplies the bread (Mark 6:32–44), reminiscent of the manna in the desert (Exodus 16:13–15). Likewise, the gift of the Eucharist enables the faithful Christian to strive and win the struggle against evil.

Jesus cleanses the area not only of unclean animals, but also of evil spirits and the fear of spiritual death. The kingdom of God is established by eliminating the forces of evil, rendering both the people and the place purified. The herdsmen flee the scene to report the miracle—a reaction quite different from the shepherds in Bethlehem who responded to the news of the birth of Jesus by going to Him (Luke 2:8ff)! Following their initial curiosity and amazement at the healing of the demoniac, the herdsmen begin to fear. However, the onlookers' fear differs from the fear of Virgin Mary (Luke 1:30), the shepherds (Luke 2:9), or even the disciples (Mark 4:41, 9:6). Human greed, the love of profit from unclean motives, prevents them from recognizing the kingdom of God and the gift of eternal life arriving in the person of Jesus in their very midst. Sadly, fearing loss of income, the townspeople request that Jesus, the Worker of miracles and Lord of life, depart from them.

The high priests of the temple in Jerusalem displayed a similar reaction, for they valued the profit coming from the money changers more than the life of Jesus, who troubled them by His prophetic appearance on Palm Sunday. The request of the Gerasenes foreshadows the nearness of the Cross. There is no room for God in self-satisfied hearts. Hunger for material prosperity can block the way to understanding the compassion and mercy of our Lord. In the prophetic gesture of the drowned swine, the people focused on their own interests preferring to stay their own course, rather than changing after encountering Christ, who alone provides eternal life.

> For when the inhabitants of that country, after having received such benefits, were driving Him away, He resisted not, but retired, and left those who had shown themselves unworthy of His teaching, having given themselves for teachers them that had been freed from the demons, and the swine-herds, that they might of them learn all that had happened; whilst Himself retiring leaves the fear vigorous in them. ... From many quarters were wafted sounds, proclaiming the strangeness of the miracle; from the cured, and from the drowned, from the owners of the swine, from the men that were feeding them.
>
> Saint John Chrysostom (344–407 AD) *Homilies on the Gospel of Matthew*, 28

The first mission of Jesus in the Gentile territory is not a complete failure. There was at least one convert to the Kingdom of God. The Gerasene ex-demoniac believes in Jesus and follows Him in obedience. Jesus commissions this first Gentile disciple to return to his people to proclaim the action of the Lord and His mercy. The cleansed man has already been liberated from the power of Satan. When the healed man acts according to the wish of Jesus and proclaims to his people the miracle of God's grace in his life, the fear of the people turns to awe and wonder. The door remains open for conversion, but the time to accept Jesus as the Son of God will wait until His death and Resurrection.

When Jesus expels demons, He demonstrates His power over evil. The Church continues the work of Jesus in driving evil out of human hearts. When people start to compromise with evil, they invite darkness into their hearts and homes. God has placed an instinct to repudiate evil in the human heart called "conscience." Remember your baptismal promises repeated each Easter: "Do you reject Satan, and all his works and all his empty promises? I do!"

Jesus worked many miracles and He still works miracles today. Jesus casts out demons and transforms lives to give glory to God the Father. Christians anchor their faith in the certainty that Jesus has won the victory over Satan, which becomes completely ours at the end of time. But, for now, Satan prowls about tempting and hassling us. Believers fight demonic forces, but never alone. Jesus assists in the struggles with darkness, discouragement, temptation, and evil. Jesus gives His Word and sacraments to sustain us. Saint James exhorts us: "Submit yourselves therefore to God. Resist the devil and he will flee from you. Draw near to God and he will draw near to you" (James 4:7–8)

1. How does Jesus demonstrate His divine sovereignty? CCC 447

2. Describe the only Old Testament reference to freeing a person from evil spirits. Tobit 6:7–8:18

3. Describe the sequence of events in the following verses.

Matthew 8:28–29	
Matthew 8:30–32	
Matthew 8:33–34	

4. In your own words, describe the events in these passages.

Mark 5:1–5	
Mark 5:6–13	
Mark 5:14–17	
Mark 5:18–29	
Mark 5:20	

5. Can you recall a time when you wanted to do something and God asked you to do something else?

6. What specific information does Saint Luke offer concerning this story in Luke 8:26–39?

7. What do Jesus' exorcisms demonstrate? CCC 550

8. Name the miracles reported in the following Synoptic accounts.

	Matthew 8:14–15	Mark 1:29–31	Luke 4:38–39
	Matthew 8:1–4	Mark 1:40–45	Luke 5:12–16
	Matthew 9:1–8	Mark 2:1–12	Luke 5:17–26
	Matthew 12:9–14	Mark 3:1–6	Luke 6:6–11
	Matthew 9:27–31	Mark 10:46–52	Luke 18:35–43
	Matthew 9:32–34	Mark 3:22	Luke 11:14–15

9. Describe different responses to the miracles of Jesus.

Mark 3:6, 22	
John 11:45	
Matthew 9:33	
Luke 17:11–19	

10. Has anyone ever witnessed to you a miraculous, life-transforming event? Explain briefly.

11. How many healing miracles do you think Jesus performed?

Matthew 12:15–16	
Mark 3:7–10	
Luke 6:17–19	

12. Please describe the one miracle of Jesus reported only by Luke. Luke 7:11–17

13. What does Jesus show in the miracle described in Matthew 8:23–27?

14. How do evil spirits respond to Jesus? Mark 3:11–12

15. In what unexpected place did Jesus encounter a demoniac? Mark 1:21–28

16. How did Jesus deliver people from demons or unclean spirits? Luke 4:33–37

17. What caution does Jesus give concerning deliverance from evil spirits? Matthew 12:43–45

18. What happens to the person who allows evil to return and dwell with him? Luke 11:24–26

19. What do the apostles reveal about the devil in the following passages?

Romans 16:19–20	
2 Corinthians 11:14	
James 4:7–8	
1 Peter 5:7–10	

**Jesus asked the Gerasene ex-demoniac to go to his friends, "and tell them how much the Lord has done for you, and how He has had mercy on you" (Mark 5:19). Write a few sentences explaining what the Lord has done for you in your life and how He has shown His mercy to you.

CHAPTER 11

Multiplication of the Loaves and Fishes

Matthew 14:13–21, 15:32–39; Mark 6:31–44, 8:1–10; Luke 9:10–17; John 6:1–13

Then he ordered the crowds to sit down on the grass; and taking the five loaves and the two fish he looked up to heaven, and blessed, and broke and gave the loaves to the disciples, and the disciples gave to the crowds. And they all ate and were satisfied. And they took up twelve baskets full of the broken pieces left over. (Matthew 14:19–20)

Miracles are events that transcend natural causes to such a degree that they can be explained only as the intervention of God. Miracles prove that our religious faith is reasonable. Jesus worked miracles. He walked on water, quieted the storm at sea, cured the blind and the lame, fed thousands by multiplying food, and raised the dead to life. Although the miracles in the Gospels are visible signs of God's power and love for His people, they never function as the primary purpose of the life and mission of Jesus. Each miracle points to a deeper spiritual reality that Jesus wants to teach.

The greatest miracle of Jesus, indeed the greatest event in all of history, is the victory of the Crucified One over sin and death, evidenced by the empty tomb. Jesus prepared His disciples for that profound miracle by raising Lazarus from the dead, which only John records (John 11:1–44). However, all of the Gospel writers recount the miraculous multiplication of the loaves and fishes. Matthew and Mark witness to two such miracles, one in the territory of Israel and another later in the land of the Gentiles, showing the deeper spiritual reality of Jesus' gift of the Eucharist for all believers.

Matthew provides the most straightforward description of the blessing and breaking of the bread, and the distribution to the people. In Mark, Jesus preaches before the miracle; in John, Jesus preaches after the miracle. No doubt both evangelists are correct. Jesus prepared the people for the miracle in some way, and, afterwards, explained it to them in a way that they could best understand this amazing spiritual gift and theological truth.

The site of the first miracle of the multiplication of loaves and fishes is the same as that of the Sermon on the Mount and the third apparition of Jesus to the disciples after the Resurrection. Here two commercial roads meet at the northwest side of the lake of Galilee at a site called *Heptapegon*, which Arabs later named Tabgha. The first Christian shrine in Galilee commemorating the feeding of the five thousand was built at the end of the fourth century along one of these roads, the Via Maris. Later, in the fifth century, Martyrios, the Patriarch of Jerusalem, who had been a monk in Egypt, commissioned a new church with three naves in the form of a cross on this site.

Some of the most beautiful mosaics in Palestine survive from antiquity in this church. In the southern part of the presbytery, a mosaic depicts life on the Nile river, including the Nilometer, a round tower with Greek letters to measure the level of the water, together with the flora and fauna of Egypt, as well as of Galilee. In biblical times, people thought the Nile was connected to the lake of Galilee. In the north transept of this church, a similar motif is enriched with Christian symbolism. The pelican, a symbol of Christ, fights a snake, the symbol of Satan. Scenes of birds, representing souls desiring to meet God, adorn the north colonnade, along with the irax, the symbol of fleshly desires. In the sixth century, a mosaic with two fishes and the Greek acronym *ichtys*, meaning "Jesus Christ, Son of God, Savior," and the basket of five loaves of bread with crosses was added under the altar in front of a protruding rock on which it is believed that Jesus performed this miracle. This sanctuary was abandoned after the arrival of Muslims in the seventh century, but today the German Benedictines care for it.

Jesus withdrew to a lonely place to pray after learning of the death of his kinsman and precursor, John the Baptist. Luke reveals that the place was Bethsaida (Luke 9:10). Mark shows the compassion of Jesus who sees the multitude as sheep without a shepherd. Mark shows Jesus teaching, while Luke focuses on Jesus healing the sick. Mark and John estimate the cost of bread at two hundred denarii. Only John suggests that Jesus was testing His disciples for He knew what He would do (John 6:6).

According to the synoptic Gospels, Jesus challenges the disciples, "you give them something to eat" (Matthew 14:16, Mark 6:37, Luke 9:13). Only Mark recalls the naive question of the disciples: "Shall we go and buy two hundred denarii worth of bread?" In Mark 6:38, Jesus asks, "How many loaves have you?" Luke and John share the same concern that the people are too numerous to be fed. Matthew and Mark estimate the crowd to be about five thousand. Remember that only adult men were counted in biblical times, so considering women and children, the number would be vast!

The Bread ~ Bread is the staff of life, as the saying goes. Not all regions of the world use bread—the Far East prefers rice—but the Holy Land is right next to the breadbasket of the ancient world. Egypt provided most of the wheat needed by the Roman world, and a very nutritious durum wheat grew there. To this day, in the absence of forks, the Arabs and Indians use bread as an indispensable part of their meal, taking the bread first and using it to grasp other foods. The Holy Land is definitely bread country. Remember that Bethlehem means "the house of bread."

Different kinds of bread were used in the area. The upper classes ate the finer wheat bread every day, while the poor commonly consumed the humble barley bread. John specifies that the loaves, which Jesus multiplied, were made of barley. Bread played an important role in the liturgical life of the Old Testament. The temple ritual involved the use of "showbread" which was conveyed on special, long spatulas. When the Romans destroyed the temple in 70 AD, they took the showbread equipment to Rome as part of the spoils of war. In the domestic rituals of the Jews, bread also was significant. For the eight-day period leading to Passover, they were allowed to eat only unleavened bread, called matzo. The last day of the festival was called "The Feast of Unleavened Bread."

When Jesus gathered His disciples for the Last Supper, He gave them unleavened bread, important in the Passover ritual, and said, "This is my body" (Matthew 26:26, Mark 14:22, Luke 22:19). Catholics may wonder why Communion bread is an unleavened host, rather than ordinary bread. Remember that the special ritual bread from the Passover was adopted for our

Eucharistic celebrations, following the example and instruction of Jesus. After the miracle of the multiplication of loaves, John adds a theological explanation in the "Bread of Life discourse" (John 6). In that sermon, Jesus explains, "I am the Bread of Life." This is a metaphoric use of the term bread. The Eucharist is not a metaphor, however. Jesus uses bread in general as a symbol of Himself, but He takes one specific loaf and says, "This is my body." In that case, symbol becomes reality.

Saint Augustine sees the five loaves of bread as the Torah, the first five books of the Bible, which nurtures those who depend on every word which comes from the mouth of God (Deuteronomy 8:3). Two fish symbolize Christ giving two commandments—love God and love of neighbor. Venerable Bede adds an interesting moral application for us. By blessing the loaves, Jesus teaches us to bless our daily bread. Like the poor barley loaves and little fish, we can offer our poor human qualities to Jesus, who can bless and transform the gift of ourselves for service to others. Moral strength comes from fellowship with Jesus who offers us healing power in the frequent reception of the Eucharist.

The Fish ~ The fish of this miracle may have been sardines, the most frequently found fish in the waters of the lake of Galilee. If the Holy Land is bread country, Galilee is fish country. People in that part of the world do not consume much red meat. Their cattle were more for milk than for meat; their sheep were more for wool than for mutton. When a prophet slaughtered his oxen during a famine, it was an act of desperation. He was eating his farm equipment and would no longer be able to farm. With the salty Mediterranean ocean on one side and the fresh-water sea of Galilee on the other, the Galileans ate a lot of fish. They made a fish paste to scoop up with bread, which constituted their most important protein source. Jesus and His apostles were very familiar with fish. After all, Jesus called at least four of His twelve apostles out of fishing boats.

The book of Tobit contained a miracle involving the use of fish. Archangel Raphael instructed Tobias to rub the eyes of his blind father with fish gall and Tobit was healed (Tobit 11:8). Fish is thus a symbol of healing and salvation as well as nourishment. In the Catacombs, the early Christians used the fish symbol to stand for Christ. This symbol may have been a secret code during periods of severe persecution.

The theological message of this miracle reveals the person of Jesus as the Messiah who has power from God to feed the hungry. Jesus is greater than Moses, who provided manna in the desert (Exodus 16:13–21) or Elisha (2 Kings 4:42–44) who prefigured Him. Jesus comes as Wisdom, offering His own flesh and blood as real food and drink, yet He remains the rejected Messiah. This miracle prefigures the institution of the Eucharist, which Jesus establishes during His Last Supper and continues to provide to the present day (1 Corinthians 11:23). Behind the symbols of bread and fish is Jesus Himself. As seed falls to the earth to die and sprout again, Jesus will bring new life (John 12:24). The Passion and Resurrection of the Lord, and the Eucharist are keys to the interpretation of this miracle.

Observe three distinct scenes of this miracle. First, Jesus, filled with compassion, teaches the crowds and heals the sick. Then, the disciples act without compassion, but rather with pragmatism, intending to dismiss the crowds and get rid of a difficult situation. Finally Jesus unites the two groups, His disciples and the hungry crowd, by blessing the bread and satisfying all. In this anticipation of the institution of the Eucharist at the Last Supper, the bread represents the body of Jesus offered for the well-being of the Church as well as the vocation of priests who consecrate the Eucharist for the People of God.

The second multiplication of loaves and fishes occurs in Matthew 15:32–39 and Mark 8:1–10. Jesus' sojourn at the lake of Galilee is interrupted by His withdrawal to the region of Tyre and Sidon in Phoenicia. On His return He traveled through the region of Decapolis—Ten Cities (see map on page 92) where He fed four thousand hungry people. Both Matthew and Mark record this miracle. The description of this miracle is shorter than the previous miracle. Here, the disciples express their amazement, but do not attempt to turn the people away. No preliminary activity of teaching or healing is recorded here. In this miracle there are seven loaves and a few small fish of undetermined number.

Whereas, in the previous miracle, twelve baskets (*kofinos*) of leftovers were collected, here there are seven baskets (*spyris*). The term *spyris* may designate a larger basket. Some interpreters associate the number twelve in the first miracle with the twelve apostles, and the number seven in the second miracle with the seven deacons who will continue the ministry of Jesus. In the Semitic world, both numbers, 12 and 7, are perfect numerals revealing the perfect sacrifice of Jesus expressed in the Eucharist. The size of the crowds differs in these miracles, where an estimated four thousand hungry people gather in the Gentile region. The exact number of people is not significant since, according to Saint Augustine, the whole of humanity is called to become the family of God in the Eucharist.

The theological message of this miracle parallels the meaning of the first multiplication of loaves and fishes. After the successful missionary journey to the Gentile territory (Matthew 15:29), Jesus goes to the mountain and gathers around Himself the church, which Origen sees as expanding through the proclamation of the Word of God. Jesus' teaching attracts passionate hearers who follow Him for three days without eating. In their faith, they are convinced that even the dogs will be able to eat the crumbs that fall from their master's table (Matthew 15:27). Witnessing the miracles of Jesus, the Gentiles, as well as the Jews, saw the mute speak and the lame walk, and they glorified God (Matthew 9:8, 14:33). The kingdom of God spreads by Jesus' authority. Signs and wonders abound.

Despite human sin, Jesus transforms people. His compassion attracts us to the Eucharist, not once or twice, but always. Participation in the Eucharist becomes the thrust of Jesus' kingdom, the goal of life in this world, and for all eternity. Elijah, strengthened by the bread offered to him by the angel, walked forty days and forty nights all the way to the mountain of God's revelation (1 Kings 19:8).

Each time we approach Jesus in the Eucharist, we show our faith in His divine Word. Some, however, are like the disciples, who, despite the repetition of the miracle, don't understand and doubt. They fail to recognize Jesus after the Resurrection on the way to Emmaus, but their eyes are finally opened in the breaking of the bread (Luke 24:30–31). We need continuous interior reform and purification on our personal journey to the heavenly Jerusalem. Paul insists that those who eat without discerning the body of Christ are weak and ill, and some already have died (1 Corinthians 11:29–30). Fortunately, the Lord is compassionate and merciful, always eager to instruct us with His Word and to strengthen us with His Body. The Church for its part offers us the sacrament of Reconciliation to purify us to receive the Eucharist worthily after the Word of God has nurtured our souls.

1. What is a miracle and what is its purpose? CCC 156

2. Who requested Jesus to perform His first miracle? What was the response? John 2:1–11

3. What do the miracles at Cana and the multiplication of loaves signify? CCC 1335

4. Can you identify some miracles from the Old Testament?

Exodus 14:21–30	
Exodus 16:15–17	
1 Kings 17:8–16	
1 Kings 17:17–24	
1 Kings 19:4–8	
2 Kings 4:14–37	

5. What did Jesus' life signify? What do Jesus' miracles reveal? CCC 515

6. What would you say to someone who doesn't believe in miracles?

7. Find the prerequisite of a miracle in the following passages.

Matthew 6:33	
Mark 9:23–24	
Luke 1:45	
Luke 5:12–13	

8. List the progression of events from the following passages.

Mark 6:34	
Mark 6:35–36	
Mark 6:37	
Mark 6:38	
Mark 6:39–40	
Mark 6:41	
Mark 6:42	
Mark 6:43	

9. How can you most accurately estimate how many people were fed by Jesus? Matthew 14:21

10. How many people did Jesus feed in His next multiplication of food? Matthew 15:32–38

11. What additional information does Luke provide in his account? Luke 9:10–17

12. Although each Synoptic offers different perspectives are there any contradictions?

13. Which apostles are mentioned in John's account? John 6:1–13

14. Compare the responses of the people in the following passages.

Matthew 14:20	
Matthew 15:37	
Mark 6:42	
Mark 8:8	
Luke 9:17	
John 6:11–14	

15. Why did some of the people follow Jesus? John 6:26

16. How does Jesus expound on the manna in the desert? John 6:31–32

17. Following the miracle, list some of the things Jesus said further in John 6.

John 6:35	
John 6:51	
John 6:53	
John 6:54	

18. How did some of the disciples react following Jesus' discourse? John 6:66

19. Had you been present at the miracle, how do you think you would have reacted?

20. Has there been a time in your life when you had a specific need and God miraculously met it?

Monthly Social Activity

This month your small group will meet for coffee, tea, or a simple breakfast, lunch, or dessert in someone's home. Please remember to "keep it simple!"

Pray for this social event and for the host or hostess. Try, if at all possible, to attend. Offer hospitality so that one of the socials is held at your home.

Activity

When you were in school, in what areas did you do well?

What is your fondest memory of your school years?

Share the funniest thing you recall from your childhood.

Peter's Profession of Faith

Matthew 16:13–20, Mark 8:27–33, Luke 9:18–22

**You are Peter, and on this rock I will build my Church,
and the powers of death shall not prevail against it.** (Matthew 16:18)

The apostles have met the Lord, answered His call, heard His message, seen His miracles, and consumed miraculous food. Now our Lord presents a test. What conclusions will they draw from these privileged experiences? Whom do they think they are following, anyway?

Now when Jesus came into the district of Caesarea Philippi, he asked his disciples, "Who do men say that the Son of man is?" And they said, "Some say John the Baptists, others say Elijah, and others Jeremiah or one of the prophets." He said to them, "But who do you say that I am?" Simon Peter replied, "You are the Christ, the Son of the living God." (Matthew 16:13–16)	And Jesus went on with his disciples, to the villages of Caesarea Philippi; and on the way he asked his disciples, "Who do men say that I am?" And they told him, "John the Baptist; and others say, Elijah; and others one of the prophets." And he asked them, "But who do you say that I am?" Peter answered him, "You are the Christ." (Mark 8:27–29)	Now it happened that as he was praying alone the disciples were with him; and he asked them, "Who do the people say that I am?" And they answered, "John the Baptist; but others say Elijah; and others, that one of the prophets of old has risen." And he said to them, "But who do you say that I am?" And Peter answered, "The Christ of God." (Luke 9:18–20)

The three synoptic evangelists each record Saint Peter's confession of faith. When Jesus asks the apostles who they think He is, Peter is the one who answers. Peter serves as the spokesman for the whole group to Jesus. Peter proclaims not just his own faith but also that of the whole believing Church.

Luke reveals that Jesus was praying alone at this time (Luke 9:18), but doesn't mention the location. Matthew and Mark identify Caesarea Philippi, at the northern tip of the Holy Land. Several miles to the west lies the archeological area of Dan (Tel el Qadi), frequently cited as the northernmost city of the Holy Land (Judges 20:1, 1 Samuel 3:20, 2 Samuel 3:10, 1 Kings 4:25, 2 Chronicles 30:5).

Caesarea Philippi lies in a mountain valley. The Jabal Shuf mountains of the Golan Heights lie to the east. To the north is Mount Hermon, at 9232 feet above sea level. The snow-capped peaks represent the purity and perfection of God Himself. Ancient Jewish tradition sees God protecting Israel from Mount Hermon. Here are the sources of the Jordan River, providing fresh water and life to the Holy Land.

This site inspired Christian iconographers. The natural beauty of Caesarea Philippi strikingly manifests the mysterious Trinitarian presence. The rock represents Jesus Christ, the Rock of our salvation. The water symbolizes the Holy Spirit and the snow on Mount Hermon lifts our spirits to contemplate God the Father.

Caesarea Philippi was originally named Paneas, after Pan, the Greek god of forests and herds. Archeologists discovered here the temples of Pan, of Caesar Augustus, and of Nemesis, the goddess of revenge. Also, a cemetery of goats, dating from Roman times, and a platform for the dance of the goats in honor of Pan were unearthed.

Several sanctuaries dedicated to Pan existed at the time of our Lord. King Herod the Great rebuilt the entire city of Caesarea Philippi and dedicated the main temple at the source of the river to the emperor Augustus. After Herod's death, his son Philip became the tetrarch of this prevalently Greek-speaking territory of Iturea and Trachonidis (Luke 3:1). His pride is evidenced in the coins with the image of himself and his wife, which he had struck. The Roman historian Josephus reports that in Caesarea Philippi there was a lack of kosher olive oil, suggesting lack of fidelity to the law.

Paneas (Caesarea Philippi) is today called "Banias" in Arabic, since Arabs do not pronounce the letter "P". During the Crusades, Banias functioned as the military outpost linked to the nearby fortress of Nimrud, protecting the road to Damascus. Today the minaret and an abandoned but relatively well-preserved Maronite Church are still visible as remnants of the Syrian village abandoned after the Six Days War in 1967.

Peter's Confession ~ Matthew's account of Peter's confession of Christ remains one of the most quoted and studied texts in Church tradition. The confession of Peter takes place after Jesus' journey into the Gentile region, which culminated in the feeding of the four thousand.

All of the Synoptics refer to the company of the disciples being with Jesus. The response to Jesus' question of His identity in Matthew elicits a broader response than the others. Only in Matthew do the disciples include Jeremiah as a possible answer, along with John the Baptist and Elijah. Mark and Luke refer to Peter, whereas Matthew provides his full name, Simon Peter. The confession of Saint Peter is most complete in the Matthean account: "You are the Christ, the Son of the living God" (Matthew 16:16). Mark simply reports, "You are the Christ" (Mark 8:29), and Luke has Peter saying rather concisely, "The Christ of God" (Luke 9:20).

Every human being must wrestle with the question of "Who is Jesus?" and the correct answer to that question defines the identity of every Christian believer. Acknowledging that Jesus is the Christ, the Son of the living God, is the first step. Allowing Jesus to be the Lord and Master of your life is the second essential step. Remember, even the demons recognized who Jesus was! The time was ripe for Jesus, compelled by His great love, to reveal His identity to the disciples. John's Gospel frequently repeats the phrase: "I am" (John 8:58, 10:11, 14:6, 15:1), corresponding to God's revelation of His identity to Moses "I AM who I AM" (Exodus 3:14–16). In the Old Testament, God is called "Yahweh" denoting the source and fullness of life. Jesus' identity is one with His Father.

Jesus did not pose the question of His identity in terms of a public opinion poll or a democratic vote. To be a Christian, a follower of Christ, demands an understanding of who Jesus really is— true God and true man. The common people had a high opinion of Jesus, regarding Him as the most legendary of the prophets. The appearance of the prophets Elijah and Jeremiah would indicate the advent of messianic times. Yet, the guessing of the people falls far short of the truth. The prophets of the past were already dead and were never appreciated in their lifetimes. To compare Jesus with the Old Testament prophets would be to assign the Author of life to the company of mere dead mortals.

Jesus' question regarding His own identity directly provokes His disciples. He expects more of them than the man on the street. Peter's emphatic answer, "You are the Christ, the Son of the living God" (Matthew 16:16), refutes the notion that Jesus could be merely a good man or a powerful prophet and becomes a turning point of the Gospels. The apostles' faith must mature in an interior transformation before they can follow Jesus to His crucifixion and Resurrection. From the northern extreme of the Holy Land, this pagan territory most distant from Jerusalem becomes the crossroad at which the disciples start to understand the depth of Jesus' love and the sacrifice which God will offer for the salvation of the world. Yet they still have a long way to explore the full reality of their initialized faith.

Theologically, the question of Jesus' identity intrigues every person. Christ is the Son of the living God, with or without Peter's endorsement. The Son of man is the divine-human messianic figure described in Daniel 7:13–14. Jesus responds "And I tell you, you are Peter," (Matthew 16:18) as emphatically as Peter confesses, "You are the Christ!" Jesus' assignment of Peter's role caused many schisms in the church, first between the east and the west, and later during the Reformation. Problems arise from refusal to acknowledge the primacy of Peter. However, problems first arise from refusing to submit to the Lordship of Jesus. Even today, people like to pick and choose those things about Jesus that they like and to dismiss the teachings of Jesus which are hard to follow.

Jesus interrogates His disciples and starts the journey toward the Holy City just after they are warned to beware of the leaven of the Pharisees and Sadducees (Matthew 16:11). The disciples' faith in Jesus must correspond to their capacity to be transparent to the questions of their Lord. Each question identifies them with a mystery, which they are asked to embrace. Faith requires answering the call of God to discover in ourselves the Spirit of God. Listening to God's Word enables us to come to know God more intimately, and then God's Word can be implemented in our lives. Faith is always a gift of God, not a by-product of human intelligence. Jesus praises Peter as "blessed" because the truth was revealed to him by God the Father in heaven. Love, however, is needed for faith to lead us in the growing desire to serve God in the beautiful gift of our lives.

Peter understands that this Galilean rabbi, actually the living God, acts among ordinary people. The mystery of the Incarnation, God becoming a man, and the relationship between the Father and the Son is revealed to Peter, whereas it is hidden from the wise and learned (Matthew 11:25). Peter drops everything to follow Jesus, spends time with Him, and dialogues with Jesus to comprehend His identity more deeply. Christianity, in essence, is not a doctrine or moral teaching, but rather a relationship with the Lord who lives in each of us and loves each of us. Saint Paul expresses this truth in the words: "it is no longer I who live, but Christ who lives in me" (Galatians 2:20).

> Jesus answered him, "Blessed are you, Simon Bar-Jona! For flesh and blood has not revealed this to you, but my Father who is in heaven. And I tell you, you are Peter, and on this rock I will build my church, and the powers of death shall not prevail against it. I will give you the keys of the kingdom of heaven, and whatever you bind on earth shall be bound in heaven, and whatever you loose on earth shall be loosed in heaven."
> (Matthew 16:17–19)

Only Matthew records the full response that Jesus gave to Peter's profession of faith. Faith is relational, a two-way street. Peter gives Jesus a response of faith, and Jesus gives Peter a commission of trust. To signify this new relationship, Jesus gives Simon a new name—Cephas (in Aramaic) or Peter (in Greek), both of which mean "Rock." The image of the rock is very powerful at the site of Banias (Caesarea Philippi). At this site, the Jordan River springs out from a huge rock over 100 feet high. Rock in the Bible is a synonym for God (Deuteronomy 32:4, Psalm 18:2, Isaiah 17:10). Isaiah 51:1–2 looks to "the rock from which you were hewn," the faith of Abraham in which we were cut. Zechariah 12:3 considers Jerusalem as an immovable rock for all the nations. Simon Bar-Jona receives a new name, a new identity, and a new mission. Peter becomes the rock because of his faith in the Son of the living God. And on this faith will be built the Church, *ecclesia*, against which no one will prevail, even the powers of death. Christ's faithfulness guarantees the security of His Church, despite the scandal of sinful members. Peter was a sinner, and his sin of betrayal and denial of Jesus is painfully recorded in the Scriptures for all to read.

The faith of Peter becomes the key, which will open the kingdom of God. Peter will need this faith to confirm his brothers (Luke 22:32). Also note the correspondence between Genesis 17:5 and Matthew 16:18–19. God gave Abram the new name, Abraham, and by his faith he became the father of many nations. Jesus names Simon Peter and upon his faith in God, Christ, the chief architect, builds the Church. The sons of Abraham are the types of those who in faith are called to follow Peter into the Church. This call to become a member of the Church is universal—catholic in nature.

The powers of death in Matthew 16:18 are the gates of Hades, in Greek, and Sheol, the "netherworld," in Hebrew. Peter receives a new name and a commission in a place with a temple to Pan, who was depicted with a human face, goat's features of a beard, horns, tail and hooves, and who was seen as living under the rocks of the Jordan riverbed—a picture that evolved into the devil in classic art.

The Lord gives Peter the keys to the kingdom of heaven in Matthew 16:19, fulfilling Isaiah's prophecy to place on the steward's shoulder the key of the house of David (Isaiah 22:22). That Jesus has the keys to death and Hades can be found in Revelation 1:18. Therefore, Jesus has the power over life and death and Jesus has the right to give these powers to whomever He chooses. The image of "binding and loosing" given to the apostles establishes the authority of the Magisterium of the Church.

The metaphors, "key" and "binding and loosing," are common in rabbinic vocabulary and denote the correct interpretation and teaching of God's Word (Matthew 28:20). This magisterial authority implies the wisdom to formulate teaching on faith and morals that are always in conformity with the Spirit of Christ contained in His Word. The power to reconcile sinners to the Church is an important mandate commissioned to the apostles after Jesus' Resurrection (John 20:21–23). Jesus gives Peter the responsibility to accept new members into the Church and to expel members from the community. While Jesus accuses the religious elite of Israel of shutting people out of the kingdom (Matthew 23:13, Luke 11:52), Petrine authority does not coerce members into tyrannical submission through absolute power, but serves believers in directing them into God's kingdom with the freedom and love of Christ. Jesus models this life of service by becoming a servant (Matthew 20:28, Luke 22:24–28).

The Roman Catholic Church preserves the primacy of Peter in the role of his successors, the popes, enduring sharp criticism and debate throughout the centuries. The Church has retained an unbroken line of popes from the time Jesus commissioned Saint Peter until Pope Benedict XVI today. Catholics accept this Scriptural text as sufficient proof of the infallibility and primacy of Peter in the tradition of the Church. This issue is very important for it concerns to whom Christ gives authority for His Church until He comes again in glory.

There is no such thing as Church authority independent from the fundamental rock who is Christ. No pope in history has ever advanced as doctrine any statement that contradicts God's Word or the example of Christ. The authority of Peter is buttressed by the love and mercy Jesus showed him and the love that Peter professed for Christ. The powers of sin and death cannot prevail over the Church because Christ has conquered sin and death on Calvary. The invisible foundation of the Church is the Risen Christ, the visible *cathedra* of Peter, and the guarantee that the Church will survive on the way to the heavenly Jerusalem. Without Peter and his successor, the pope, there is no stability or permanence in the Church. The pope preserves the unity of Christ's universal Church.

> The Catholic Church affirms that during the 2000 years of her history she has preserved in unity, with all the means with which God wishes to endow His Church, and this despite the often grave crises which have shaken her, the infidelity of some of her ministers, and the faults into which her members daily fall. The Catholic Church knows that, by virtue of the strength which comes to her from the Spirit, the weaknesses, mediocrity, sins and at times the betrayals of some of her children cannot destroy what God has bestowed on her as part of His plan of grace.
>
> John Paul II, *Ut Unum Sint* (May 25, 1995), I.11

Only by grace can we humbly recognize the relationship between Christ, Peter, and his successors. But scripture leaves no doubt about the primacy of Peter. In John 21:15–19, despite Peter's recent denial of our Lord, Jesus commissions Peter to feed and tend His lambs and sheep. Peter is mentioned 195 times in the New Testament. The next most frequently mentioned apostle is John, who is mentioned 29 times. Peter is always listed first among the apostles and Judas is listed last. Peter is present at the Transfiguration (Matthew 17:1) and at the healing of Jairus' daughter (Mark 5:37). Peter is the first to confess the identity of our Lord in these passages and he reaffirms the identity of Jesus in the Eucharistic discourse (John 6:68–69). The Risen Christ appears first to Peter and then to the other disciples (Luke 24:34, 1 Corinthians 15:5).

Although John is younger and reaches the empty tomb first, he defers to Peter, respectfully allowing the elder to examine the tomb first. The beloved apostle, Saint John, depicts Peter as the prominent figure in the last dialogue of Jesus in the Gospel of John. In that dialogue, Jesus presses Peter on the quality of his love. Even though Peter cannot match the height of Jesus' sacrificial love on the Cross, *agape*, our Lord, nonetheless, demands assurance that Peter is committed in love to serve the members of the Church. Peter must love with the warm, personal, friendly love expressed by the word *filea*. Jesus speaks about sacrificial love at the Last Supper; He demonstrates it on Calvary, and continues to instruct His disciples after His Resurrection.

In the end, genuine human love becomes truly sacrificial love, which Jesus demonstrates for all eternity. The powers of death cannot prevail against a love that is "strong as death" (Song of Solomon 8:6). Love is the essential prerequisite of a disciple of Christ. Human willpower cannot provide all that is necessary for discipleship. Good intentions and warm feelings cannot sustain love. Faith working through grace enables the apostles to love their enemies and pray for their persecutors.

The events of Christ's death and Resurrection in Jerusalem are foretold to the disciples immediately after the awesome experience in Caesarea Philippi (Matthew 16:21, Mark 8:31, Luke 9:22). In the accounts of Matthew and Mark, Peter takes Jesus aside and begs Him not to suffer or die. But if Jesus does not die, Peter will not be saved, nor anyone else! Peter argues against the interests of the whole human race—against the whole purpose of Jesus' mission on earth. Peter feels love, but he stumbles. So soon after being named Rock, Peter suffers a moment of embarrassing humiliation.

> It is important to note how the weakness of Peter and of Paul clearly shows that the Church is founded upon the infinite power of grace. Peter, immediately after receiving his mission, is rebuked with unusual severity by Christ. ... How can we fail to see that the mercy which Peter needs is related to the ministry of that mercy which he is the first to experience?
>
> Pope John Paul II, *Ut Unum Sint* (May 25, 1995), III, 91

Jesus' stern rebuke, "Get behind me, Satan! You are a hindrance to me; for you are not on the side of God, but of men" (Matthew 16:23), must have stung Peter and shocked the other disciples. Despite Peter's sin and weakness, he perseveres. Peter gets it wrong many times and Jesus rebukes and corrects him. But, Peter doesn't give up and throw in the towel. He doesn't get mad and storm away to follow someone else. Peter denies Jesus three times, but Jesus never denies Peter, never gives up on Peter, never gives his job to somebody else. Certainly there were more learned, more eloquent, more attractive men in the Holy Land at that time. But, Jesus chose Peter and He never abandoned His choice. Jesus predicted the martyrdom that Peter would endure in John 21:18 and Peter did not object. Peter learned the way of humble love and service of others, which qualified him to become the *servus servorum Dei* (the servant of the servants of God).

The exchange between Jesus and Peter at Caesarea Philippi proves to be foundational for the life of the Church as well as the turning point of Christ's public life. Now, from the northern limits of the Holy Land, Jesus starts His pilgrimage to Jerusalem, the heartland of the country. The geography of the land underscores the theological message of Jesus. Jesus must walk the long way of the Cross and descend into the underworld in order to bring eternal life. Peter learned a great lesson at Caesarea Philippi, to be transmitted to the whole Church by all his successors. He already loved Jesus, and now he learns that he must love His holy Cross.

> Let no man therefore be ashamed of the honored symbols of our salvation, and of the chiefest of all good things, whereby we even live, and whereby we are; but as a crown, so let us bear about the cross of Christ. Yea, for by it all things are wrought, that are wrought among us. Whether one is to be new-born, the cross is there; or to be nourished with that mystical food, or to be ordained, or to do anything else, everywhere our symbol of victory is present. Therefore both on house, and wall, and windows, and upon our forehead, and upon our mind, we inscribe it with much care. For of the salvation wrought for us, and of our common freedom, and of the goodness of Our Lord, this is the sign … when therefore thou signest thyself, think of the purpose of the cross, and quench anger, and all other passions. When thou signest thyself, fill they forehead with all courage, make thy soul free.
>
> Saint John Chrysostom (344–407 AD), *Homily on Matthew*, 54.

1. What can you learn about Peter from the following passages?

Family	John 1:40–42	
Hometown	John 1:44	
Standing	Matthew 4:18–20	
Marital Status	Matthew 8:14	
Mission	Galatians 2:7–8	

2. What question does Jesus pose to His disciples? How do the disciples answer the question?

Matthew 16:13–14	
Mark 8:27–28	
Luke 9:18–19	

3. What question does Jesus ask in Matthew 16:15?

4. Who answers Jesus question? What answer is given?

Matthew 16:16	
Mark 8:29	
Luke 9:20	

5. How would you answer the question: Who is Jesus for you?

6. What response does Jesus give to Peter's answer in Matthew 16:17?

7. List three (3) things stated in Matthew 16:18.

8. How is God depicted in the following passages?

Deuteronomy 32:4	
2 Samuel 22:2–3	
Psalm 18:1–3	
Psalm 31:2–3	
Psalm 62:1–7	
Isaiah 17:10	

9. What can you learn about the term "rock" from these verses?

Matthew 7:24–25	
Luke 6:46–48	
Romans 9:33	
1 Corinthians 10:4	
1 Peter 2:7–8	

10. On what did Christ build His Church? CCC 424

11. How did Jesus respond to Peter's confession of faith? CCC 440

12. Who has the authority to start a church? Matthew 16:18

13. What does Jesus give to Peter?

Isaiah 22:22–23	
Matthew 16:19	
Revelation 1:17–18	

14. What do the following terms designate? Matthew 16:19

power of the keys	
power to bind and loose	

15. What power does Jesus impart in Matthew 16:19? CCC 1444

16. How would you explain Peter's primacy among the apostles?

Matthew 17:1–2	
Luke 5:1–8	
Matthew 14:28–30	
Mark 16:6–7	
Luke 24:32–34	
1 Corinthians 15:3–5	

17. What place and unique mission does Peter hold? CCC 552

18. How does Jesus govern His Church? CCC 869

19. Which of the following statements does Jesus make in the Bible? Cite the chapter and verse.
_____ "Upon this rock, I will establish a group of loosely affiliated fellowships with divergent doctrines and a council of churches. Choose whichever one you like best."
_____ "When I am gone, write this down in the Bible. The Bible alone is all you will ever need to understand faith and morals."
_____ "Pick a church with the best music, warmest fellowship, and most inspirational preaching, because, what makes you happy, makes God happy."
_____ "You are Peter and upon this rock I will build My Church."

20. What comfort would a Catholic derive from Matthew 16:16–19?

Chapter 13

The Transfiguration

Matthew 17:1–9, Mark 9:2–10, Luke 9:28–36

**This is my beloved Son, with whom I am well pleased;
listen to him.** (Matthew 17:5)

The Gospel writers don't record an exact geographical site for the Transfiguration, but early Christians chose Mount Tabor, a traditional site defended by Origen as early as the 3rd century. Mount Tabor remains the most plausible site for this important event which signified the final departure of Jesus from Galilee for Jerusalem.

The word *Tabor* in Hebrew refers to the navel or umbilicus. Mount Tabor, about 1700 feet high, abuts three biblical tribal territories: Zebulun to the northwest, Isaachar to the southwest, and Naphtali to the north. Local Arabs call the mountain Tur, which means the sacred point where the divine and human touch. The victory of Barak and Deborah, the prophetess, over Sisera (Judges 4–6) occurred in this area. Psalm 89:12 presents Tabor praising God's name. The prophet Jeremiah compares the might of Nebuchadnezzar to the strength of Tabor (Jeremiah 46:18).

The Byzantines built three chapels on the mountain to honor Jesus, Moses, and Elijah, and later a chapel commemorating the descent of Jesus and the three disciples from the mountain. During the Crusades, the Benedictines built an extensive monastery and the Church of the Transfiguration on the top of Mount Tabor. After the battle at Hattin in 1187, the monks left the monastery and Muslims built a fortress on this strategic position on Tabor. Christian pilgrims rarely ventured to visit this forbidden place. Emir Fakhr ed-Din allowed the Franciscans to return to Mount Tabor in the 17th century, but their presence was short lived, due to his assassination. When the Turks left the Holy Land in 1917, the Franciscans bought property on the mountain and built a new church and monastery.

Today pilgrims visit the basilica of the Transfiguration, designed by the architect Antonio Barluzzi and completed in 1924. The east oriented sanctuary has two towers and three interior naves with a crypt reserved for the Eucharist. Pilgrims may touch or kiss the presumed place of the Transfiguration in the crypt. Some pilgrims leave prayers written on paper. The central mosaic depicts the scene of the Transfiguration in the crypt. A familiar motif to observe is the peacock, the symbol of immortality. In an adjacent chapel, dedicated to Moses, is a heavy cross which one Bavarian pilgrim in the 20th century brought on his shoulders first to Rome and then to the Holy Land. Pope Paul VI visited this holy place on January 5, 1964. Historians say that the Holy Father remained immersed in prayer for an unusually long time. Interestingly, Pope Paul VI died on August 6, 1978, the Feast of the Transfiguration of our Lord.

| After six days Jesus took with him Peter and James and John his brother, and led them up a high mountain apart. And he was transfigured before them, and his face shone like the sun, and his garments became white as light. (Matthew 17:1–2) | After six days Jesus took with him Peter and James and John, and led them up a high mountain apart by themselves; and he was transfigured before them, and his garments became glistening, intensely white, as no fuller on earth could bleach them. (Mark 9:2–3) | Now about eight days after these sayings he took with him Peter and John and James, and went up on the mountain to pray, and as he was praying, the appearance of his countenance was altered, and his raiment became dazzlingly white. (Luke 9:28–29) |

All three Synoptics link the Transfiguration with the first prediction of Jesus' passion and the conditions of discipleship, which follows the confession of Peter in Caesarea Philippi. Only Matthew and Mark bring forth the dialogue of Jesus with His disciples regarding the coming of Elijah, but all three of them narrate the subsequent event of the healing of a boy possessed by an evil spirit. According to Matthew and Mark, the Transfiguration occurs six days after the preceding narratives. Luke says "about eight days," an expression of the fullness of days in relation to Jesus' Passion and Resurrection, implying one week plus the first day of the week. Saint Gregory of Nyssa suggests that this represents the final goal of creation. Matthew and Mark name James before John, while Luke names John first. Luke alone mentions that Jesus was praying on the mountain.

Matthew and Mark both use the verb *metamorfoo* for "transfigure," Matthew and Luke speak about the altered countenance of Jesus' face, which shone like the sun. Only Mark points out that Jesus' clothes were brighter than any fuller on earth could bleach them. Mark also shows his predominant interest in Elijah by putting him before Moses, in contrast to Matthew and Luke.

| And behold, there appeared to them Moses and Elijah, talking with him. And Peter said to Jesus, "Lord, it is well that we are here; if you wish, I will make three booths here, one for you and one for Moses and one for Elijah. (Matthew 17:3–4) | And there appeared to them Elijah with Moses; and they were talking to Jesus. And Peter said to Jesus, "Master, it is well that we are here; let us make three booths, one for you and one for Moses and one for Elijah." For he did not know what to say, for they were exceedingly afraid. (Mark 9:4–6) | And behold, two men talked with him, Moses and Elijah, who appeared in glory and spoke of his departure, which he was to accomplish at Jerusalem. Now Peter and those who were with him were heavy with sleep, and when they wakened they saw his glory and the two men who stood with him. And as the men were parting from him, Peter said to Jesus, "Master it is well that we are here; let us make three booths, one for you and one for Moses and one for Elijah"—not knowing what he said. (Luke 9:30–33) |

Luke points out that Peter and the others with him were heavy with sleep, anticipating the disciples' weariness and inability to stay awake and pray at the time of Jesus' agony in the Garden of Gethsemane (Luke 22:39–46). Peter's address to Jesus with the title *kyrie* or "Lord" in Matthew 17:4 is the most theologically advanced. Mark 9:5 employs the term *rabbi* and Luke 9:33 uses *epistata*, "master." In Matthew's account, Peter politely addresses Jesus with "if you wish" and there is no hint of Peter's confusion as in the Marcan and Lucan accounts.

Several important connections to the Old Testament appear in this narrative. For example, Luke uses the Greek word *exodus*, or "departure" (Luke 9:31), recalling the biblical exodus of the Jewish people from slavery in Egypt. Jesus fulfills the spiritual exodus by liberating humanity from the slavery of sin. The presence of the two most remarkable figures of the Old Testament, Moses, the author of the Law, and Elijah, the father of the prophets, underlines Jesus' decision to bring about the new exodus.

A striking parallel is seen between Jesus and Moses. When Moses approaches the mountain to speak to the Lord, Aaron, Nadab, and Abihu are allowed to worship only at a distance. Moses alone is permitted to approach the Lord when the cloud covers the mountain (Exodus 24:1–18). The shining face of Jesus parallels the radiant face of Moses, as well as the commands of God: "listen to him" and "him shall you heed" (Deuteronomy 18:15).

Jesus functions as the new Moses and the new Elijah, the fulfillment of the law and the prophets. Moses and Elijah's previous ascents on Mount Horeb (Exodus 19:20, 1 Kings 19:8) prefigure the key event of salvation history, which Jesus chooses to accomplish. Malachi, the last Old Testament prophet, provides another important link between the authority of Moses and Elijah and the coming of the day of the Lord, which is fulfilled in Jesus Christ. Malachi proclaims, "Remember the law of my servant Moses, the statutes and ordinances that I commanded him at Horeb for all Israel. Behold, I will send you Elijah the prophet before the great and terrible day of the Lord comes. And he will turn the hearts of fathers to their children and the hearts of children to their fathers" (Malachi 4:4–6). Malachi's conviction, originating in Jewish tradition, is confirmed in the dialogue at the Transfiguration.

The steadfastness of Jesus contrasts with the wavering faith of the disciples. Peter's bold confession of Jesus as the Christ (Matthew 16:16) seems distant as Jesus announces His impending passion and death (Matthew 17:12). Luke's irony in describing the disciples with the Greek verb *barreo*, "heavy with sleep," indicates their unwillingness to comprehend the spiritual truth behind the scene as well as physical weariness. The disciples immediately awaken when they see Jesus in all His glory.

Linguistically *skene* (booth) sounds similar to *shekinah* (God's glorious presence in the cloud). This sad play on words reveals how the human person is prone to see only the pleasant realities of God's revelation and to reject what is painful and difficult to understand. The three booths recall the Jewish feast of Tabernacles, also known as the Feast of Booths, the harvest feast. Peter speaks for all humanity when he says, "Lord, it is well that we are here." Peter desires the eschatological solution of salvation history, but without suffering. The desire for Easter Sunday without any Good Friday is typically human, and so Mark and Luke avoid using the word "Lord" in Peter's remark. Saint Jerome sees the need to prepare a tabernacle, a booth in the inner sanctum of the human heart, to make a place for Jesus to dwell.

The Old Testament also references the cloud. A luminous cloud guides the people in the desert (Exodus 14:19) and, later, identifies the divine presence over the Tabernacle (Exodus 40:34–36,

Numbers 9:15, 1 Kings 8:10–12). Even today, Orthodox Jews believe that the presence of God remains firm, although invisible, at the temple mount in Jerusalem. Moses enters the cloud at the climax of the Exodus when he is entrusted with the gift of the Decalogue. For Elijah, the cloud on Mount Carmel brings the rain, the symbol of blessing and fertility (1 Kings 18:44).

| He was still speaking, when lo, a bright cloud overshadowed them, and a voice from the cloud said, "This is my beloved Son, with whom I am well pleased; listen to him." When the disciples heard this, they fell on their faces, and were filled with awe. But Jesus came and touched them saying, "Rise, and have no fear." And when they lifted up their eyes, they saw no one but Jesus only. (Matthew 17:5–8) | And a cloud over-shadowed them, and a voice came out of the cloud, "This is my beloved Son, listen to him." And suddenly looking around they no longer say any one with them but Jesus only. (Mark 9:7–8) | As he said this, a cloud came and over-shadowed them; and they were afraid as they entered the cloud. And a voice came out of the cloud, saying, "This is my Son, my Chosen; listen to him!" (Luke 9:34–35) |

The climax of the Transfiguration is marked by the voice which comes out of the cloud. The imperative, "listen to Him," recalls and completes the revelation of Jesus' divine identity at His Baptism (Matthew 3:13–17). To follow Jesus means to fully accept the authority of the Incarnate Word. The face of God is discovered by completely trusting in the word of the Son. The obedience of listening prepares for the sonship of baptism. The Christian puts off the works of darkness to become a child of the day.

Only Matthew refers to the cloud as "bright," in parallelism to the "garments white as light." While, only Luke speaks about the disciples entering the cloud. The words from the cloud are briefest in Mark, with Matthew adding "with whom I am well pleased," and Luke adding "my chosen." As He did at the Baptism of Jesus at the Jordan, God the Father affirms Jesus to be His Son and allows us an insight into the relationship between the persons of the Blessed Trinity. The Father also answers decisively the question of "Who is Jesus?" At the Baptism of our Lord the Holy Spirit was present as a dove, here as a cloud.

Matthew expounds on the immediate aftermath of the revelation of the voice from the cloud. Only in Matthew's account do the disciples fall on their faces. Jesus then touches them with the words: "Rise and have no fear" (Matthew 17:7).

| And as they were coming down the mountain, Jesus commanded them, "Tell no one the vision, until the Son of Man is raised from the dead." (Matthew 17:9) | And as they were coming down the mountain, he charged them to tell no one what they had seen, until the Son of Man should have risen from the dead. (Mark 9:9) | And when the voice had spoken, Jesus was found alone. And they kept silence and told no one in those days anything of what they had seen (Luke 9:36) |

Only Luke reports that the disciples obediently kept silent about what they had seen. Mark and Matthew both report Jesus' command not to speak about the Transfiguration until after His

Resurrection. Mark provides the solitary reference to the disciples questioning among themselves the meaning of the resurrection from the dead.

The Transfiguration confirms Jesus' journey toward Calvary. Jesus anticipates the glory of His Resurrection in this event, which serves to strengthen the faith of the apostles. The disciples' faith will soon be tested when they will be asked to follow Jesus to the Cross and to share in His destiny. The revelation of the glory of the Son and the voice of the Father are intended to help the disciples understand the necessity of suffering and embrace the Cross.

The Transfiguration demonstrates the anticipated glory of Jesus in His Resurrection and invites us to contemplate the hope of our future resurrection at the end of salvation history. Meanwhile, we are challenged by God to listen attentively to the word of the Gospel and be transformed by God's Word. We should listen, like the disciples who with unveiled faces beheld the glory of the Lord, and be transformed into His likeness through the Spirit (2 Corinthians 3:18). Beyond our own daily commitments, God offers each of us our own mount of Transfiguration. The Lord invites us, in the inner sanctum of our baptized souls, to climb the holy mountain with Him. Each time we transcend the earthly realities to gaze upon the glory of the Lord in the Eucharist, we are drawn into greater intimacy with Him. Jesus comes down from the mountain to dwell in the communicants and gives us grace to embrace the crosses of our lives with dignity and faith.

Strive for a personal, intimate relationship with the Lord. The masters of the spiritual life recommend daily prayer in silence. Through holy contemplation, you can become united with the transfigured Lord. Even when we meditate on the crucifix or make the Way of the Cross, we, like John, hold in our minds the memory of the Transfiguration of our Lord and the anticipation of the Resurrection.

Tradition also connects Mount Tabor to the last farewell of Jesus (Acts 1:9). The disciples hear the command to go to the whole world to spread the Gospel, making other disciples. The blessing and success of missionary work in the Church, to bring more people to God's plan of salvation, is God's commission to all of us. Are we ready to listen and respond?

Peter never forgot the mystical experience on the mountaintop. Decades after the Transfiguration, Peter gives us a fourth recounting of the Transfiguration in his second letter—the only account left by an eye-witness! John was there but did not leave an account in his extensive writings, nor did James. Only Peter, the first Pope, gives us this precious recollection. Our faith in the divine identity of Jesus and our hope for our own ultimate transformation comes from this apostolic testimony.

For we did not follow cleverly devised myths when we made known to you the power and coming of our Lord Jesus Christ, but we were eye-witnesses of his majesty. For when he received honor and glory from God the Father and the voice was borne to him by the Majestic Glory, "This is my beloved Son, with whom I am well pleased," we heard this voice borne from heaven, for we were with him on the holy mountain. And we have the prophetic word made more sure. You will do well to pay attention to this as to a lamp shining in a dark place, until the day dawns and the morning star rises in your hearts. First of all you must understand this, that no prophecy of scripture is a matter of one's own interpretation, because no prophecy ever came by the impulse of man, but men moved by the Holy Spirit spoke from God. (2 Peter 1:16–19)

1. Which apostles observed the Transfiguration of our Lord? Matthew 17:1–2.

2. What does Luke say Jesus was doing before his appearance changed? Luke 9:29

3. What is the aim of the Transfiguration? CCC 568

4. Who talked with Jesus and how did they appear? Luke 9:30–31

5. Describe the presence in the following verses.

Exodus 13:21–22	
Exodus 24:15–18	
Number 9:15–17	
1 Kings 8:10–12	
Isaiah 19:1	
Matthew 17:5	
Mark 9:7	
Luke 9:34–35	
Revelation 14:14	

6. Compare Peter's statements in the following passages.

Matthew 17:4	
Mark 9:5	
Luke 9:33	

7. Compare the following passages.

Exodus 34:29	
Matthew 17:2	

8. When does God the Father solemnly speak in the Gospels? What does God say?

Matthew 3:17	
Matthew 17:5	

9. What does the title "only Son of God" affirm? CCC 444

10. What does the Transfiguration intend to show? CCC 554

11. What can you learn from the following passages?

Deuteronomy 34:5–12	
2 Kings 2:9–12	

12. How did the disciples react to the Transfiguration? Matthew 17:6

13. How do you think you would react to seeing the glorified Lord?

14. Complete the following explanations. CCC 555

| Moses and Elijah ... |
| The Law and the Prophets ... |
| The cloud ... |
| Your disciples ... |

15. Who is "Elijah to come?" Matthew 11:11–14, CCC 717, 719

16. What is the work of "Elijah who must come"? Mark 9:12, CCC 718

17. What two things did Jesus do?

| Matthew 17:7 | |
| Mark 9:9 | |

18. What does the Transfiguration do for us? CCC 556

19. What is happening to us right now? 2 Corinthians 3:18

20. How can you cooperate with God's grace to gaze upon His glory? CCC 1378–1380

CHAPTER 14

The Rich Young Man

Matthew 19:16–22, Mark 10:17–22, Luke 18:18–23

If you would be perfect, go sell what you possess and give to the poor, and you will have treasure in heaven; and come follow Me. (Matthew 19:21)

The Synoptic Gospels present Jesus' encounter with the unnamed rich young man on Jesus' way to Jerusalem. At the time of our Lord, four different routes between Galilee and Jerusalem were used by merchants, military personnel, travelers, and pilgrims. The shortest but most dangerous way, Via Media or Mountain Road, passed through central Samaria. Abraham and Jacob traveled this road from Sechem to Bethel, then to Bethlehem, Hebron, and finally to Beer Sheva (Genesis 12:8–9, 35:15–27). Hence, this road is also called the Road of the Patriarchs.

The Gospel writers report several encounters of Jesus on this road. John describes Jesus speaking with the Samaritan woman at Jacob's well (John 4:1–42). Luke presents a conflict with an inhospitable Samaritan village when Jesus sends messengers ahead of Him to them (Luke 9:51–55), and a later encounter with ten lepers, who Jesus healed as He was passing between Samaria and Galilee on the way to Jerusalem (Luke 17:11–19).

Another well-traveled road in Palestine in antiquity was Via Maris (the Way of the Sea), also called the Way of the Philistines. This road, linking Syria with Egypt, crossed from the plain of Esdrelon through the Carmel mountains at Megiddo and on to the Mediterranean coast. Saint Paul traveled this route from Jerusalem to Caesarea (Acts 23:31–33).

The corridor of the Jordan Valley provided another popular route for pilgrims. Many travelers avoided this road in summer, because of the scarcity of villages and dangers lurking from the desert. It was used in the spring when larger groups traveled together on pilgrimage to Jerusalem for Passover, affording greater safety for the pilgrims.

The last known road, an international King's highway (Numbers 20:17), linked Syria with the Transjordan and Red Sea area. At the time of Jesus, the region from Damascus to Philadelphia (today's suburb of Amman, Jordan) was known as Decapolis, which contained Greek-speaking cities with large Jewish populations. Since Matthew and Mark mention this region (Matthew 4:25; Mark 5:20, 7:31), there is reason to believe that Jesus often chose this peaceful route, the King's highway, for pilgrimage to Jerusalem. If the final pilgrimage of our Lord passed through the Transjordan, He would have crossed the place of His baptism of water in the Jordan River on His way to His baptism of blood in Jerusalem. The final entry of Jesus into the Holy Land presents Him as the new Joshua, the liberator of the human soul.

The Rich Young Man ~ Among the Synoptics, Matthew elaborates most extensively on the encounter of Jesus with the rich young man. All three Synoptics sandwich this event between the account of Jesus blessing the children and His teaching on riches and the rewards of discipleship. Only Mark reports that the man ran to Jesus and knelt before Him (Mark 10:17).

Luke says that he was a ruler, *"archon."* Matthew adds that he was young and interjects Jesus' condition "if you would enter life" (Matthew 19:17), keep the commandments. Mark is the only source to add "do not defraud" to the list of commandments. And Matthew emphasizes "you shall love your neighbor as yourself" (Matthew 19:19), which is not part of the Decalogue, but obviously the focus of Christ's teaching and example. Mark provides unique information reporting that Jesus, looking upon the young man, loved him.

Jesus presents two conditions, "if you would enter life" and "if you would be perfect," prior to His directive to the young man and His invitation to discipleship. These two conditions are reminiscent of Jesus' teaching from the Sermon on the Mount; "You, therefore, must be perfect as your heavenly Father is perfect" (Matthew 5:48).

Mark and Luke reveal that something is lacking in the rich young man, despite his insistence that he has kept all the commandments since his youth. What prevents the rich young man from abandoning everything to follow Jesus, as the apostles did? Is it pride, greed, attachment to things, or love of money? Whatever the obstacle, Mark uses the idiom, "his countenance fell," to show the obvious disappointment of the young man. Luke explains that the man was very rich and Mark divulges that he had great possessions. Perhaps his possessions possessed him!

The young man senses that there is a connection between moral good and the fulfillment of his own destiny. He is a devout Israelite, raised as it were in the shadow of the Law of the Lord. If he asks Jesus this question, we can presume that it is not because he is ignorant of the answer contained in the Law. It is more likely that the attractiveness of the person of Jesus had prompted within him new questions about moral good. He feels the need to draw near to the One who had begun His preaching with this new and decisive proclamation: "The time is fulfilled and the kingdom of God is at hand; repent, and believe in the Gospel" (Mark 1:15).

People today need to turn to Christ once again to receive from Him the answer to their questions about what is good and what is evil. Christ is the Teacher, the Risen One who has life in Himself and Who is always present in His Church and in the world. It is He who opens up to the faithful the books of the Scriptures.

"Come, follow Me" (Matthew 19:21) ... is an invitation, the marvelous grandeur of which will be fully perceived by the disciples after Christ's Resurrection, when the Holy Spirit leads them to all truth.

It is Jesus Himself who takes the initiative and calls people to follow Him. ... *Following Christ is thus the essential and primordial foundation of Christian morality:* just as the people of Israel followed God, who led them through the desert toward the Promised Land (cf. Exodus 13:21), so every disciple must follow Jesus, toward whom he is drawn by the Father himself (cf. John 6:44).

This is not a matter only of disposing oneself to hear a teaching and obediently accepting a commandment. More radically, it involves *holding fast to the very person of Jesus*, partaking of his life and his destiny, sharing in his free and loving obedience to the will of the Father.

To imitate and live out the love of Christ is not possible for man by his own strength alone. He becomes *capable of this love only by virtue of a gift received.*

Pope John Paul II, *Veritatis Splendor* (August 6, 1993), I.8, 19, 22.

From the Gospels, one may sense that this encounter between Jesus and the rich young man was rather brief. The discourse concerning observation of the commandments presupposes that the young man was Jewish. Jesus' invitation to the rich young man to sell everything, give to the poor, and then follow Him is found nowhere else in the Gospels.

After the man departs, Jesus, as He had done in the previous discussion on divorce, focuses His attention on His disciples. The apostles are astonished when Jesus says that "it is easier for a camel to go through the eye of a needle than for a rich man to enter the kingdom of God" (Matthew 19:24). What seems impossible to them is made possible by God. Not only those, like the disciples, who don't understand Jesus, but also the rich can be saved. The followers of Jesus are expected to restore God's order in love and marriage and abandon themselves to God's Will.

The Old Testament presents riches and wealth as blessings to be shared with others. Riches attract friends (Proverbs 14:20; 19:4), bring honor (Sirach 10:30), provide security (Proverbs 10:15), and afford the opportunity to practice almsgiving (Tobit 12:8). Still, the happiness of the wealthy is often fleeting. Many texts remind the rich that treasures cannot be brought into the next world. Job, a once wealthy man who lost everything, states "Naked I came from my mother's womb, and naked shall I return" (Job 1:21). The Bible warns that the love of money and the hoarding of wealth can lead to sin. The prophets condemn social injustice, especially the exploitation of the weak and needy (Isaiah 10:2, Amos 4:1), and the oppression of widows and orphans (Ezekiel 22:7).

The wisdom literature of the Bible cautions against excessive concern over wealth (Sirach 31:1; Ecclesiastes 2:4–11, 5:10). Moreover, the Sacred Scriptures warn that those who love money will be led astray by it and come to ruin (Sirach 31:5–6). Whereas in antiquity, people believed that the rich were blessed and the poor cursed, the Bible seems to favor the poor. "Better is a little that the righteous has than the abundance of many wicked" (Psalm 37:16). The focus is not on money, but on righteousness. The fear of the Lord surpasses any consideration of wealth or poverty.

Jesus asks His apostles to give up everything to follow Him and embrace their vocation. Jesus embraces poverty and the twelve apostles freely share the discipline of poverty in order to be at the service of God's Word. Disciples must be free to serve and share with others. Attachment to wealth chokes the Word of God and renders it unfruitful (Mark 4:18–19).

Jesus teaches not only about relationships with others, but also about relations with the things of this world. Riches are not the goal, but a means of sharing with others freely and generously. Whatever we hold for ourselves, divides us from others. Whatever we share, unites us with them. We are free and sons of the Father when we serve others. But, we can become slaves when greed prompts us to become subject to created things. Everything is the gift of God. He freely gives everything to us and invites us to be generous as well.

Only God is good. Man contemplates the absolute goodness of God and measures himself by that supreme standard. What is the way of life? Is it love and service to God demonstrated by the life of Jesus Christ, or service to mammon (Matthew 6:24)? The Christian loves freely and unconditionally. The new law of love, presented by Jesus in the Gospel, requires a new heart capable of grasping how much one is loved by God. Only God's love and grace make it possible to love others. Humanly speaking, it is impossible to love as God loved. No one can embrace God's call without supernatural grace. With sacramental grace, all things are possible!

The rich young man was loved by Jesus and offered an invitation to embrace a vocation. He did not come to Jesus with evil intent, but he came with a weak will. Obedience and abandonment to the will of God are requisites to discipleship. Whether an individual has many possessions or few, it is important to practice detachment from material things. God gives blessings to be enjoyed in this life. But, attachment to material things may prevent one from obtaining treasures in heaven.

Prior to meeting the rich young man, Jesus blesses the children. They don't possess anything and they are insignificant in the eyes of the world. Children represent the gift of life from God and they belong to the Father. The rich young man sets his values on wealth and his heart belongs to mammon. Hence, he finds faith exceptionally hard. Zacchaeus also had great wealth, but a heart open to repentance (Luke 19:1–10). Zacchaeus understands that the way of salvation for him demands the sharing of his wealth with the poor and generous compensation to those whom he has defrauded. He concludes that almsgiving will help to atone for the sins of his past life. While some abandon wealth and still fail to follow the Savior, Zacchaeus repents of his greed and is free to receive Jesus with joy. Unwillingness to completely trust Jesus results in isolation and sadness.

The Acts of the Apostles offers an image of the ideal community, in which Christians are of one mind and one heart, sharing everything in common (Acts 4:32–35). The Old Testament prefigures this principle of sharing when God calls for the forgiveness of debts in the holy year of Jubilee in Israel (Leviticus 25:8–17). The Israelites were to live in the promised land with the blessings of offspring and security. They were to control their greed and leave something for the poor to glean.

Jesus' beatitude, "Blessed are you poor, for yours is the kingdom of God" (Luke 6:20) reminds Christians of God's love for the poor. James promises that the poor are rich in faith and heirs of the kingdom (James 2:2-6). Throughout Church history, many outstanding men and women have chosen evangelical poverty, freely consecrating their lives for the kingdom of heaven. The disciplines of poverty, chastity, and obedience provide a radical Christian testimony of dedicating one's self and resources entirely to love God and neighbor. Everyone has a special call from God. Saint Francis of Assisi called poverty his sister. Mother Teresa placed her life at the service of the poorest of the poor, whom she served with such dignity that the whole world observed and was blessed.

Love for the poor means freedom and service. Some impoverished people may be guilty of greed, because their hearts are fixed on the imaginary wealth which they covet. Yet even the poor can be generous to those who have less. Those who have more are required to be more generous as their means allow for the sake of Christ. Jesus was very poor. He emptied Himself and became the servant of everyone (Philippians 2:6-11). The Catholic Church follows the ideals of Jesus, responding to the call to become the salt of the earth and the light of the world (Matthew 5:13). "Our Lord Jesus Christ, though He was rich, yet for your sake He became poor, so that by His poverty you might become rich" (2 Corinthians 8:9). Jesus withheld nothing, but offered everything to save us!

Jesus praised the poor widow who gave out of her poverty (Mark 12:42–43). Each of us is called by Jesus and invited to offer something beautiful for God. God gives each of us life. He gives faith and salvation. God gives each of us time, talent, and treasure. Let us sit at the feet of Jesus and ask the Holy Spirit to prompt us to respond generously to God's love. With God's grace it is possible even for the rich to enter the kingdom. With God's grace, no one should walk away sad.

1. Compare the question of the rich young man from these passages.

Matthew 19:16	
Mark 10:17	
Luke 18:18	

2. How does Jesus respond in Mark 10:18?

3. Jesus refers to the Decalogue from Exodus. Write the commandments. Star the ones Jesus lists.

Exodus 20:2–3	
Exodus 20:7	
Exodus 20:8	
Exodus 20:12	
Exodus 20:13	
Exodus 20:14	
Exodus 20:15	
Exodus 20:16	
Exodus 20:17	
Exodus 20:17	

4. What new commandment does Jesus add? Matthew 19:19

    Is it really new? Leviticus 19:18

5. How could you sum up the commandments of God? Romans 13:8–10

6. Compare the man's response in these passages. Find one question in one response.

Matthew 19:20	
Mark 10:20	
Luke 18:21	

7. With what emotion does Jesus relate to the young man? Mark 10:21

8. Identify the following from Luke 18:22.

Jesus' observation or evaluation	
Jesus' first instruction	
Jesus' second directive	
Jesus' promise	
Jesus' call or invitation	

9. Did the young man accept Jesus' invitation? Matthew 19:22 What emotion results?

10. What emotion results from accepting God's invitation in Luke 19:6

11. What teaching does Jesus give the disciples in Mark 10:23–27?

12. Who else proclaimed this truth of God's omnipotence? Luke 1:35–37

13. What can you learn from these passages?

Psalm 37:16	
Psalm 41:1–3	
Psalm 49:16–21	
Proverbs 19:1–4	
Proverbs 30:8	
Wisdom 7:7–12	
Sirach 11:17–21	
Sirach 27:1	
Sirach 31:1–7	
Sirach 31:8–11	
Isaiah 10:1–3	
Jeremiah 5:25–29	
1 Timothy 6:10	

He who loves money, never has enough of it!

14. What does God do when someone walks away or rejects Him? CCC 30

15. How do people seek happiness, and where can happiness be found? CCC 1723

16. What is the Catholic Church's attitude toward the poor? CCC 2444–2445

17. What is necessary for entrance into the kingdom of heaven? CCC 2544

18. Recall a time in your life when you were in need and someone met that need.

19. In what ways do you share your time, talent, and treasure for the kingdom of God?

20. What does God promise in Proverbs 3:9–10?

** Some fear giving money to the poor lest it be used on alcohol, drugs, or cigarettes. Brainstorm ways that you could be generous to the poor and insure that needs are met, i.e. gift certificates to a grocery store or to a restaurant, serving in a soup kitchen, other.

CHAPTER 15

Triumphal Entry into Jerusalem

Matthew 21:1–17, Mark 11:1–19, Luke 19:28–48

Hosanna to the Son of David!
Blessed is he who comes in the name of the Lord! (Matthew 21:9)

The final entry of Jesus into Jerusalem is associated with the Mount of Olives. This mountain, 810 meters or 2650 feet high, is east of Mount Zion and is the highest point in the immediate vicinity of historical Jerusalem. The Kidron Valley separates the Mount of Olives from Mount Zion, where the temple of Jerusalem was built. The Mount of Olives derives its name from the olive trees that have been cultivated in the area from ancient times.

Geographically, a two miles long mountain range, which includes the Mount of Olives, closes the holy city from the east. To the north, the present site of the Hebrew University, Mount Scopus or *Har ha-Zophim* in Hebrew, called the Mount of Lookout, is the best place to observe the city of Jerusalem. The holy city was laid under siege about 50 times in her long history and was conquered about 40 times. Foreign invaders from Pharaoh Sheshonq in 925 BC to Nebuchadnezar in 587 BC, and from Titus in 70 AD to Moshe Dayan in 1967 encamped on the northern slope of the Mount of Olives to breach and invade the walls of Jerusalem on the unprotected north side.

The location of the Mount of Olives with respect to Jerusalem has a spiritual significance linked to the first and second coming of the Messiah (Zechariah 9:9, 14:1–5). Zechariah predicted that the Messiah would come to the temple area from the Mount of Olives. Joel prophesied that the last judgment would take place in the valley of Jehosaphat below the mountain (Joel 3:2ff). Ezekiel prophesied that the glory of God would abandon the city of idolatry and stop on the mountain east of it (Ezekiel 11:22). Partially these prophecies were fulfilled when Jesus entered the temple by way of the Mount of Olives. Christian pilgrims, reconstructing the events of Palm Sunday, stop at Bethphage, a town on the route to Jerusalem from the Mount of Olives. Here our Lord mounted the mother of the colt to enter the Holy City (Matthew 21:1–11). A small church in Bethphage reminds one of the extreme humility of Jesus who used the animal associated with submission and obedience rather than the horse used by kings or generals in military conquest.

Today, the steeple of the Russian Orthodox Church of the Ascension of Jesus on the Mount of Olives provides a breathtaking view of Jerusalem. Another pilgrim church on the Mount of Olives, *Dominus Flevit,* "Our Lord Wept," recalls Jesus' weeping over Jerusalem (Luke 19:41–44). The architect Antonio Barluzzi designed the sanctuary in the form of a tear, recalling that our Lord wept over the hardness of the human heart and the lack of response to His invitation to repent. The weeping of Jesus also anticipates the destruction of Jerusalem in 70 AD. Today, Jewish tombs cover the western slope of the Mount of Olives. Jews desire to be buried there for an eschatological reason—they want to be the first, ready to greet the Messiah, at the resurrection of the dead.

The descent to the valley of Kidron is marked by the Russian Orthodox Church of Mary Magdalen and then by the Basilica of the Agony of Jesus. Before crossing the brook in the Kidron valley, our Lord passed by the grotto of Gethsemane where Judas would betray Him with a kiss. The east gate of the temple mount is called the Gate of Susa, Golden Gate, Gate of Eternity, Gate of Judgment, Gate of Messiah, or Double Gate. Byzantine Christians identified this as the Beautiful Gate, which was mentioned in the miracle of Peter recorded in Acts 3:1–8. Muslims walled and sealed today's entrance to the temple mount at the Golden Gate to prevent the coming of the Jewish Messiah. The placement of the cemetery on the western slope would also be a cause of defilement for a Jew coming into Jerusalem through the Gate of the Messiah. Even today, Orthodox Jews wait for the Messiah under the Golden Gate in the Kidron valley during the Feast of Tabernacles. Tradition holds that Jesus will come again in glory during this feast at the end of harvest.

Jesus' entry to the Holy City caused turmoil among the inhabitants. Zechariah, the Old Testament prophet, says that the Mount of Olives will be split in two when the Lord comes (Zechariah 14:4). Jesus' solemn entry into the Jerusalem temple created division among the people. If Jesus overturned the money changers' tables at the west side of the temple compound, He had to cross the whole platform erected by King Herod the Great. Its entire length of about 900 feet from the east entrance of the valley of Josaphat would have provided a dramatic effect for Jesus' solemn entry.

All the evangelists record the entry of our Lord into Jerusalem. Matthew and Mark present the event immediately after Jesus heals two blind beggars, one of whom Mark calls Bartimaeus, on the road from Jericho to Jerusalem. Luke presents the triumphal entry of Jesus after the healing of a blind beggar, the encounter with Zacchaeus, and the parable of the pounds. Of the Synoptics, only Luke records the lament of Jesus over Jerusalem. Mark describes Jesus spending a day in Bethany, while Matthew proceeds directly to the cleansing of the temple. John presents the entry of Jesus into Jerusalem in the final stage of Jesus' public life but recounts the cleansing of the temple in the beginning of his Gospel.

One difference between Matthew and the other two Synoptic Gospels concerns the number of animals involved. Matthew refers to an "ass and a colt." Mark and Luke simply mention the colt and Luke adds on which "no one has ever sat." Only the first Gospel recalls the Old Testament prophecy, "Lo, your king comes to you; triumphant and victorious is he, humble and riding on an ass, on a colt the foal of an ass" (Zechariah 9:9). Luke's account of Jesus' entry to the city describes Jesus as being set on the colt, rather than seating Himself as in Matthew and Mark. Luke omits the branches which Matthew says the crowd cut from the trees to spread on the ground before Jesus. Mark notes that the branches were cut from the fields. Only Luke refers to the descent from the Mount of Olives and "the whole multitude of the disciples began to rejoice and praise God with a loud voice for all the mighty works that they had seen" (Luke 19:37).

The exclamation of the multitudes differs among the versions. Luke doesn't mention "Hosanna," but reports the greeting as "Peace in heaven and glory in the highest." Only Luke refers to Jesus emphatically as "king," which is also echoed in John 12:13. Matthew hails Jesus as the "Son of David." Mark points to the "kingdom of our father David that is coming." Luke reports the Pharisees demanding that Jesus rebuke the disciples, which goes unnoticed by Matthew and Mark.

Along with the cleansing of the temple, Matthew adds Jesus' healing the blind and lame, and drawing the indignation of the chief priests and scribes. Mark's observation of the cleansing of the temple is closer to John's than to the other Synoptics. Luke, the shortest narrative, reports the negative attitude of the religious leaders. Matthew uses the term "temple of God." According to Mark, Jesus would not allow anyone to carry anything through the temple. John describes different groups of animal sellers, who are driven out by Jesus with the whip of cords. Jesus shows little leniency except to the pigeon sellers, whom He verbally scolds. Only John reveals Jesus' motivation; "Zeal for thy house consumes me" (Psalm 69:9). Only Matthew tells of the crying of the children, "Hosanna to the Son of David." Luke points out that the accusers of Jesus made the temple a den of robbers.

Jesus' triumphal entry into the holy city of Jerusalem symbolizes His attempt to conquer the human heart. He first travels through the village of Bethany, which symbolizes friendship. Here Jesus would stop on His pilgrimages to Jerusalem to visit Martha, Mary, and Lazarus. Next on the route is Bethphage, the "house of figs." Jesus curses the fig tree at Bethphage (Mark 11:12–14). The leaves, which covered the shame of Adam and Eve, failed to provide fruit for Jesus. The curse of the fig tree symbolizes the rejection of those who refuse Jesus' call to faith and, in turn, crucify Him. Merely existing without yielding fruit is not the purpose for which people are given the gift of life. The lack of fruit of the fig tree is in opposition to the fruit of the Cross. This unique fruit of salvation comes from the naked and disfigured body of Jesus on the Cross in contrast to the green leaves of the barren fig tree.

Jesus sends two of His disciples to untie the ass, symbolizing everyone who accepts the Word of the Gospel and thus is freed from the bonds of ignorance and sin. The sacrament of Baptism unties the bonds of sin and brings the believer to Jesus. The donkey, the familiar domestic animal of the Middle East, is the symbol of obedience, simplicity, and fertility. In obedience, Jesus carried the burden of the Cross which brought spiritual fruit for those who accepted Him. Jesus our King began His life humbly in a manger in Bethlehem and now concludes His work by humbly riding a colt into Jerusalem. Zechariah 9:9, quoted by Matthew, emphasizes humility—a necessary condition, as we invite Jesus to sit on our own personal "donkey" and as we lay our "garments" on the road in front of Him.

Recall Psalm 118:27, quoted in the prayer of Hallel for the feast of Tabernacles, which calls the people to "bind the festal procession with branches, up to the horns of the altar!" The Jewish people gave thanks to God that when the gift of manna ceased, new life began, and they enjoyed the first fruits and harvest of the Holy Land. The olive growing on the Mount of Olives reveals the reconciliation of man with God.

Only John refers to the "palm" branches which the people used to welcome the Lord. Jesus demonstrates His love for us in His death as well as His life. Hence, Luke 19:38 ends the prayer of the crowd for salvation (this is the meaning of "hosanna") with the invocation for peace.

The arrival of Jesus affects people. Matthew reports that the "city was stirred" (Matthew 21:10) when Jesus made His triumphal entrance. This is reminiscent of Christ's birth when all of Jerusalem "was troubled" (Matthew 2:3). Only this time the authorities resolve to eliminate Jesus for good. Note the fickleness of the crowd who cry out "Hosanna to the Son of David! Blessed is he who comes in the name of the Lord!" (Matthew 21:9) now, but then cry out "Let him be crucified" (Matthew 27:22), just a few days later.

Jesus' cleansing of the temple is reminiscent of Simon Maccabeus who, after defeating the Hellensists in 142 BC, cleansed and re-dedicated the temple (1 Maccabees 13:51).The Lord claims ownership of the sacred edifice which ought to function as a house of prayer. Jesus quotes Isaiah 56:7 and Jeremiah 7:11 to justify His behavior and explain His actions. His prophetic gesture becomes the key to understanding the eschatological events. In His person the arrival of God's kingdom is announced (Mark 1:15). A new moment in salvation history is proclaimed by God in the person of Jesus. He is the true spiritual temple. Through the gift of the Holy Spirit, we put our faith in Him (1 Corinthians 6:19) and belong to Him.

The overturning of the tables of the sellers and money changers contrasts with the healing of the blind and the lame (Matthew 21:14). The beginning of Jesus' public life was marked with the prophecy of Isaiah where the Lord intends to recover the sight of the blind (Isaiah 61:1–2, Luke 4:18). The mission of Jesus was not simply to restore the liturgical order of the temple in Jerusalem or to renew liturgical ritual, but to heal spiritual blindness and paralysis. To allow this to happen, we must allow Jesus to enter the "temple" of our inner being and let Him cleanse us from everything which defiles us. Jesus purifies the temple of the defilement of progressive secularization. The basic problem behind the objection of the chief priests and scribes concerns the problem of faith (Matthew 21:16).

Do people really believe that God alone is sufficient to meet their spiritual, emotional, and material needs? Even in the culture of biblical Israel, the people were tempted to depend on human abilities rather than relying totally on God. The same temptation faces us today. Pushing God in the background, contemporary people can trust in their own talents, education, job, social security, personal savings, or the stock market as the source of their security.

This concern plagues all Christians, not just the laity. An Old Testament prophecy speaks about the need for the purification of the priesthood, like refining of gold and silver, so they may present right offerings to the Lord (Malachi 3:2–3). Shifting the focus from personal discipline and virtue to secularism, even the priests risk abandoning God's mercy and compassion and can themselves become like the cursed fig tree or the temple abandoned by God.

In light of Jesus' solemn entry to Jerusalem, there is an urgent need to get our lives and our Church in order. Since we no longer live in a Judeo-Christian society which once promoted a moral ethic based on natural law and the commandments of God, we must strive to learn and live out what God desires in a secularized society. The ignorance and knowing rejection of what God has made known through the revelation of his Son, Jesus of Nazareth, calls for prayerful action. Every serious practicing Catholic is responsible and accountable for the temple of his or her immortal soul and the example given.

The genuine reform of the Christian to become "the salt of the earth" and "the light to shine before men" (Matthew 5:13, 16) requires serious, regular study of God's Word. The Holy Spirit, the divine Author of the Word of God, prompts the soul of the believer in the study of Sacred Scripture. To avoid receiving the wrath of Jesus, displayed to the sellers and money-changers in the temple, the Catholic returns to the sacraments of Reconciliation and Eucharist on a regular and frequent basis.

The temple sellers may have been surprised by Jesus. They may have thought they were doing God's will and behaving appropriately. Perhaps they didn't recognize the greed that had crept into their lives. Frequent Confession helps guard against deceiving ourselves that all is well. Penance helps deal soberly with sins of omission and commission that can rob us of intimacy with God. This week, pray to the Holy Spirit and discern how often you should celebrate the sacrament of Reconciliation. Then, do it! Each Catholic wants to be pure and spotless when Jesus comes again in glory.

———

1. Compare the following verses.

Isaiah 62:11	
Zechariah 9:9	
Matthew 21:3–5	
Mark 11:1–5	
Luke 19:28–34	

2. Describe the geography of Jesus' journey. Luke 19:28–30

3. Relate something special about Bethany? John 11:1–5

4. What event can you predict from the geography of these verses?

Joel 3:1–2	
Zechariah 14:4–5	
Mark 13:7–27	
Revelation 21:2–4	

5. What does Hosanna mean? CCC 559, Matthew 21:9

6. When do Catholics recite the verse from Matthew 21:9 at Mass?

7. Compare the following verses.

Matthew 21:9	
Mark 11:9–10	
Luke 19:38	

8. What did the Pharisees demand of Jesus in Luke 19:38–39?

9. How did Jesus respond to the Pharisees?

Habakkuk 2:11	
Luke 19:28–40	
Psalm 8:2	
Matthew 21:16	

10. Explain the situation in Luke 19:41–44

11. How did Saint Peter advise the early Christians to behave so as to glorify God on the day of visitation? 1 Peter 2:11–12

12. What does Jesus' entry into Jerusalem show? CCC 560

13. How did the crowds interpret Jesus' entry into Jerusalem? Matthew 21:10–11

14. Compare and contrast the following accounts.

Matthew 21:12–14	
Mark 11:15–18	
Luke 19:45–48	
John 2:13–17	

15. Why did Jesus react so violently? Psalm 69:9

16. What can you learn from these Old Testament passages?

Isaiah 56:7	
Jeremiah 7:11	

17. How did the people respond to Jesus' words? Luke 19:48

18. Why should someone cling to God's Word?

Psalm 119:11	
Psalm 119:33–34	
Psalm 119:103–105	
Psalm 119:114	

19. How can Catholics make the Bible come alive for them? CCC 108

20. Nobody should experience the wrath of God like the temple moneychangers did. The sacrament of Reconciliation enables Catholics to ensure that the temple of the Holy Spirit remains pure (1 Corinthians 6:19–20). What is essential to this sacrament? CCC 1424

** When was the last time you celebrated the sacrament of Reconciliation? How about this week?

If you have been away from the sacrament of Reconciliation for a while, ask your group to pray for you that you might receive the grace to make a good confession soon.

CHAPTER 16

Controversies

Matthew 22:15–23:39, Mark 12:1–40, Luke 20:1–47

**He who is greatest among you shall be your servant;
whoever exalts himself will be humbled,
and whoever humbles himself will be exalted.** (Matthew 23:11–12)

According to the famous Jewish scholar David Flusser, there were about twenty four religious movements in Israel at the time of Jesus. Several are mentioned in the New Testament and in the writings of Josephus Falvius. These Jewish groups demonstrated tremendous diversity of doctrine and religious practice. They disputed among themselves, but it was all "in the family." Sometimes family disputes are bitter, and in this spirit we consider the controversies between Jesus and the religious leaders.

The "Zealots" were the political revolutionaries responsible for bringing disaster down upon the Jewish people. The Zealots' militant rebellion against the Roman forces increased until the Pentecost festival of 66 AD when the Jewish revolt began. By November 66 AD, the Jews expelled the Roman prefect Gersius Florus, the successor of Pontius Pilate, from Judea. Rome retaliated and Jewish fortresses and cities fell until the summer of 70 AD when the temple of Jerusalem was burned and the city sacked. This disaster destroyed the continuity of Jewish life in the Holy Land, and the diversity of religious movements disappeared, leaving only normative Rabbinic Judaism and Christianity.

Luke identifies the tenth of the twelve apostles as "Simon who was called the zealot" (Luke 6:15). Jesus chose Simon from among these militants who would later spark the Jewish war with Rome. The traditional date for the martyrdom of Saint Simon the Zealot is February 70 AD, when the Jewish war was raging and the siege of Jerusalem was about to begin.

Disaster fell on many groups because of the Jewish rebellion. Among the first to suffer were the Samaritans, whom General Vespasian massacred at their holy mountain Gerizim in May 67. The following summer, Vespasian's forces burned the monastery of the Essenes at Qumran on the shore of the Dead Sea. Fortunately, the monks hid their precious scrolls in eleven nearby caves. When the scrolls were discovered in 1947, they fleshed out our knowledge of first-century Judaism.

The Essenes, stern orthodox Jews awaiting the coming of Messiah, were known in Qumran. The discovery of the Dead Sea Scrolls provided writings of the Essenes themselves and scholars have identified features of Essene life that have parallels in Christianity, such as a ruling council of twelve, like the twelve apostles. The Essenes used a different calendar than the one used by the high priests in Jerusalem, which could explain some differences in holy week chronology in the four gospels.

The ruins of the monastic complex at Qumran reveals a number of bathing pools used for their extensive ritual bathing practices. John the Baptist, who lived "in the wilderness of Judea"

(Matthew 3:1), not far from Qumran, may have been an Essene. At least two of the disciples, including Andrew the brother of Peter, were disciples of John the Baptist before they came to Jesus (John 1:40). Saint John's frequent theme of light and darkness is also found in the writings of the Essenes, showing some interdependence. When Qumran was sacked, the Essenes disappeared from the face of the earth, while no amount of persecution would prove sufficient to destroy Christianity.

Leaders from several different religious groups appear in the New Testament in Matthew 22, Mark 12, and Luke 20 to interrogate Jesus. The leaders bring their agendas with them, and their interplay with Jesus reveals their beliefs and clarifies the doctrines of Christianity. The Pharisees first approach Jesus in tandem with the Herodians.

> The Pharisees went and took counsel how to entangle him in his talk. And they sent their disciples to him, along with the Herodians, saying, "Teacher, we know that you are true, and teach the way of God truthfully, and care for no man; for you do not regard the position of men. Tell us, then, what you think. Is it lawful to pay taxes to Caesar, or not?" But Jesus, aware of their malice, said, "Why put me to the test, you hypocrites? Show me the money for the tax." And they brought him a coin. And Jesus said to them, "Whose likeness and inscription is this?" They said, "Caesar's." Then he said to them, "Render therefore to Caesar the things that are Caesar's, and to God the things that are God's." When they heard it they marveled; and they left him and went away. (Matthew 22:15–22)

Of the three gospels which report this incident, Matthew's is the most compelling, because Matthew had been a tax collector for the Romans before his call to be an apostle. He gives the correct name for the Roman coin—the denarius. Matthew had been treated as an outcast because of his previous line of work, handling coins with the imperial likeness and inscription on them. "Render to Caesar what is Caesar's and to God what is God's" is a foundational concept in Western Civilization. To no one, however, did it resonate more than to the evangelist who had once been a tax collector.

The Pharisees and Herodians created a conundrum for Jesus. If He advised against paying the tax, it would put Him in league with the zealots and in disfavor with Rome. If He insisted that one must pay the tax, it would make the zealots His enemies. It was a "no-win" situation. Yet, Jesus cuts through the dilemma with consummate skill. He doesn't just extricate Himself; He provides the teaching principle that saints, scholars, and ordinary believers have used for two millennia to establish right proportionality in the treatment of things sacred and profane. Even His enemies were impressed.

The Herodians had the trust of the Romans, collecting taxes and administering portions of the holy land. Jesus' answer seems to exonerate the Herodians from blame in their business. Since the Herodians were responsible for the beheading of John the Baptist, the citizens of the tribal coast of the middle East would have expected Jesus to seek vengeance for His kinsman. Here, Jesus practices what He preaches and forgives His enemies. Ultimately, Jesus will die on the Cross to forgive their sins.

Another group, the Sadducees, who did not believe in the resurrection since it was not found in the Law of Moses (Matthew 16:1–12), come to see Jesus with a hypothetical situation advancing their beliefs. Luke 20:27–40 describes the question concerning whose wife would a woman be, who had married seven brothers and been widowed seven times, while remaining childless.

Now, the Sadducees were a priestly group, overseeing the Temple establishment in Jerusalem. They were influenced by Greek ways of life and thought. The Greeks scorned the idea of a bodily resurrection at the end of time, because they thought of the body as inherently imperfect and inferior to the mind. A goal of Greek philosophy was to escape from the body's limitations. The Greeks saw death as a liberation from the body, so why would they want to get a body back?

The Pharisees held the doctrine of bodily resurrection. Now, the Sadducees, seeing Jesus disputing with the Pharisees, approach Jesus hoping to enlist support for their belief in a fleshless life after death. Here Jesus does not avoid taking sides as He did in the case of the tax. Jesus aligns Himself squarely in league with the Pharisees on the question of the resurrection. The doctrine of the Pharisees helps set the groundwork for Jesus' own Resurrection, while the belief of the Sadducees would undermine the truth. Saint Paul explains, "For if the dead are not raised, then Christ has not been raised. If Christ has not been raised, your faith is futile and you are still in your sins" (1 Corinthians 15:16–17).

Following the Pharisees, Herodians, and Sadducees, another representative steps forward to question Jesus. Matthew calls him a lawyer and Mark a scribe. A lawyer was knowledgeable in the Torah, the Law of Moses. A scribe was literate and able to read and write. The Scribes, responsible in the Old Testament for keeping military, government, legal, and financial records, did not represent any particular religious establishment in Israel at the time of our Lord. They belonged either to the Pharisees or Sadducees. The Scribes were professional copiers of God's Word, legal experts, and teachers of the Law. They made their living interpreting the Law and teaching applications of oral traditions. Mark 12:28–34 reports a scribe asking Jesus about which is the first commandment.

The Mosaic Law contained 613 separate commandments, including ethical, cultural, social, and hygienic rules. With this large body of Law, one question frequently discussed by the early rabbis was "Which commandment is the first of all?" (Mark 12:28). The response that Jesus gives, that love of God is first and love of neighbor second, is indeed the shared conclusion of the rabbis. Christianity and Judaism stand side by side here on the same solid ground of divine love and human compassion. Jesus' words to the scribe, "You are not far from the kingdom of God" (Mark 12:34) are similar to His words on the Cross to the good thief; "Today you will be with me in Paradise" (Luke 23:43). This meeting of minds between Jesus and the scribe depicts a relationship of mutual respect founded on good principles and shared values, a perfect model for Jewish-Christian relations.

No one can deny the conflict between Jesus and religious leaders of His time. However, debate does not always sunder relationships, but sometimes is a means of arriving at shared truth. Jews argue about important things, precisely because they are so important. Jesus demonstrates His Jewishness in holding His own with the best of them. These debates resolve important religious questions—the relationship between the sacred and the secular, the truth of the bodily resurrection, and the love of God and neighbor over any other law or religious observance.

Only the Sadducees stood in opposition to one of these doctrines, and they disappeared with the destruction of the Temple.

In view of the doctrinal consensus established between Jesus and the Pharisees, it is quite jarring to read on. The tone of Matthew 23 is exceptionally harsh in contrast to the kindness of Jesus through the rest of the Gospels. Matthew gives the speech against the Scribes and Pharisees considerably more space than his Synoptic counterparts, thirty-six verses in Matthew compared to two or three in Luke and Mark. In Matthew 23:1–36, our Lord warns the disciples not to be like the religious leaders and articulates their condemnation.

Jesus does not condemn the doctrine of the Pharisees, but criticizes their practices. Their teaching is correct, but they do not model good behavior—a criticism that religious leaders of every time must take care not to deserve. Having right doctrine is not enough; it must be lived in a deeply interior way and in charity. Matthew 23 constitutes the climax of Jesus' rejection of the superficial spirituality of the Pharisaic establishment which failed to bring holiness to Israel.

Each of us shares the stigma of the religious leaders if we arrogantly grasp the Word, desiring only to appear intelligent and revered, without trying to commune with the Author of the Word. Without the Holy Spirit, observation of the Law can become a pretext for human pride. Church leaders who acclaim the places of honor (Luke 20:46) follow the pattern of the Pharisees. For example, Paul confronts Peter in Antioch for his hypocrisy, in trying to save face in front of the Judeo-Christians (Galatians 2:11ff).

The seat of Moses in this text has both literal and metaphorical meaning. The Moses seat, an elevated throne, is still visible in the excavated synagogue of ancient Corazin. Archeologists found a Moses seat in Tiberias, but it was later stolen. Rabbis sat on such seats when they taught in the synagogues. "Moses seat" also refers to the authority in interpreting the Law, which the Scribes and Pharisees arrogantly exercised. Jesus points out that the Pharisees do not practice what they preach.

The second part of Jesus' warning concerns the practice of the Scribes and Pharisees in drawing attention to themselves as teachers. The danger of hypocrisy comes from the imposition of personal interest over the Gospel call for repentance. The Law of the Spirit does not gratify human pride (Galatians 5:17), but requires discernment lest we become slaves of our selfishness. Christ forms the new disciples into Christian teachers with pure hearts and genuine love for God and the brothers and sisters.

In Greek theater, actors wore masks to display a variety of attitudes. The word "hypocrite" means "one who acts or pretends." God does not accept pretending or play-acting in matters of faith. Jesus shows that the religious leaders hid behind masks of superficial godliness, concealing hearts of bitterness, envy, and pride. External observance of the Law failed to bring about genuine repentance. Saint Clement of Rome offers a saying of Jesus not recorded in the Gospels, that when two things become one, the exterior as the interior, then the kingdom will come.

The Pharisees avoided ritual uncleanness at all costs. The central focus of their lifestyle was to stay ceremonially clean. Jesus criticizes their failure to combine external correctness with internal purity of heart. The cup of the soul must be cleansed from the inside out. Greed and self-indulgence preclude righteousness. Repenting of pride enables one to regain a pure heart and become sensitive to human misery. Jesus accuses the religious leaders of hypocrisy. As in the Sermon on the Mount, Jesus obeys the Law of Moses (Matthew 5:17–19), but criticizes the leaders' narrow and duplicitous interpretation of the Law, insisting that others obey man-made rules, which they themselves disregard. Our Lord sees the heart and judges their behavior as hypocritical because in obeying the rules, they honor themselves rather than God.

Jesus presents seven woes or denunciations against the religious leaders. "Woe" expresses Jesus' sorrow for the evil committed. The hypocrite seeks self-approval and personal gratification rather than the glory of God the Father. Instead of relying completely on divine Providence, the religious leaders place heavy burdens on the shoulders of the weak. The blind guides lack pure hearts. Overzealous legalism concerning tithes of herbs and spices highlights the hypocrisy of the Pharisees, because there is no requirement in the Mosaic Law to tithe these foods. In their extreme interpretation of the Law, the Scribes and Pharisees neglect justice and mercy.

Compare these Woes with the Beatitudes.

Woe	Beatitude
You shut the kingdom. (Matthew 23:13)	Theirs is the Kingdom. (Matthew 5:3)
You make him a child of hell. (Matthew 23:15)	They will be called sons of God. (Matthew 5:9)
Woe to you, blind guides. (Matthew 23:16)	They shall see God. (Matthew 5:8)
Pharisees neglect mercy. (Matthew 23:23)	Blessed are the merciful. (Matthew 5:7)
First cleanse the inside. (Matthew 23:26)	Hunger for righteousness. (Matthew 5:6)
Tombs—dead men's bones. (Matthew. 23:27)	Blessed are those who mourn. (Matthew 5:4)
How will you escape hell? (Matthew 23:33)	They will inherit the earth. (Matthew 5:5)

Jesus accuses the religious leaders of murderous intent, which has roots in the past. The bloody history of man starts with the murder of Abel by his brother, Cain. Zechariah, the prophet, was stoned by the people in the court of the house of the Lord, when he spoke the Word of the Lord and rebuked the people for their sin (2 Chronicles 24:20–22). Cain is the first murderer in the Bible and 2 Chronicles closes the historical books of the Bible. Therefore, innocent blood marks the whole history of Israel from the beginning to the end, climaxing with the murder of Jesus.

Matthew 23 closes with a warning that corresponds with the one given at the beginning of the first Gospel (Matthew 3:7). Woe to you, serpents and vipers, parallels the ancient serpent from the Garden of Eden, a murderer from the beginning and the father of lies (John 8:44). Jesus recalls the murderers of the prophets of old, while at the same time alerting His disciples about the persecution to come.

Matthew himself was once a scribe. As a tax-collector, Matthew laid heavy burdens on men's shoulders (Matthew 23:4) and used his wealth to put on feasts (Matthew 23:6). Matthew shows humility in recording this speech of Jesus which may have pointed directly at him!

Jesus' great commission, sending disciples to the whole world, requires faith and determination even to this day. Accepting the challenge of Jesus requires not only hope in the future coming of the Lord at the end of salvation history (Matthew 23:39), but also the testimony of the faith of the martyrs of the past. Jesus challenges us today as He did the people of that time.

As Christians do we seek the places of prominence? Do we impose burdens on others, without offering to help? Do we examine our consciences nightly and repent of our wrongdoing? Do we seek the mercy of God for ourselves and offer that mercy to others? Without the love of Christ in our hearts and the power of the Holy Spirit, Christianity will not appeal to anybody. Beg God for the grace to encounter His love and share it with those who most need the love of Christ.

---

1. To whom was Jesus speaking in Matthew 23:1?

Jesus spoke to the crowds and to disciples.

2. What did Jesus tell the disciples to do concerning the Pharisees? Matthew 23:2–3

The scribes and Pharisees have taken their seat. therefore, do not follow their example,

3. Find a contemporary application of Matthew 23:4. How do people do this now?

they Tie heavy Burdens. and hard to carry and they Lay them on people shoulders. but they will not LIFT a finger TO Help.

4. Identify the motive of the Pharisee's good deeds. Matthew 23:5–7

all their works are performed To be seen they love places. of Honor. at banquets. in marketplaces.

5. What commonality can you find in the following verses?

	in haven
Matthew 23:9–11	*Call no one on earth father but the one*
James 3:1–2	*not many of you should became Teachers.*

6. Compare and contrast the following verses.

Genesis 26:24	Isaac the Lord appeared and said I'm the father of Abraham
Jeremiah 3:19	Condition for forgiveness
Luke 16:24	Lazarus and Rich man, cried out, for father abraham for help
James 2:21	Body without a spirit is dead also without works is dead
1 Timothy 5:1	Do not rebuke older man, but appeal to him a father.

7. What do the following verses teach?

Matthew 20:26–27	But it shall not be so among you
Matthew 23:11–12	
Mark 12:38–40	

8. Identify the seven woes of Jesus.

Matthew 23:13–14	
Matthew 23:15	
Matthew 23:16–20	
Matthew 23:23–24	
Matthew 23:25–26	
Matthew 23:27–28	
Matthew 23:29–35	

9. Describe the drama in the following situations.

Genesis 4:8	Cain and his brother. Cain killed is brother
2 Chronicles 24:20–22	
Luke 11:49–51	
Revelation 18:23–24	

10. What type of death is foretold in Matthew 23:34?

11. Describe the scenario in Mark 15:22–27.

12. How did the disciples explain their disappointment? Luke 24:18–21

13. What happened to these disciples of Jesus?

Acts 7:54–60	
Acts 12:1–3	

14. After denouncing the Pharisees to whom does Jesus point in Mark's account?

Mark 12:38–40	
Mark 12:41–44	

15. Identify the woes that Luke records.

Luke 11:42–43	
Luke 11:44	
Luke 11:45–46	
Luke 11:47–51	
Luke 11:52	

16. How did the Pharisees respond to Jesus' criticism? Luke 11:53–54

17. What terms does Jesus use at the beginning of this Gospel and here?

Matthew 3:7–12	
Matthew 23:33	

18. What emotion does Jesus show at the end of this chapter? Matthew 23:37–38

19. Compare the following verses.

Jeremiah 12:7	
Hosea 9:15	

20. How can you avoid hypocrisy in your own life? 1 Peter 5:5–7

Monthly Social Activity

This month your small group will meet for coffee, tea, or a simple breakfast, lunch, or dessert in someone's home. Please remember to "keep it simple!"

Pray for this social event and for the host or hostess. Try, if at all possible, to attend. Offer hospitality for one of the socials to be held at your home.

Activity

Share about a recent movie you've seen or book you've read.

Does this book or movie have a theme that you could connect with a story from the Gospel?

CHAPTER 17

End Times Discourse

Matthew 24:1–25:46, Mark 13:1–37, Luke 21:1–36

**When the Son of man comes in glory, and all the angels with him,
then he will sit on his glorious throne. Before him will be gathered all the nations,
and he will separate them one from another as a shepherd
separates the sheep from the goats.** (Matthew 25:31–32)

Eschatology is the study of the ultimate or last things—death, judgment, heaven, and hell. With increasing emphasis, after Peter's proclamation of Jesus as the Christ in Caesarea Philippi (Matthew 16:13–28), Jesus speaks about a glorious conclusion of salvation history.

Jesus Prophesies the Destruction of the Temple ~ The Synoptic authors tackle this theme of the last things as Jesus' answer to the disciples' two fold question: "When will this be, and what will be the sign of your coming at the close of the age?" (Matthew 24:3). Jesus answers the second question by pointing out the signs that will appear at the end of the world. He doesn't answer the first question, for it is not the will of God the Father to provide divine revelation concerning the time or the hour. Jesus simply alerts His followers to be watchful and ready.

The eschatological discourse of Jesus in the Synoptic Gospels provides the last of a series of instructions given by Jesus. This speech becomes the last will and testament of Jesus in which He strengthens the faith of His disciples before His trial and crucifixion. Jesus delivers this discourse immediately before His Passion as the final sayings of His public teaching.

Here, as elsewhere in Matthew, Jesus frequently used the title "Son of man," pre-figured by the heavenly figure in Daniel 7:13. Saint Augustine noted that the title "Son of man" is the one most associated with Jesus' Passion and death.

Death ~ This world is passing away. The Greek thinker Heraclitus taught that the one constant in the universe was change. All living things are on a trajectory toward death, and even the "everlasting" hills erode and change in the span of geological time.

There are two kinds of death: 1) the body's death at the end of our time on earth, and 2) the soul's death at the moment of mortal sin. The book of Revelation identifies this soul-death by the term "the second death" (Revelation 2:11, 20:14, 21:8).

You may wonder. Why does death of either kind exist? How final is death? Is anything more powerful than death?

The Bible provides answers to those questions, teaching that:
† "God did not make death" (Wisdom 1:13).
† "Do not fear those who kill the body but cannot kill the soul" (Matthew 10:28).
† "Love is strong as death" (Song of Songs 8:6).

When Christ came the first time, He conquered the world's death by means of His death on the Cross. When He comes a second time, the mortality of the body will end. "Death shall be no more, neither shall there be mourning nor crying nor pain any more" (Revelations 21:4).

Therefore Saint Paul says, "Death is swallowed up in victory. O death, where is thy victory? O death, where is thy sting" (1 Corinthians 15:54–55).

The second coming of Christ will transform the futility and decay brought about by sin and rebellion against God. The realm of death will be overcome with the resurrection of the dead (1 Thessalonians 4:14), and all things will be subjected to Christ so that God may be everything to everyone (1 Corinthians 15:28). The Cross is the interpretive key to this text. The revelation of God on the Cross demonstrates the holiness of God. The Cross is the power and wisdom of God, but to this world the Cross is folly, a stumbling block (1 Corinthians 1:23). Jesus' death on the Cross and His Resurrection from the dead are the bases of the Christian faith. The final events of the history of the world were prefigured in the crucifixion of Jesus Christ, when Jesus defeats the power of evil by His supreme sacrifice of love. The glory of God revealed on the Cross calls every person to repent. So, the appropriate human response to the Cross of Christ is sorrow for personal sin and vigilance in following Jesus. The Cross embraces all of human history in revealing the wondrous love of God. The second coming of Christ will bring the eschatological completion of creation into full communion with God. The Church on earth continues to lift up the Cross as the sign of Jesus' love for all and the testimony of faith, and will continue to do so until the final event announced in the promises of Jesus.

Judgment ~ There are two stages of judgment:
† the particular judgment that each person will experience at the moment of death, and
† the general judgment that the entire human race will share on the last day.

At the end of our lives, we will be judged on how well we have loved. Our refusal to love and to serve others alienates us from God. Our moral and ethical choices now will determine our plight for all eternity. By God's grace, the goal of our lives should be the happiness of full communion with God forever in heaven.

We ask Mary's assistance for our particular judgment when we ask: "Pray for us sinners now and at the hour of our death." We pray for a "good death," meaning access to the grace of God.

When there is danger of death, a priest should be called so that as many sacraments as appropriate can be administered—the sacraments of Reconciliation, Anointing, and Holy Communion which is called "viaticum," spiritual food for the journey. Other sacraments may also be needed—Baptism, Confirmation, even the blessing of a marriage. The Church sees so much value in receiving the sacraments when death draws near that she relaxes some of her regulations. For example, even a laicized priest may give sacraments to the dying.

Pope Paul VI extended to every dying person a plenary indulgence, provided he or she had been in the habit of saying at least one prayer on a regular basis. (An indulgence is the remission before God of the temporal punishment due to sins whose guilt has already been forgiven.) Even in the absence of a priest, God's mercy can reach out to one who is sorry for sin and has a habit of prayer. These graces prepare the dying person for the particular judgment that will usher him or her into heaven, hell, or purgatory.

The great religions of Judaism, Christianity, and Islam all teach that there will be a final judgment of the entire human race on the last day. Just as particular judgment follows the death of the individual, so general judgment will follow the death of the world.

Many missed the revelation of God in the first coming of Christ. The second coming will be unmistakable. Jesus, who appeared on the Cross in dishonor, will then appear in majesty and power upon His throne of glory. The final reunion with God offers everlasting life. However, this gracious gift requires purification from any defilement of sin. Jesus will judge all people and separate them according to each person's individual response to Him and the conduct of his or her life. Jesus warns us to keep alive the moral message of the Gospel. In eschatological parables He emphasizes the Christian's responsibility to persevere over time. *Kairos*, the critical time of human response, demonstrates the urgency of action as the decisive criteria of approval or rejection of the servant left in charge (Matthew 24:47–51). The wise and foolish virgins, and the servants entrusted with talents underscore personal responsibility for action.

Last Judgment, Matthew 25:31–46 ~ When the history of this world is concluded and the Son of man comes in glory in the company of the angels to judge the living and the dead, the supreme Shepherd will gather humanity and separate the sheep from the goats. Sheep are the righteous people—gentle, patient, harmed by others, but bearing injury without resistance. Goats, on the other hand, refer to the sinners who are capricious, proud, and belligerent.

Jesus evaluates people according to their response to the poor. Works of mercy impact final judgment. Our present response, in our critical time of challenge, determines the verdict of our future. We prove ourselves by how we show compassion to others. The underlying theology of this text lies in the unconditional love of God for the world and His commandment to love one another as He has loved us (John 13:34).

Jesus came into the world in a poor family and identified with the downtrodden. The poor often respond generously to the Gospel, becoming disciples of Jesus. Through love and service to others, we love and serve Christ Himself. The suffering Servant on the Cross identifies with the hungry, thirsty, stranger, naked, sick, and prisoners. Approaching the needy with compassion, we find the sign of the Cross in their suffering and the way to our personal salvation.

The Passion of Christ continues in the suffering of the little ones until the end of the world. We are called to share the Cross in love for the sake of the Church (Colossians 1:24). Faith sustained by works of mercy overcomes fear of judgment. God's grace enables evangelization in the world. Embracing the love and mercy of God propels us to become disciples of Jesus. The surprising reaction of those on the left of the shepherd, oblivious to how they offended God, warns us of the seriousness of our sins of omission.

Hell ~ Matthew speaks about hell more often than any other New Testament writer—nine times in all, including three times in the Sermon of the Mount (Matthew 5:22, 29, 30).

Matthew uses the classical Greek word *Hades* twice:
† "And you, Capernaum … You shall be brought down to Hades" (Matthew 11:23).
† "On this rock I will build my church, and the [gates of Hades] will not prevail against it" (Matthew 16:18).

The Book of Revelation uses the word *Hades* four times, each in tandem with the word "death":

† "I died, and behold I am alive for evermore, and I have the keys of Death and Hades" (Revelation 1:18).
† "Behold, a pale horse, and its rider's name was Death, and Hades followed him" (Revelation 6:8).
† "Death and Hades gave up the dead in them, and all were judged by what they had done" (Revelation 20:13).
† "Then Death and Hades were thrown into the lake of fire" (Revelation 20:14).

According to ancient witnesses, Matthew wrote his Gospel originally in Hebrew. If so, it is not surprising that, instead of the Greek word *"Hades,"* Matthew prefers the Hebrew word *"Gehenna,"* which he uses seven times (Matthew 5:22, 5:29–30, 10:28, 18:9, 23:15, 23:33). *Ge* is the Hebrew word for "valley," and the *Hinnom* is the proper name of a valley which runs along the southern edge of Jerusalem far below Mount Zion. The Jerusalemites dumped their refuse there, and garbage fires were always burning. The fires of *"Ge-Hinnom"* became a symbol for the perpetual fires of hell. Jesus Himself teaches that at the final judgment, those on His left will be told: "Depart from me, you cursed, into the eternal fire prepared for the devil and his angels" (Matthew 25:41).

That hell is a real place and that some will be consigned there for all eternity, is a biblical truth, a defined doctrine of the Church, and a frequent theme in the visions of the saints. The fear of hell is sufficient impulse for good contrition—"I detest all my sins, because I dread the loss of heaven and the pains of hell." But there is a better impulse yet—"because they offend You, my God, who are all good and deserving of all my love." Our refuge is the goodness of God, and the place of that refuge is heaven.

Heaven ~ The stars fall and the heavens are shaken. The sun and the moon are darkened. These are images of the end of the world. With the passing of this world everything turns upside down. The signs in the skies should be viewed in the light of Jesus' death on the Cross. The glory of the Cross imposes a new order in which evil is forever obliterated, sin is forgiven, and the world is created anew through the power of God's forgiveness and redemption.

The New Testament mentions heaven more often than hell. Matthew references hell nine times, but heaven 74 times. The words "sky" and "heaven" are the same in Hebrew and Greek. The Bible speaks sometimes of the final heaven of the saints and sometimes of the this-worldly sky above our heads. The latter will pass away (Revelation 21:1). The stars, powers, signs, and clouds seem to refer to the skies of this world (Matthew 24:29), but the elect and the angels (Matthew 24:31) surely point to an other-worldly heaven. Matthew makes clear that after the end of history there will be a heaven for the just (Matthew 25:34).

Saint Paul says of that heaven: "[N]o eye has seen, nor ear heard, nor the heart of man conceived, what God has prepared for those who love him" (1 Corinthians 2:9), seeming to refer to the prophet's statement "from of old no one has heard or perceived by the ear, no eye has seen a God besides thee, who works for those who wait for him" (Isaiah 64:4). Certainly, however, by the end of the New Testament period, one set of eyes have indeed seen: "And I saw the holy city, new Jerusalem, coming down out of heaven from God" (Revelation 21:2).

We hope for heaven for ourselves, and all people, even the most hardened of sinners. To exclude anyone from the hope of heaven is "theological hatred," while extending the hope of heaven to another demonstrates the proper exercise of the theological virtue of charity. To give every gift this world offers but to deny heaven would be hatred not love. As God loves us, He offers us the promise of heaven; "Rejoice and be glad, for your reward is great in heaven" (Matthew 5:12).

> Knowing then these things, let us not be offended, neither let us be confounded at any of the things that happen, nor bring in upon us the storm of thought, but giving place to God's providence, let us give heed to virtue, and flee vice, that we may also attain to the good things to come, by the grace and love towards man of our Lord Jesus Christ, by whom and with whom be glory unto the Father together with the Holy Spirit, now and always, and world without end. Amen.
>
> Saint John Chrysostom (344–407 AD), *Homilies on Matthew*, 75.

1. What can you learn from these Old Testament verses?

Genesis 18:25	
Psalm 7:7–8	
Psalm 96:13	
Psalm 110:5–7	

2. Compare the following verses.

Matthew 24:29	Mark 13:24–25	Luke 21:25–26

3. What does Jesus advise and foretell in Matthew 16:24–28?

4. Identify any distinct information from these passages.

Matthew 24:30–31	
Mark 13:26–27	
Luke 21:27–28	

5. To whom does Jesus foretell the second coming in Mark 14:61–62?

6. Describe the situation in 1 Thessalonians 4:15–18.

7. What can you learn from the following Old Testament prophets?

Isaiah 13:9–11	
Ezekiel 32:7–8	
Joel 2:10–13	
Amos 8:9	

8. To whom do the following verses point?

Daniel 7:13	
Acts 7:55–56	
Revelation 1:13	
Revelation 14:14	

9. What two things can you learn from the following verses?

Revelation 15:4	
Revelation 16:7	

10. How could you identify the Last Judgment?

Zechariah 9:14	
Matthew 24:29–31	
1 Corinthians 15:51–52	
1 Thessalonians 4:16	

11. What will be brought to light on the last day? CCC 678

12. How could someone risk condemnation?

CCC 679	
Matthew 25:31–46	
2 Timothy 4:3–4	

13. Explain these parables.

Matthew 24:45–51	
Matthew 25:1–13	
Matthew 25:14–30	

14. Compare these verses.

Ezekiel 34:17	
Matthew 25:31–33	

15. Salvation is a free gift. Is it possible to renounce your salvation? Hebrews 6:4–6

16. What encouragement can you find in the following verses?

Isaiah 58:6–9	
Matthew 25:34–40	
James 1:27, 2:15–17	
Hebrews 13:1–3	

17. Identify the promise in these verses.

Proverbs 19:17	
Mark 9:41	
Hebrews 6:10–12	

18. What does Jesus teach in the following verses?

Matthew 5:22	
Matthew 5:29–30	
Matthew 10:28	
Matthew 18:7–9	
Matthew 23:13–15	

19. Do you think hell is real? Matthew 25:46, CCC 1033

— How could one avoid ending up in hell? Matthew 7:13–14, CCC 1036–1037

20. What hope can you glean from the following passages?

Psalm 73:25–26	
Psalm 84:1–2, 10–11	
Mark 16:19	
John 14:1–3	
Colossians 3:1–4	
1 Peter 3:21–22	

CHAPTER 18

The Last Supper

Matthew 26:17–29, Mark 14:12–25, Luke 22:7–20, 1 Corinthians 11:23–26

Now as they were eating, Jesus took bread, and blessed, and broke it, and gave it to the disciples and said, "Take, eat; this is my body." And he took a cup, and when he had given thanks he gave it to them saying, "Drink of it, all of you; for this is my blood of the covenant, which is poured out for many for the forgiveness of sins." (Matthew 26:26–28)

Matthew and John were both present at the Last Supper to experience Jesus instituting the sacraments of the Eucharist and Holy Orders. Mark and Luke were not physically present, but, like us, they received the benefits of those sacraments, and they are spiritually present at the Last Supper along with us in the celebration of the Holy Mass. All four Gospels give an account of the Last Supper, and, in addition, Paul gives an account in his First Letter to the Corinthians. Taken together, then, five documents of the New Testament present Jesus' last meal with His disciples, and that is a sign of its importance for us.

The site of the Last Supper at the southwest part of Mount Zion was well documented by the unknown pilgrim of Bordeaux (333 AD) and by a nun, Egeria (380 AD), as well as by the Madaba map of the Holy Land from the 6th century. Archeological excavations unearthed extensive remnants of a church called "the Mother of all Churches," which was destroyed during the Persian invasion of 614 AD.

Saint Francis of Assisi obtained rights to this site, the Cenacle, from the sultan during his visit to the Holy Land in 1219–1220. Shortly after the death of Saint Francis, Pope Clement VI formally commissioned the Franciscans to establish themselves at the Cenacle on Mount Zion and to care for it. However, in the 14th century, the Muslims confiscated the church and converted it into a mosque commemorating the tomb of David. After the war of 1948, the Muslim presence was replaced when Israel took the church and established a synagogue.

The Cenacle, as built by the Crusaders, has a lower floor, which originally housed the chapel of the washing of the disciples' feet (John 13:1–16) and the tomb of David. The architect divided the upper room into the chapel of the Holy Spirit and the chapel of Thomas. Pilgrims visiting this holy site recall the Last Supper, the institution of the Eucharist and the priesthood, Jesus' appearance after His Resurrection giving His apostles the authority to forgive sins, the story of doubting Thomas (John 20:19–29), and the coming of the Holy Spirit on Pentecost (Acts 2:1–4).

The Cenacle, practically the first Church in Christian history, was recently restored by the community of Saint Egidio of Milan in hopes that the State of Israel would return it to the Catholic Church. During his visit to Israel in January 1964, Pope Paul VI was not allowed to celebrate a Mass in the Cenacle. However, in March 2000, Pope John Paul II obtained permission and celebrated Mass there. Recall that at this site of so much division, Jesus prayed for the unity of the Church (John 17:20). Ecumenical prayers are said here each year in January.

All three evangelists mention the context of the Jewish feast of Passover. The whole life of Jesus fulfills the meaning of the Jewish Passover. The liberation of the Jews from Egyptian slavery prefigures our redemption from the slavery of sin and death that was won by Jesus. Ezekiel 12 tells of the angel of the Lord passing judgment on the Egyptians' first born, while sparing the first born of the Jews, who marked their homes with the blood of the lamb. Saint Paul writes: "Christ, our paschal lamb has been sacrificed" (1 Corinthians 5:7b). Christians are saved by the sacrifice of our Lord, which is celebrated in the mystery of the Eucharist. With Jesus we start a new and final exodus, which liberates us from the final enemy, death (1 Corinthians 15:54–57), and leads to the fullness of life in God.

The narrative of the Last Supper of Jesus unfolds in four parts: 1) the preparation (Matthew 26:17–20), 2) the foretelling of Judas' betrayal (Matthew 26:21–25), 3) the Last Supper and the institution of the Eucharist (Matthew 26:26–29), and 4) the prediction of Peter's denial of our Lord (Matthew 26:30–35). Focus now on the preparation and institution of the Eucharist.

Now on the first day of Unleavened Bread the disciples came to Jesus, saying "Where will you have us prepare for you to eat the passover?" He said, "Go into the city to such a one, and say to him, 'The Teacher says, My time is at hand; I will keep the passover at your house with my disciples.'" (Matthew 26:17–18)	And on the first day of Unleavened Bread, when they sacrificed the passover lamb, his disciples said to him, "Where will you have us go and prepare for you to eat the passover?" And he sent two of his disciples, and said to them, "Go into the city, and a man carrying a jar of water will meet you; follow him. … And he will show you a large upper room furnished and ready; there prepare for us." (Mark 14:12–15)	Then came the day of Unleavened Bread, on which the passover lamb had to be prepared. So Jesus sent Peter and John, saying, "Go and prepare the passover for us, that we may eat it. … Behold, when you have entered the city, a man carrying a jar of water will meet you; follow him into the house which he enters, and tell the householder, 'The teacher says to you, where is the guest room, where I am to eat the passover with my disciples?' And he will show you a large upper room furnished; there make ready." (Luke 22:7–13)

The preparation for the Last Supper began in the mind of God. In creating the world, God made the raw materials for the banquet—the wheat to become bread and grapes to become wine. When God spoke to Moses, he instituted the celebration of the Passover meal. When God came to earth in the Person of Jesus, He called His twelve disciples, to be the first congregation at the celebration. By teaching them for three years, He prepared their minds. By working miracles, especially the multiplication of the loaves and fishes on not one but two occasions, He prepared their hearts. By preaching repentance, He prepared their souls—the most important preparation of all, because it cleared a space within them for the gift to be received.

Jesus remains in control of every detail leading up to His trial and crucifixion. Jesus sends two disciples to untie the colt, because He has need of it. He sends the two most trusted disciples, Peter and John, to prepare the Passover, which He will share with His disciples (Luke 22:15).

Matthew's account is shorter than Mark's, which doesn't happen very often. In Matthew, Jesus just sent off "disciples;" in Mark he sends off "two disciples," and Luke names them, "Peter and John." Jesus highlights the importance of this event by sending two of his greatest disciples, his highest-ranking apostle, Peter and His beloved, John, who is also the youngest. For the Seder, the youngest male present (the one who had most recently made his bar-mitzvah at age twelve) asks the questions about the meaning of the meal.

Matthew simply writes "Go into the city to a certain one," While Mark and Luke specify that the disciples are to search for a man carrying a water jar. The significance is that a poor man's wife would go get the water herself, but a rich man's wife would send a maid servant, and a very wealthy man's wife would send a man servant. The upper room was a first class accommodation.

During the time of Passover, Jerusalem was filled to overflowing with pilgrims, and there was a shortage of banquet facilities, particularly the cheaper ones. Perhaps the more expensive ones could still be had. However, there is no mention of payment here, and the offering of hospitality to an important rabbi and his disciples is something that a wealthy patron might especially want to do at Passover time. Part of the Passover discipline is welcoming the poor so that they are not excluded from the feast.

Since Jesus takes such care to prepare the Last Supper for His disciples, it makes sense for us to prepare each and every time that we attend Mass and receive the Eucharist. Setting the table for the divine banquet requires clearing the table of our souls of any unworthy stain, impulse, fantasy, or memory. When we invite God in, we should prepare a clean place for Him.

The very act of receiving Holy Communion brings forgiveness for venial sins. However, before receiving the Eucharist, the sacrament of Reconciliation is required for mortal (grave) sins. Both sacraments should be available to the faithful as often as possible, ideally daily. Priests themselves should set the standard of being humble penitents and vivid examples of Eucharistic adoration. Fr. Raniero Cantalamessa advises priests to celebrate Mass in a way that they themselves would be willing to assume the passion of Christ in their own bodies.

The consecrated bread and wine, changed into the Body and Blood of Christ, are offered to those who have repented and believe. Frequent communion, joined with the purification by the Holy Spirit in the grace of Confession, enables the gift of faith to grow despite difficulties and enables the Christian to be faithful in missionary endeavors. Not availing oneself of the sacrament of Reconciliation exposes one to be at risk of profaning the Body and Blood of the Lord, thus bringing judgment upon oneself (1 Corinthians 11:27–29).

And when the hour came, he sat at table, and the apostles with him. And he said to them, "I have earnestly desired to eat this Passover with you before I suffer; for I tell you I shall not eat it until it is fulfilled in the kingdom of God." And he took a cup, and when he had given thanks he said, "Take this, and divide it among yourselves; for I tell you that from now on I shall not drink of the fruit of the vine until the kingdom of God comes." (Luke 22:14–18)	Now before the feast of Passover, when Jesus knew that his hour had come to depart out of this world to the Father, having loved his own who were in the world, he loved them to the end. (John 13:1)

Jesus institutes the Eucharist within the context of the Seder meal of the Passover celebration. In the Seder meal, there are four ritual cups of wine, and Jesus consecrated one of these. Luke tells us that at least one of the ritual cups was passed among those at table (Luke 22:17) prior to taking "a cup after supper," over which Jesus says the words of consecration (Luke 22:20).

Matthew describes Jesus as "blessing" the bread, whereas Luke speaks of "giving thanks," a term very descriptive of the Hebrew form of blessing, which is directed upwards to God. Saint John Chrysostom writes: "And He gives thanks, to teach us how we ought to celebrate this sacrament, and to show that not unwillingly does He come to the passion, and to teach us whatever we may suffer to bear it thankfully, thereby also suggesting good hopes." (Saint John Chrysostom [344–407 AD], *Homilies on Matthew*, 82).

Jesus speaks of His yearning to share this meal with His disciples. And we, like the apostles at the Last Supper, desire to receive Jesus. It is in Holy Communion that these two desires meet— our need and His providence. As John points out, love is the basis of these desires (John 13:1). Because Jesus loved the disciples, He wished to give Himself fully to them. What a consolation it was to Jesus as true man to know that He had left such an excellent gift to the apostles whom He was leaving behind. When Jesus gave this Eucharistic gift, He empowered the apostles to go out to the world and share it.

The best reason for wanting to receive Holy Communion is to please God the Father and our Lord and Savior Jesus Christ. Every time we receive, we demonstrate that this great gift was not given in vain. We enable Christ to have the satisfaction of a Giver who knows His gift is appreciated. He yearned to bless us, and we should yearn to please Him by receiving the gift worthily and with thanksgiving.

Now as they were eating, Jesus took bread, and blessed, and broke, and gave it to the disciples and said, "Take, eat; this is my body." And he took a cup, and when he had given thanks he gave it to them, saying "Drink of it, all of you; for this is my blood of the covenant, which is poured out for many for the forgiveness of sins. I tell you I shall not drink again of this fruit of the vine until that day when I drink it anew with you in my Father's kingdom." (Matthew 26:26–29)	And as they were eating, he took bread, and blessed, and broke it, and gave it to them, and said, "Take; this is my body." And he took a cup, and when he had given thanks he gave it to them, and they all drank of it. And he said to them, "This is my blood of the covenant, which is poured out for many. Truly, I say to you, I shall not drink again of the fruit of the vine until that day when I drink it anew in the kingdom of God." (Mark 14:22–25)

The narrative of the Last Supper itself is virtually identical in Matthew and Mark. Remember that Matthew was an eye-witness. It is commonly assumed that Mark's account depends on the eye-witness account of Peter. Here two eye-witnesses give the same testimony, one speaking first-hand and the other quoted second-hand. The statements "This is my body" and "This is my blood" are unparalleled in any world religion. There is nothing like this in Judaism, Islam, or anywhere else.

Christianity is a religion based on the truthfulness of Jesus Christ. If we believe that He is God, and that the world takes its existence from Him, then everything is what it is because He wills it to be so in the first place. If, then, He wishes to redefine the reality of something, so that it is no longer what it was or what it appears to be, that is entirely His right and within His power. The Catholic term for the transformation here is "transubstantiation," which was formally defined as a doctrine of the Church by the Fourth Lateran Council in 1215 AD. We believe that what was really and truly bread and wine becomes really and truly Christ—Body, Blood, Soul, and Divinity. Christ remains undivided, un-fragmented into parts, whole and entire in each and every perceivable drop or particle of either species.

The Holy Mass, celebrated every day throughout the world except on Good Friday, is a participation in the reality of the Last Supper. The Holy Spirit makes present upon the altar, through the words of the priest, the same reality that came about during the Last Supper through the words of Christ. Those who believe in this Real Presence are Eucharistic Christians, and they could never find complete spiritual satisfaction without this manna from heaven, this food for the journey home. The tragedy of the Christian community is that many of its members seem unaware of this great treasure of the Body, Blood, Soul, and Divinity of our Lord really present in the Eucharist.

And he took bread, and when he had given thanks he broke it and gave it to them, saying "This is my body which is given for you. Do this in remembrance of me." And likewise the cup after supper, saying, "This cup which is poured out for you is the new covenant in my blood." (Luke 22:19–20)	For I received from the Lord what I also delivered to you, that the Lord Jesus on the night when he was betrayed took bread, and when he had given thanks, he broke it, and said, "This is my body which is for you. Do this is in remembrance of me." In the same way also the cup, after supper, saying, "This cup is the new covenant in my blood. Do this, as often as you drink it, in remembrance of me." For as often as you eat the bread and drink the cup, you proclaim the Lord's death until he comes. (1 Corinthians 11:23–26)

Luke's account and Paul's in First Corinthians have a lot in common in the two verses that they share. They both mention that the consecrated cup was after supper, and they both contain the memorial imperative "Do this in memory of me." Luke has the imperative only after the first consecration, while Paul repeats the imperative after each of the two consecrations.

The consecration of the cup has different wording in each of the four narratives:
✝ For this is my blood of the covenant, which is poured out for many for the forgiveness of sins. (Matthew)
✝ This is my blood of the covenant, which is poured out for many. (Mark)
✝ This cup which is poured out for you is the New Covenant in my blood. (Luke)
✝ This cup is the New Covenant in my blood. (Paul)

This variety of expression indicates that, in the early Church, there were several approved phrasings for the celebration of Mass, just as we have four major Eucharistic prayers for the Mass today. Paul not only gives us the words "Do this … in memory of me" twice, he also has an extended memorial acclamation (1 Corinthians 11:26).

Throughout the history of the Church, the Last Supper of Jesus has been repeated in the continuous celebration of the Eucharist, every day all around the world. Christians throughout the world believe that the Eucharist is a re-presentation of Christ's sacrifice, the Lamb slain but still living, and an opportunity to consume the Body and Blood of the Lord Jesus Christ in Holy Communion.

None of the four accounts indicate that the Eucharist is only for those physically present at the Last Supper. Indeed the statement "Do this in memory of me" in Luke and Paul empowers the apostles to do the same thing that Jesus has done—to extend the reality of the Last Supper by their own celebrations, as we see them doing right away in Acts: "And day by day, attending the temple together and breaking bread in their homes, they partook of food with glad and generous hearts, praising God" (Acts 2:46–47). Christ's redemptive death became the eschatological reality, which is open to every person of every race, not just the Jewish people.

The Messianic expectation of the Jewish nation reaches its climax in Jesus. The Old Covenant is fulfilled in the New Covenant, represented by the broken bread and the cup of eternal salvation. The essential difference between the Old and the New Covenant consists in the value of the sacrifice. In the Old Testament, the priest sacrificed an animal, an offering separate from himself. In the New Covenant, Jesus offers His own Body and Blood in sacrifice. Hence, the Eucharist commemorates Jesus' death and Resurrection.

There is a missionary aspect to the Eucharist. Christ died on the Cross to offer salvation to every human being, so He wishes that everyone be given the opportunity to draw sustenance from the gift of His Body and Blood. Knowing this, we cannot be satisfied just receiving Holy Communion ourselves. Because we love our children, we want them to receive. As we love our neighbors, we want to invite them as well. When we receive Christ's Person, we acquire Christ's own zeal for souls.

After His death on the Cross, Jesus rises by the power of God and invites people to participate in this victory over death and the joys of heaven. Creation is joined with the Creator in the Eucharist through the symbol of nature and sustenance—bread. When we eat this sacred "bread," mystically we are united more intimately to Christ and become part of a higher order, the members of Christ's body, His brothers and sisters. The destiny of our Master is shared in the Eucharist by His disciples. In the Liturgy of the Eucharist in every Mass, the priest says "By the mystery of this water and wine may we come to share in the divinity of Christ, who humbled Himself to share in our humanity." Therefore, the Eucharist deifies us. On the other hand, it bestows on us an awesome responsibility to offer ourselves humbly in the example of Jesus.

The Eucharistic banquet invites us to share the spiritual fruit of Jesus' death and Resurrection with the community of believers. The mercy of God through the sacrifice of Jesus is universal. The Eucharist provides solidarity of the individual with Christ and with the Christian community. Jesus also prays for the unity of the Church during the Last Supper (John 17:20–25).

"Partaking of the Body and Blood of Christ, you become united in body and blood with Him. For thus do we become Christ-bearers, His Body and Blood being distributed through our members. And thus we become, according to the blessed Peter, sharers of the divine nature" (Saint Cyril of Jerusalem [315–386 AD], *Mystagogic*, 4.3). The very meaning of Christian life is to carry on the sacrifice of Jesus through fraternal service in thanksgiving, which gives blessing to all our endeavors and makes us free in Christ. Christ's sacrifice on Calvary bestows the strength we need to persevere in any trial that we will face in life. Christ invites us to participate in His work by living a life worthy of the sacrifice embraced by Jesus.

The Eucharistic banquet described by the Synoptics is eschatological. The consecration presents the new and eternal covenant. The Eucharist is the anticipation of heavenly glory and it is both a pledge and a sign of the "new heavens and the new earth" that are to come (cf. CCC 1402–1405). It is the food for our journey in this life and our hope for life eternal.

> Lo! The angel's food is given to the pilgrim who has striven;
>   see the children's bread from heaven, which on dogs may not be spent.
> Truth the ancient types fulfilling, Isaac bound, a victim willing,
>   Paschal Lamb, its life blood spilling, manna to the fathers sent.
> Very bread, Good Shepherd, tend us, Jesu, of Thy love befriend us,
>   This eternal goodness send us in the land of life to see
> Thou who all things canst and knowest, who on earth such food bestowest,
>   Grant us with Thy saints though lowest,
>   Where the heav'nly food Thou showest fellow heirs and guests to be. Amen. Alleluia.

> Saint Thomas Aquinas, *Ecce Panis Angelorum*

1. Before the Last Supper, what did Jesus say to His disciples? Matthew 26:1–2

2. Describe an act of kindness offered to Jesus by a woman in Matthew 26:6–13.

3. Compare the following verses. Find some new information in each passage.

Matthew 26:14–16	Mark 14:10–11	Luke 22:2–6

4. What can you learn about Judas' motivation from John 12:3–8?

5. To whom do you think the following Psalms refer?

Psalm 41:9–10	
Psalm 55:12–14	

6. Identify some unique information from each of the following passages.

Matthew 26:17–19	Mark 14:12–17	Luke 22:7–14

7. Why did Jesus institute the Eucharist at the Last Supper? CCC 1323

8. Explain the Eucharist is three different ways.

CCC 1324	
CCC 1325	
CCC 1326	

9. Write each of the following verses in entirety. Meditate on each of them for a while.

Matthew 26:26–29
Mark 14:22–24
Luke 22:17–20
John 6:53–56
1 Corinthians 11:23–26

10. What should precede worthy reception of the Eucharist? 1 Corinthians 11:27–29

11. How did the early Christians worship? Acts 2:42, 46–47

12. When you receive Holy Communion, what do you proclaim? 1 Corinthians 11:26

13. Explain Exodus 12:21–30.

14. What did Moses institute in Exodus 13:3?

15. Explain Jesus' role in the New Covenant. Hebrews 9:11–22

16. What does Jesus give us in the Eucharist? Matthew 26:28, CCC 1365

17. Explain how Christ's sacrifice is re-presented in the Eucharist. CCC 1366

18. What is contained in the Eucharist? CCC 1374

19. What is the purpose of the tabernacle? CCC 1379

** Seek an opportunity to spend extra time in adoration of the Blessed Sacrament this week.

CHAPTER 19

Agony in Gethsemane

Matthew 26:36–46, Mark 14:32–42, Luke 22:39–46

**And going a little farther he fell on his face and prayed,
"My Father, if it be possible, let this cup pass from me;
nevertheless, not as I will, but as thou wilt."** (Matthew 26:39)

The "agony," the mortal struggle of Jesus in the garden of Gethsemane, is the prelude to His arrest, trial, crucifixion, and Resurrection. All the evangelists report this event. John speaks about the "hour" of Jesus (John 19:27). The theological significance of the agony involves Jesus' free decision to accept His Father's will for the sake of human salvation. Prayer and submission girds Jesus' spiritual and moral strength, providing the most profound proof in the New Testament of our Savior's obedience (Hebrews 5:8).

A visit to the garden of Gethsemane is a highlight of any Christian pilgrimage to the Holy Land. The word "Gethsemane" in Hebrew refers to the olive press used to squeeze the precious oil from the olive crop. The Gospels give no hint as to the owner of the olive grove, whether the disciples paid rent to use this place during their pilgrimage to Jerusalem, or whether the owner just generously offered his garden to Jesus. This location offered proximity to the temple Mount and Gihon spring, as well as privacy for Jesus and his entourage from curious crowds and vindictive authorities. During His last pilgrimage to Jerusalem, Jesus probably kept a very low profile, using the olive press of Gethsemane as a meeting place (John 18:2). Judas' betrayal and his key role in leading the chief priests, elders, and crowds there confirm this fact.

Currently, the grotto of the olive press is still very well preserved. About 333 AD, the unknown pilgrim of Bordeaux identified it as the place of Jesus' betrayal. The first Christians left graffiti on the walls of the interior of a nearby cave, which unfortunately are now illegible. A tomb, with damaged mosaic inscription, was found near the cisterns where the pressed oil was gathered. The grotto also bears traces of the Crusaders presence. They adorned the walls of the sacred place with frescoes which have been partially restored. The Franciscan fathers have strengthened the grotto with columns and erected an altar to celebrate Mass for pilgrims.

The present Basilica of Jesus' Agony is just a "stone's throw" (Luke 22:41) south of the grotto of Gethsemane. Eight ancient olive trees on the north side of the church have been examined by the universities of Jerusalem and Lisbon to try to determine their age. The olive tree, one of the most resilient plants in the world, can even survive when its trunk is cut off. Only uprooting the tree will destroy it. The historian Josephus reports that Titus cut off all the trees around the city to make crosses for the Jewish insurgents in Jerusalem. Since the city was destroyed in 70 AD, the olive trees in the garden of Gethsemane today were probably not witnesses to Jesus' agony.

Today's Basilica of the Agony of Our Lord was built in 1926 by the well-known architect, Antonio Barluzzi. Perhaps this church is his masterpiece. The building consists of three naves with dark interiors reflecting the mystery of Jesus' passion. When the crusaders replaced the Byzantine church with a new church, they changed the orientation more to the east. Barluzzi preserved this eastern orientation. In front of the altar of the basilica, pilgrims venerate the rock believed to be the place of Jesus' mortal struggle and victory in favor of our redemption from sin. Sixteen nations donated funds to build this sanctuary, and, for this reason, the church is also called The Basilica of the Nations. However, this name impoverishes the theological significance of the event—Jesus' anguish and turmoil.

A spectacular mosaic adorns the front exterior of the church. Jesus kneels in the center with outstretched arms, the obedient Son offering His heart to the will of His Father. The crowd on the left side of the mosaic represents those who would not receive the revelation of the Gospel—the people of "ignorance." On the right side are the faithful followers worshiping Jesus. There are three gardens near the church. You can view the mosaic from the garden across the street and the Franciscan fathers have another garden in the back that may, upon request, be used by pilgrims for private prayer. The guardians of the basilica also offer pilgrim groups the opportunity for evening adoration inside the church so that they can respond to Jesus' request to Peter: "Could you not watch with me one hour?" (Matthew 26:40).

Catholics meditate on "The Agony in the Garden" in the first sorrowful mystery of the Rosary. The Gospel accounts present this struggle immediately after the Last Supper. The betrayal of Judas and arrest of Jesus follow the prayer of Jesus in Gethsemane. Luke refers to the Mount of Olives (Luke 22:39), while his two Synoptic counterparts identify the place as Gethsemane. The Lucan address of Jesus to the disciples "Pray that you may not enter into temptation" (Luke 22:40) contrasts with Matthew 26:36 and Mark 14:34 in which Jesus asks them to sit and watch, while He prays. Matthew and Mark report that Jesus took Peter, James, and John with Him. And being sorrowful, even to death, He asked them to remain with Him and watch. Only Mark reveals Jesus' anguish in praying, "if possible, the hour might pass from Him" (Mark 14:35).

Only Luke presents the appearance of the angel to strengthen Jesus and the progressive agony culminating in the sweat which "became like great drops of blood falling down upon the ground" (Luke 22:43–44). Concerning Jesus' question to Peter "Could you not watch with me one hour?" (Matthew 26:40), Jesus seems to exhort all disciples with the words: "Rise and pray that you may not enter into temptation" (Luke 22:40, 45–46).

Matthew and Mark emphasize three attempts by Jesus to pray and contrasts them with three occasions of drowsiness on the part of the disciples. Matthew emphasizes Jesus' turmoil, yet submission to the Father's will: "My Father, if this cannot pass unless I drink it, thy will be done" (Matthew 26:42). Mark reveals that the disciples seem to be embarrassed by their somnolence and inability to stay alert to watch and pray with the Master (Mark 14:40).

This mortal struggle of Jesus in the garden of Gethsemane was decisive for the redemption of the world. It functions as the Christological key for all that follows: Jesus' arrest, trial, and crucifixion. Before His Passion, Jesus courageously decides to submit to the Father's will in contrast to the weakness and crises of faith of His disciples. By His act of perfect obedience, Jesus atones for the sin of Adam's disobedience. The relationship with God, whom Jesus calls "Abba" in His prayer, is the dominating theme of Jesus' agony in the garden. Jesus embraces the way the Father has ordained for Him in order to redeem the world through His love.

Similarities can be found between the Transfiguration of Jesus on the mountain and the agony in the garden. The mountain in both instances symbolizes closeness with heaven. In both situations Jesus comes to strengthen His commitment to His Father's plan through prayer. In each case, there is the negative counterpart in the hesitant faith of the same three disciples, Peter, James, and John. One difference can be observed in that on the mountain of Transfiguration, the Father calls Jesus His Son; while in Gethsemane, Jesus calls God His Father. The Transfiguration identifies Jesus with the divinity of His Father; the agony identifies Jesus with the horror of sinful humanity.

Night in the garden recalls the darkness of the world when God created light and brought order out of the chaos. In the night of Jesus' agony, the eternal light of God's love overcomes the darkness and chaos of man's rebellion against God. Jesus faces His impending death in all its drama. The sinless Son of God embraces death, which is the wage of sin (Romans 6:23). Nonetheless, Jesus chooses to embrace fallen humanity with all His heart. The mystery of redemption in the agony in the garden troubles the sorrowful soul of Jesus even unto death (Matthew 26:38). The infinite ocean of divine love is measured by the great expanse of His suffering.

In the curse and anguish of sin, Jesus hurls Himself into the arms of His Father. The mysticism of Jesus' suffering in Gethsemane defies human comprehension. The horror of all the sins committed by humanity before and after the redemption, as well as the indifferent attitude of many, imposed a terrible burden upon the Son of God. Willingly, in His Passion, Jesus becomes the sinner abandoned by God. Jesus solves the irresolvable mystery by committing His will to the will and wisdom of the Father. Overwhelmed by the tragedy of sin, assuming it upon His body (1 Peter 2:24), Jesus falls into the arms and will of His Father as He collapses to the ground and prays (Matthew 26:39, Mark 14:35).

Prayer dominates the agony in the garden in the Gospel of Luke. Six key elements of Jesus' prayer serve as a model for every sincere Christian prayer.

1) Jesus demonstrates communal prayer in commanding the disciples to pray in order not to enter into temptation and inviting them to remain with Him in prayer. This instruction matches "where two or three are gathered in my name, there am I in the midst of them" (Matthew 18:20).

2) Jesus withdraws from His disciples for privacy. Jesus treaded the winepress of suffering alone, and each believer must learn the importance of solitude in order to listen to God. There is a time for communal prayer and a time for private prayer in the Christian life.

3) Jesus prays on His knees, demonstrating the humble position of one who kneels before the sovereignty of the Father (Luke 22:41). If Jesus, who is divine and true God, could kneel before the Father, any serious Christian should kneel in humble prostration before the majesty of God.

4) The prayer of Jesus is concise, sincere, and trusting. Jesus affectionately addresses God as His Father, Abba, for He truly is the Son of God. In the finding in the temple, Jesus told His mother that He must be about "His Father's business." In His agony in the garden Jesus submits totally to the will of the Father. The will of the Father and the Son are one. It is recorded in Hebrews:

"In the days of his flesh, Jesus offered up prayers and supplications, with loud cries and tears, to him who was able to save him from death, and he was heard for his godly fear" (5:7).

5) The prayer of Jesus in Gethsemane is concentrated. He doesn't speak much during prayer. Many words are not needed to emphasize His decision to submit to the will of His Father. An intense struggle between the human and divine nature of Jesus emerges here. The request that this cup pass from Him reveals the human frailty and fear in Jesus of Nazareth. The image of sweat, like great drops of blood falling to the ground, prefigures His flagellation. After the fall, Adam had to sweat for his daily bread (Genesis 3:19). Through His bloody sweat, Jesus heals Adam and brings him back to the garden. The prayer of abandonment brings victory to the agony of Jesus. In a garden where olives are pressed, our Lord experiences the immense pressure of the weight of human sin. The oil of His blood falling on the ground, instead of sin, prefigures the anointing of the sick with oil for forgiveness of sins and healing (James 5:13ff).

6) Finally, Jesus models perseverance in prayer. Three times, Jesus asks His disciples to remain with Him in prayer. They fail, but Jesus perseveres in prayer. When Jesus is at a distances from them, they then are tempted to fall asleep instead of persevering in prayer. In our own need, we should heed Jesus' advice to pray and not lose heart (Luke 11:8, 18:1).

In light of the agony of Jesus in the garden of Gethsemane we can examine our own prayers. Do we tell God our needs, or also the solutions we expect to receive, especially in times of trial and suffering? Favors not granted should not lead to loss of faith, but rather to humble submission to the will of God. Sometimes, God doesn't answer our prayers because we ask wrongly (James 4:3). In other situations, God brings forth a mysterious greater good from our cross, as in the case of Job. The answer to Job's trial was beyond human understanding. In submitting his suffering to God's will, Job learns that God will not be called to account to anyone for His actions. In divine providence, Job ultimately receives more blessings than he had before his great adversity.

The prayer of Jesus in the garden of Gethsemane provides an example of the effectiveness of prayer for healing from fear. Saint James tells us that "the prayer of a righteous man has great power in its effect" (James 5:16). Jesus, the righteous man, obtained our salvation through His prayer and sacrifice. Jesus accomplished the redemption of the world. Despite the strong human instinct for survival and self-preservation, Jesus willingly gives up His life for our sake. God does not always meet our expectations. But there is a greater and more comforting truth—God does hear every prayer and He answers those prayers that correspond with His will on earth as it is in heaven (Matthew 6:10).

God's thoughts are above our thoughts. God wants what is best for each of His children. Even though your prayer might not be answered today, God may have a more wonderful answer to that prayer just around the corner. Submitting to the will of such a good God, who did not spare His own Son but freely gave Him up for us, proves that we can depend on the goodness of God just like a trusting child resting in his parent's lap.

1. How did Jesus prepare for His impending death? Matthew 26:36–39

2. Who did Jesus take with Him? Mark 14:32–34

3. Describe the events in Luke 22:39–46.

4. Compare the following verses.

Matthew 26:38	
Psalm 42:6–12	

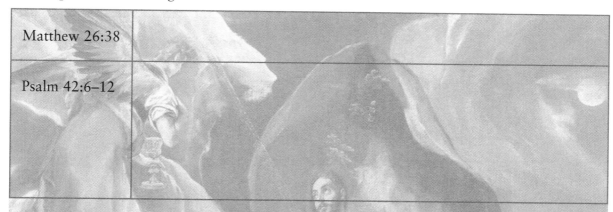

5. Who came from where to help Jesus? What help was given? Luke 22:43

6. Did Jesus know that He was going to die? Mark 14:41–42

7. What can you learn from the following verses?

Matthew 26:39
Mark 14:35–36
Luke 22:41–42
Philippians 2:5–8

8. What do the following passages tell you about Jesus?

Hebrews 5:7–10
Hebrews 10:9–10

9. Jesus faced a battle and a victory through prayer. What does He urge of us? CCC 2849

10. If you knew you only had a few days to live, what example of Jesus could you embrace?

11. Why did Jesus consent to die for our sins?

CCC 536	
Matthew 26:39	

12. Why did God the Father allow this suffering and agony of Jesus? John 3:16–17

13. Did Jesus have to die?

Hebrews 4:14–16	
CCC 612	

14. What manner and duration of prayer did Jesus request in the garden?

Matthew 26:40	
CCC 2719	

15. Describe three traditional types of prayer.

CCC 2700	
CCC 2708	
CCC 2714–2715	

16. Describe some difficulties disciples have encountered in prayer.

Luke 22:45	
CCC 2729	
CCC 2731	
Luke 22:40	
CCC 2733	

17. How can you persevere in prayer? Ephesians 6:18

18. How and why should you pray? 1 Thessalonians 5:16–18

19. What are the biggest obstacles you face in persevering in prayer?

** Share with your group some ways that help you to be faithful and persevere in prayer!

CHAPTER 20

The Trials of Jesus

Matthew 26–27, Mark 14–15, Luke 22–23

"I adjure you by the living God, tell us if you are the Christ, the Son of God."
Jesus said to him, "You have said so. But I tell you,
hereafter you will see the Son of man seated at the right hand of Power,
and coming on the clouds of heaven." (Matthew 26:63b–64)

The two most famous trials of antiquity were the trial of the Greek philosopher Socrates and the trial of Jesus of Nazareth. Both legal processes were apparent travesties, leaving a poor impression of the administration of justice in those days. Nonetheless, there is no transcript of these court proceedings, and we know of the trials only from the followers of the condemned. The earliest trial for which we have a complete verbatim transcript is the trial of Saint Joan of Arc in the 15th century. In the case of Jesus there are only fragmentary reports, which do not give a complete sense of the legal issues.

Complicating the matter, the Holy Land under Roman occupation had overlapping legal systems:

1) Mosaic law administered by 71 members of the greater Sanhedrin and the lesser Sanhedrins,
2) Roman martial law administered by the Roman prefect and his military court, and
3) Jewish secular law enforced by King Herod the Great and his sons after him.

Sometimes problems arose in establishing jurisdiction. When an act was criminalized in one of the three systems, then that system could take care of it. But when two or three of them forbade the act, it might be a matter of who apprehended the criminal and got to him first. Jesus appears before each of these tribunals—religious, military, and secular—in the course of his night of trial. Each jurisdiction has the opportunity to exonerate him, but each fails to do so.

The word "trial" in Greek is the same as the word "temptation." The three legal trials remind us of the three temptations Jesus underwent in the desert:

1) The Sanhedrin wants to license Jesus and commission Him to teach only under their authority. If He throws Himself at their feet, He can teach their truths. But He is the truth and cannot be subjected.
2) Pontius Pilate represents the emperor of all the kingdoms of the earth. Jesus does not worship this kind of authority, for He has His own kingdom which is not of this world.
3) Herod Antipas wants Jesus to entertain him with a miracle, like turning stones into loaves of bread. If Jesus had complied, He could have become a court jester instead of the Savior of the universe.

Jesus could have saved Himself from death if only He had been willing to become Herod's fool, Pilate's sycophant, and the Sanhedrin's puppet. Since Jesus planned to save humanity instead of Himself, He allowed Himself to be judged by these inherently flawed tribunals.

The Trial before the Sanhedrin ~ The Synoptic Gospels are briefer than the Gospel of John in describing the events of that shameful night. Only John 18:13 informs readers that Jesus was first taken to the house of Annas, the former high priest and the father-in-law of the current high priest. The site of the house of Annas can be found in the modest church in the Armenian quarter of the Old City of Jerusalem. The Armenian community also owns the unfinished church of the house of Caiaphas, south of the Zion gate of the Old City near the Armenian quarter.

Jesus is detained there while all seventy-one members of the great Sanhedrin are called to the house of the high priest Caiaphas (Matthew 26:57–68, Mark 14:53–64, Luke 22:54–71). This was not an entirely legal session, because Jewish law required courts to meet only during the daytime. There are other elements of this trial that are contrary to Mosaic law: no one could be condemned to death without the testimony of two credible witnesses, and no one could testify against himself in a capital case. The hearings were held in chamber, with only the Sanhedrin members and guards present. Nicodemus and Joseph of Arimathea, members of the tribunal, probably provided the post-trial accounts we have.

Despite ongoing disputes among the experts, the only plausible site in Jerusalem for the first stage of Jesus' trial is the present day Church of Saint Peter in Gallicantu (the chant of the rooster). Archeological excavations reveal a large house from the Roman period of Jerusalem. Excavators also found two Christian churches from the Byzantine period nearby. In the dungeons were found crosses on the walls and an ancient fresco of a person praying on his knees with outstretched arms. This pit was probably the prison where Jesus would have been kept during His imprisonment by the Jewish authorities. Nearby prisons could have been used for flagellations, as indicated in Acts 5:40, where this torture was imposed without any Roman authorization. This suggests that Jesus may have been scourged in two different places, once by His own people, probably forty lashes minus one, and then a much more brutal scourging by the order of Pontius Pilate (cf. Matthew 27:26 ff).

To the north of the present sanctuary of Saint Peter in Gallicantu, an ancient path, which connected the upper city with the Gihon spring, was discovered. A possible scenario would have Jesus using this path after the Last Supper, descending into the Kidron valley to the garden of Gethsemane, and then, immediately after His arrest, being dragged from the Kidron valley to the houses of Annas and Caiaphas in the upper city.

The story of Jesus' trial before the Jewish council of elders intertwines with Peter's denial of Christ, which Luke places before Caiaphas' verdict condemning Jesus to die. Luke chronicles Peter's weakness during the evening of Jesus' arrest, while the sentencing occurs the following day. Matthew and Mark record both events following each other during the night of the arrest. John's Gospel presents the drama of Peter's denial along with the interrogation of Jesus by the Sanhedrin (John 18:15–27).

Luke provides information about Peter sitting by the fire in the middle of the courtyard (Luke 22:55). The order of those who press Peter about being with Jesus differs slightly. Matthew and Mark speak of a maid speaking to Peter, while Luke refers to a maid and then two men (Luke 22:58–59). The suspicion against Peter intensifies in Matthew and Mark since bystanders hear the second and third denials. Peter's reaction against his accusers intensifies with an oath in the second denial and cursing against himself and swearing in the third (Matthew 26:72–74). Only

Luke reports that the cock crowed while Peter was still speaking and that the Lord turned and looked at him (Luke 22:60–61).

Matthew elaborates on the court hearing of the Sanhedrin more than the other Synoptics, explicitly stating that "false testimony" was sought against Jesus so they might put Him to death (Matthew 26:59). The witnesses to Jesus' claim about destroying the temple came at last, and Mark 14:59 reports that their testimonies did not agree.

The reaction of the high priest to the silence of Jesus is most dramatic in Matthew, where the high priest says, "I adjure you by the living God, tell us if you are the Christ, the Son of God" (Matthew 26:63). Mark puts it similarly but without any adjuring, while Luke offers the most concise version; "If you are the Christ, tell us" (Luke 22:67). On the other hand, Luke offers the most exhaustive answer of Jesus to the elders. Mark doesn't single out the person of the high priest in interrogating Jesus, but has all the assembly of elders involved. Luke divides the self-revelation of Jesus in two parts. First, Jesus reproves the Sanhedrin for their lack of faith. Then, Jesus quotes Daniel 7:13 concerning the Son of man coming with the power of God. The other Synoptics complete the reference with "coming on the clouds of heaven" (Matthew 26:64).

Only Matthew reveals that the high priest tore his garment, emphasizing the blasphemy for which Jesus was condemned to die. Luke has no reference to the verdict of death reached by the Sanhedrin. Matthew and Mark report them spitting in Jesus' face.

Who was responsible for putting Jesus to death? Consider this question through the prism of its theological implications, embracing the spiritual perspective of God's redemption of all from sin. From the spiritual viewpoint, every person is culpable because all alike are under sin (Romans 3:9). Considering the text from a literary historical perspective, several groups of people are interested in getting rid of Jesus. The high priests represent the interests of political religious power. The elders concern themselves with economic matters. The scribes are ideological. Pontius Pilate represents the oppressive Roman occupation. Herod Antipas, a puppet tetrarch incapable of reaching a judgment of his own, fails to oppose the injustice against Jesus. Masses of people demand the release of a guilty man and demand crucifixion for the innocent Jesus. Jesus was betrayed by Judas, denied by Peter, and abandoned by His disciples. Ultimately, we all share responsibility for the death of Jesus.

> My adorable Jesus, it was not Pilate, no, it was my sins that condemned Thee to die. I beseech Thee by the merits of this sorrowful journey, to assist my soul in its journey toward eternity. I love Thee, my Beloved Jesus; I love Thee more than myself; I repent with my whole heart for having offended Thee. Never permit me to separate myself from Thee again. Grant that I may love Thee always, and then do with me what Thou wilt.
>
> Saint Alphonsus Liguori, *The Way of the Cross*

Why would the high priest violate one of the Ten Commandments, the law against false testimony (Exodus 20:16, Deuteronomy 5:20), to secure a death sentence for Jesus? Perhaps the greatest irony of the trial of Jesus is that the death sentence comes when Jesus reveals His true identity as "the Christ, the Son of man seated at the right hand of Power and coming on the clouds of heaven (Matthew 26:63–64)."

The identity of Jesus helps to discover the identity of God the Father. God revealed His name "I am," to Moses in the desert, starting the Exodus. Through the exodus of Calvary, God again reveals Himself in the humiliated body of Jesus. The hidden God became visible in Jesus. The Old Testament prohibited making images of God. The New Testament allows this one, the Cross—Jesus Christ crucified. There, Jesus is God "I am" (Exodus 3:6) saving, justifying, and loving every human being. The merciful God on the Cross appears in weakness and humiliation. The challenge of Christian faith is to accept God in weakness, as well as God in power. Jesus doesn't denounce Peter after his denial. How could Jesus renounce His bride, the Church, which often, due to human weakness, betrays Him? The supreme mercy of God, Jesus dying on the Cross for our sins, becomes God with us, Emmanuel.

Luke gives us a highly accurate summary of the proceedings in the religious courtroom: "And they spoke many other words against him, reviling him" (Luke 22:65). Jesus had His sympathizers like Joseph of Arimathea and Nicodemus on the tribunal, but they were not numerous enough to carry the day. Perhaps they were able to prevent a condemnation on the spot, and so the high priest tears his robes and takes the drastic action of sending Jesus to Pilate. A prosecutor asks for a change of venue only when he thinks he might be facing a hung jury!

The Second Trial before Pontius Pilate ~ The high priest knew that he was transferring Jesus from a tribunal that had to respect His rights to another tribunal that would not respect them. The Romans had one system of law for Roman citizens and another for non-citizens. Saint Paul was a Roman citizen, so when he was condemned to death he was beheaded, the right of a swift death for a citizen. Others could be persecuted and tortured in any way seen fit by the tribunal. Also there was no standard of proof in accusing non-citizens. Simple denunciation could lead to an agonizing public death. Jesus was not tried under Roman civil law as a citizen, but under Roman martial law as a non-citizen.

Pilgrims searching for the place of the trial of Jesus by Pontius Pilate visit the site of the Roman military garrison called Antonia, named after Marc Antony, on the Via Dolorosa in the Old City of Jerusalem. Two churches are dedicated to this event in the same location. The church of the Flagellation, built by Antonio Barluzzi, has beautiful stained glass windows. In the dimmed light of the presbyterium of the church, the visitor can recognize the humiliated figure of Jesus in the center with a jubilant Barabbas on the right and Pilate washing his hands on the left.

The other sanctuary is the chapel of the Condemnation of Jesus. There are remnants here of a Byzantine structure and even pavement from the public market from the 2nd century AD. Believing that this may be the place where Pilate sentenced Jesus to die on the Cross and handed Him over to be scourged, pilgrims start their Way of the Cross here. Many pray and, perhaps, carry a cross while following in Jesus' footsteps on His way to the Cross, sincerely desiring reconciliation with the Lord and peace in their hearts. For centuries, people have followed Jesus lonely walk toward Calvary.

John describes Jesus' trial before Pilate more dramatically than the Synoptics. Matthew reveals that they "bound" Jesus before delivering Him to Pilate. Luke starts the trial with three false accusations and a crime of "stirring up the people." Matthew and Mark reveal that Jesus was silent before Pilate and report the custom to release one prisoner during the feast. Mark specifies that Barabbas was a murderer. Pilate calls Jesus "Christ" in Matthew and "King of the Jews" in Mark. Only Matthew reports the incident of Pilate's wife warning her husband not to do anything to this righteous man because she suffered over Him in a dream.

Luke records that Pilate desired to release Jesus. All Synoptics deliver the third intervention of Pilate with the ironic question: "What evil has He done?" Luke expands on the conviction of Pilate concerning the innocence of Jesus in that Pilate found no crime in Him deserving death, intending, therefore, to chastise and release Him. Matthew offers unique information concerning Pilate's washing of his hands and the chilling response of the crowd that "His blood be on us and on our children!" (Matthew 27:25). Matthew and Mark recount the scourging of Jesus; Matthew reveals that the soldiers put a reed in Jesus' right hand, while Luke describes the mockery of the soldiers.

The theological significance of Jesus' trial before Pilate concerns the identity of Jesus. Pilate accepts Jesus self-revelation as "King of the Jews," and judges that He is innocent and attempts to set Jesus free. Pontius Pilate probably misunderstood Jesus' royalty but recognized that the Jewish crowd saw the title "King of the Jews" in a messianic sense. Despite Pilate's conviction that Jesus is the innocent "King of the Jews" and Herod's inability to find any wrong in Him, both the leaders and the crowd are culpable of the injustice. Pilate with his acquiescence becomes guilty of condemning Jesus. The Roman soldiers, despite their mockery of Jesus, will ultimately confirm the truth proclaimed by Pilate.

The Third Trial before King Herod ~ The Gospel of Luke is the solitary source for Jesus being sent to Herod (Luke 23:6–12). Luke, excellent researcher that he is, finds a significant clue to the nature of the proceedings on that night. There was a third legal entity in the Holy Land at that time—the continuing kingdom of the Herodian dynasty. When Pilate finds that Jesus is no threat to Roman authority, he changes the venue by sending Jesus, a Galilean, over to King Herod the tetrarch, the ruler in Galilee.

Herod the Great's palace was located at the citadel near today's Jaffa Gate. Only the ruins of the once beautiful palace remain at the place where Jesus faced Herod's son, Antipas. The Herodians were a bloodthirsty family. Herod the Great killed several of his own relatives, and Matthew reports that he slaughtered the innocent baby boys of Bethlehem. Saint Joseph took the holy family into Egypt to flee from Herod and, after his death, had to settle in Nazareth, outside the territory ruled by his son, Archelaus. Herod Antipas, the tetrarch, imprisoned and beheaded John the Baptist.

Who were these Herodians? They were puppet monarchs set up to rule in the Holy Land by the Romans. They were of mixed blood and were not from the family of David. Therefore, it seems from evidence in the New Testament that there was an ongoing feud between the Herodians and the Davidians. The former had might, and the latter had the right. The crucifixion of Jesus was one of a series of strategic assassinations designed to keep Herodians on top.

The Sanhedrin did not object to Jesus being king. They favored the restoration of the Davidic monarchy, as long as it was in the traditional mode. The Romans did not object to the idea of a Jewish king from any family whatsoever, as long as he was on a Roman leash. The Herodians were the ones who found any attention to Davidic bloodline a threat to be exterminated at any cost, and they had already demonstrated their ruthless willingness to do whatever they could to prevent that threat from becoming a reality.

Jesus speaks quite civilly to Pontius Pilate, and is hardly confrontational with the Sanhedrin. But He refuses to open His mouth before Herod Antipas the tetrarch, the murderer of His cousin, John the Baptist. At this tribunal, the prophecy is fulfilled, "Like a sheep that before its shearers is dumb, so he opened not his mouth" (Isaiah 53:7b, quoted in Acts 8:32). On the last day, when Jesus is judge, all the courts of every land will appear before Him to be judged. Time will tell and God will judge!

> Jesus in the palace is the image of a man who surrendered his authority to God. He atoned for all abuses of freedom we have committed and are still committing, the untouchable freedom which is nothing else but enslavement of ourselves. We should remember well this episode in the palace of the governor because, also for us will come a day when we will be powerless in body or in spirit—caused by others or by age—that only Jesus will help us to understand and will bring in our new freedom. We may achieve a certain intimacy with Christ when we are close to Him, in His and our hour of shame when we also bear the abuse He endured (Hebrews 13:13). How many people are bound by illness or struck by immobility similar to that of Christ in the palace of the governor and spend their lives in the wheel chair or in bed! Jesus reveals the mysterious greatness hidden in those lives if they are lived in connection to Him.
>
> Fr. Raniero Cantalamessa, *La Vita in Cristo*

1. Describe the betrayal and arrest of Jesus.

Matthew 26:47–56	Mark 14:43–52	Luke 22:47–53

2. What was foretold and what became of the betrayer of Jesus?

Psalm 41:9–10	
Matthew 27:3–10	

3. Explain Peter's behavior from the following accounts.

Matthew 26:69–75	Mark 14:66–72	Luke 22:56–62

4. What was foretold of Peter's action? Matthew 26:30–35, Mark 14:26–31, Luke 22:31–34

5. To whom was Jesus taken first, and with what type of testimony? Matthew 26:57–59

6. Compare the following verses. What can you learn from them?

Mark 14:61	
Isaiah 53:7	
Matthew 26:64	
Psalm 110:1	
Daniel 7:13	

7. What was Jesus falsely accused of and what was the penalty?

Matthew 26:65	
Leviticus 24:16	

8. When was Jesus taken to Pilate? Describe the trial before Pilate in detail.

Mark 15:1–5	
John 18:29–38	

9. Describe the input that three different sets of people gave to Pilate concerning Jesus.

Mark 15:1–5	
Matthew 27:19	
Luke 23:13–25	

10. Why was Jesus subjected to a third trial? Luke 23:6–8

11. Why was Herod Antipas, the tetrarch, glad to see Jesus? Luke 23:8–10

12. How did Herod and his soldiers treat Jesus? Luke 23:11

13. What can you recall about Herod's father, Herod the Great? Matthew 2:7–8, 16–18

14. Why was Herod curious about Jesus? Luke 9:7–9

   What had Herod's attitude been toward Jesus during His public ministry? Luke 13:31–33

15. Identify two serious sins of Herod from Mark 6:17–29 or Matthew 14:3–12.

16. Recall the previous trials of Jesus.

Matthew 4:1–4	
Matthew 4:5–7	
Matthew 4:9–11	

17. How did Jesus defend Himself in each trial?

Before the Sanhedrin	Mark 14:60–62	
Before Pilate	Matthew 27:11	
Before Herod	Luke 23:9	

18. Why did Jesus allow Himself to be subjected to these trials? CCC 609

19. Who was responsible for the death of Jesus? CCC 597–598

20. What did Jesus accomplish by His obedience? CCC 615

** Can you think of a time in your life when you offered up a trial for the love of God?

Monthly Social Activity

This month your small group will meet for coffee, tea, or a simple breakfast, lunch, or dessert in someone's home. Please remember to "keep it simple!"

Pray for this social event and for the host or hostess. Try, if at all possible, to attend. Offer hospitality so that one of the socials is held at your home.

Activity

Share about one thing you learned in Bible study this year.

Try to share the Good News of Jesus with someone.

Pray for three people that you could invite to Bible study next time.

CHAPTER 21

Crucifixion and Death of Jesus

Matthew 27:31–56, Mark 15:20–41, Luke 23:26–49

Then Jesus, crying with a loud voice, said,
"Father, into thy hands I commit my spirit!"
And having said this he breathed his last.
(Luke 23:46)

The Gospel of John provides the only eyewitness account of the final sufferings of Jesus. The three Synoptic narratives of the Passion rely upon good second-hand testimony. Matthew's excellent reporting skills enable him to gather information about what he missed when he ran away from the arrest. Mark seems to report Peter's reconstruction of the events. Luke gathered multiple sources in his usual thorough investigative reporting. The Church uses John's narrative on Good Friday because of his faithfulness in witnessing everything with his own eyes, but the Synoptics are read on Palm Sunday.

The narrative of the crucifixion of Jesus in the Synoptic Gospels occurs in six literary units.
1. The Road to Golgotha (Matthew 27:31b–32, Mark 15:20–21, Luke 23:26–32)
2. The Crucifixion (Matthew 27:33–37, Mark 15:22–26, Luke 23:33–34)
3. The Derision of Jesus on the Cross (Matthew 27:38–43, Mark 15:27–32, Luke 23:39–43)
4. The Two Thieves (Matthew 27:44, Mark 15:32, Luke 23:39–43)
5. The Death of Jesus (Matthew 27:45–54, Mark 15:33–39, Luke 23:39–43)
6. The Witnesses to the Crucifixion (Matthew 27:55–56, Mark 15:40–41, Luke 23:49)

The final sufferings of Jesus took place in a geographical swath of about two thousand feet (a little less than half a mile) that runs across the city of Jerusalem. Christian pilgrims have often walked the "Via Dolorosa" to remember Christ's Way of the Cross. Since Crusader times, the Franciscan Order has had the Papal mandate to keep custody of the these holy places, and to erect Stations of the Cross in churches and oratories throughout the Catholic world as a means of promoting devotion.

To this day scholars dispute the exact point of origin of the Way of the Cross. The brutal destruction of Jerusalem in 70 AD and again in 135 AD, with its subsequent reconstruction, challenges the authenticity of specific historical sites of antiquity. Fortunately, there is consensus about where the Way of the Cross ended. Two thousand years of the uninterrupted presence of Christians at the site of the crucifixion and Resurrection provide support for the authenticity of this historical landmark.

Jesus started the humiliating march to Calvary, the distance of about two thousand feet of upward slope, at the *praetorium*, the central courtyard of the procurator's palace at the fortress Antonia. The roads at the time of Jesus were probably narrow, crooked, and dirty. Jesus laboriously climbed this terrain after the severe scourging and loss of blood He had endured.

The Stations of the Cross

I.	Jesus Is Condemned to Death
II.	Jesus Bears His Cross
III.	Jesus Falls the First Time under His Cross
IV.	Jesus Meets His Afflicted Mother
V.	Simon of Cyrene Helps Jesus Carry His Cross
VI.	Veronica Wipes the Face of Jesus
VII.	Jesus Falls the Second Time
VIII.	Jesus Consoles the Daughters of Jerusalem
IX.	Jesus Falls the Third Time
X.	Jesus Is Stripped of His Garments
XI.	Jesus Is Nailed to the Cross
XII.	Jesus Dies on the Cross
XIII.	Jesus Is Taken Down from the Cross
XIV.	Jesus Is Laid in the Tomb

Today's Way of the Cross follows the Via Dolorosa from the chapel of the Condemnation of Jesus through the Arab and Christian quarters of the old city. The first two stations, *Jesus is Condemned to Death* and *Jesus Bears His Cross,* begin at the *praetorium.* Underneath the convent of the Sisters of Zion is a well-preserved pavement with markings such as those made by Roman soldiers. One symbol relates to a form of torture they used called "crowning the king." Outside the convent, the pilgrim passes under the arch of *Ecce Homo,* "Behold the Man," (cf. John 19:5) built during the reign of Hadrian a hundred years after Jesus' death.

Between the third and fourth stations, *Jesus Falls the First Time* and *Jesus Meets His Mother,* there is an Armenian Catholic chapel with a mosaic of the sandals of the Virgin Mary who waited for her Son on the way to Calvary. Though not mentioned in the scriptural accounts until the foot of the Cross, the Blessed Mother was certainly among the sizable entourage which followed Jesus to Golgotha (Luke 23:27–31).

At the fifth station, *Jesus is Helped by Simon,* there is a chapel in a house described as the house of Simon of Cyrene. All three Synoptics mention this Simon as "a man of Cyrene," which is part of modern-day Libya. He may have worshipped at the synagogue of Roman freedmen from Cyrene and Alexandria mentioned in Acts 6:9. Mark adds biographical details that this Simon was the father of Alexander and Rufus, to distinguish him from other Simons, such as Simon Peter or Simon the Zealot.

Here the Way of the Cross turns sharply to the west and steadily climbs to the level of the present main market throughway. Outside the convent of the Little Sisters of Jesus of Charles de Foucauld, one can see a round pillar stone with the inscription "Veronica," marking the sixth station, *Veronica Wipes the Face of Jesus.* Jesus continues to weaken, because now He falls again even though Simon is helping to carry the Cross. The seventh station, *Jesus Falls a Second Time,* is on the market street, marked by a Catholic chapel. Just a short flight of steps brings one to the eighth station, *Jesus Consoles the Women of Jerusalem,* recounted by Luke (23:27–31).

Returning to the market street, pilgrims follow the steps to the Coptic Patriarchate, a building owned by the Egyptian Coptic Church, for the ninth station, *Jesus Falls a Third Time*. This last station outside the Basilica of the Holy Sepulcher is marked by a round bronze sign installed in March 2000 on the occasion of the visit of Pope John Paul II. Pope Paul VI also followed the Way of the Cross here during his pilgrimage in January 1964. These are the only two popes since Saint Peter reported to have made the Way of the Cross in Jerusalem, but every year, on Good Friday, the Way of the Cross is also commemorated at the Colosseum, the site of many early Christian martyrdoms.

All of the remaining Stations of the Cross are inside the Basilica of the Holy Sepulcher within striking distance of one another. Eastern Christians call this church the *Anastasis*, meaning "The Resurrection." Western Christians call it the "Basilica of the Holy Sepulcher," meaning "the Tomb."

Mosaics of the Old Testament prophets who foretold the Passion of Messiah, David, Isaiah, Daniel, and Zechariah, mark the tenth station, *Jesus is Stripped of His Garments*. The eleventh station, *Jesus is Nailed to the Cross*, has an altar with a powerful mosaic of Jesus being nailed to the Cross. The figures of the Madonna, Mary Magdalene, and John emerge beyond Jesus and His torturer.

The Greek Orthodox Church controls the site of the crucifixion and the Holy Sepulcher. Golgotha at the time of our Lord was an abandoned stone quarry. The place of crucifixion was located at a protruding rock. Archeologists recently discovered the hole where the vertical beam of the Cross was fixed to the ground. Pilgrims may touch the rock, the place of Jesus' death, through an opening under the altar at the twelfth station, *Jesus Dies on the Cross*. Nearby, life size icons of Mary and John beholding Jesus on the Cross are covered by silver. Just left of the altar is the monument to our Lady of Sorrows, marking the thirteenth station of the Cross, *Jesus Is Taken Down from the Cross*.

The tomb of Jesus, the fourteenth station, *Jesus is Laid in the Tomb*, is commemorated by two chapels in the Basilica of the Holy Sepulcher. In the Chapel of the Angel, one may gaze under the glass near the altar to see pieces of the original rock which covered the tomb of Jesus. A second chapel houses the marble slab above the original one on which the body of Jesus was laid to rest. This is undoubtedly the most holy ground on the surface of our earth. Despite all the distractions of the present Way of the Cross, the pilgrim may realize the depth of the spiritual scar made by God to shake us from within. The death and Resurrection of Jesus is the beginning of life for us!

Great artists down through history have portrayed the death and Resurrection of Jesus Christ. Rubens, Michelangelo, El Greco, Salvador Dali, and so many others have implanted their artistic images into the hearts of believers. The Passion of Jesus synthesizes the entire human experience of suffering.

Catholic devotions are not just visual, however. There is a long tradition of meditation upon the "Seven Last Words of Christ." The old Good Friday service involved the preaching of seven sermons, one on each of the final sentences of Christ. Great composers, like Franz Joseph Haydn and Theodore Dubois, have set to music these seven texts.

> ## The Seven Last Words of Christ
>
> I.   Father, forgive them; for they know not what they do. (Luke 23:34)
> II.   Truly, I say to you, today you will be with me in Paradise. (Luke 23:43)
> III.   Woman, behold, your son! ... Behold your mother! (John 19:26–27)
> IV.   Eli, Eli, lama sabachthani (My God, my God, why has thou forsaken me?). (Matthew 27:46)
> V.   I thirst. (John 19:28)
> VI.   It is finished. (John 19:30)
> VII. Father, into thy hands I commit my spirit! (Luke 23:46)

The first words of Jesus from the Cross, "Father forgive them; for they know not what they do" (Luke 23:34), set the tone for the entire Passion. Jesus came to forgive the world's sins. Jesus redeems sinful humanity with no hatred, bitterness, or resentment toward any of the guilty parties, present or absent. Later, the first Christian martyr, Saint Stephen, repeats this sentiment as he is being stoned to death, "Lord, do not hold this sin against them" (Acts 7:60). The challenge of martyrdom involves dying for Christ and also forgiving those who are in the very act of taking one's life. Only by grace can one rise above the instinct to fight or flee in such cases. Saint Maria Goretti expressed it well to her attacker, "Aren't you afraid of going to hell if you do this?" She was more concerned about the salvation of the soul of her attacker than the safety of her own body.

None of the words of Jesus on the Cross relate to His kingship, but clearly He is creating a world different from that ruled by ordinary kings, where retaliation and vengeance are the rule rather than forgiveness. Over His head, meanwhile, is the reminder that this is a dying King, "Jesus of Nazareth, the King of Jews" (John 19:19), written in Hebrew, Latin, and Greek.

Mark 15:29 reveals that the people passing by derided Jesus, wagging their heads. Among the mockers Matthew 27:41 identifies the chief priests, scribes, and elders. The Synoptics each offer different words of taunt toward Jesus, presumably all of them intended to hurt Him. Luke offers the most details on the two thieves being crucified alongside Christ. Mark suggests that both thieves reviled Jesus (Mark 15:32). Luke reveals the repentance of the good thief, and Jesus' subsequent promise, "Truly, I say to you, today you will be with me in Paradise" (Luke 23:43), which are the most touching of Jesus' word of mercy reported by the evangelists.

Matthew and Mark record only one sentence from Jesus on the Cross, "Eli, Eli, lama sabachthani?" that is, "My God, my God, why hast thou forsaken me?" (Matthew 27:46, Mark 15:34). Both evangelists report the words in Aramaic and Greek. Jesus quotes the beginning of Psalm 22, and we may understand that He recalled the entire psalm, which contains other identifying details, such as: "They have pierced my hands and my feet" and "They divide my garments among them, and for my raiment they cast lots" (Psalm 22:16, 18). The beginning of Psalm 22 sounds like an expression of ultimate despair, but by the end of the psalm faith triumphs. "I will tell of thy name to my brethren; in the midst of the congregation I will praise thee!" (Psalm 22:22). From the Cross Jesus prophesies the Resurrection! Millions of martyrs have emulated Him.

Jesus may have recited psalms in Hebrew as well. Bystanders may have had to struggle to understand Him, in view of the horrific beating He had taken about His face and body, and that He is suspended from a Cross, struggling for breath as the lungs collapse in the chest cavity. Yet Jesus continues to pray through His agony.

The final words of Christ according to Saint Luke, "Father, into thy hands I commit my spirit" (Luke 23:46), recall Psalm 31: "Into thy hand I commit my spirit" (v. 5). Jesus begins this prayer using His favorite prayer word, "Abba! Father!" Psalm 31, like Psalm 22, is a prayer of hope in a time of tribulation.

Again, Jesus intends to call to our minds the entire psalm or long parts of it from the Cross, which includes "Blessed be the LORD, for he has wondrously shown his steadfast love to me. ... Be strong, and let your heart take courage" (Psalm 31:21, 24).

During the recitation of the Lord's Passion on Palm Sunday and Good Friday, at the moment when life leaves the body of Jesus, the entire congregation kneels for a moment of silence. Matthew describes the actual scene at the time as anything but quiet.

"And behold, the curtain of the temple was torn in two, from top to bottom; and the earth shook, and the rocks were split; the tombs also were opened, and many bodies of the saints who had fallen asleep were raised" (27:51–52). Luke reveals that many return home beating their breasts.

The mood of the soldiers changes dramatically. The Romans were great believers in signs in nature, such as earthquakes (Matthew 27:51). Immediately following the death of Jesus, the presiding centurion says the last word, a profession of faith, and is joined by the rest of the soldiers.

The Witness of the Centurion
Certainly this man was innocent! (Luke 23:47)
Truly this man was the Son of God! (Mark 15:39)
Truly this was the Son of God! (Matthew 27:54)

From Luke's quotation, "Certainly this man was innocent!," we learn only that the officer in charge regarded the actions he had to take as unjust. Matthew and Mark tell us more—the centurion had come to a belief in the divinity of Jesus: "Truly this was the Son of God!" The centurion reminds us that we must read about the death of Christ with a spirit of faith and thanksgiving. Without faith, it was just another dreary episode in the long saga of man's inhumanity to man. God has stepped into the equation, however, and made this suffering salvific.

With chilling authenticity the Synoptics report the death of Jesus, the greatest tragedy in recorded history—the innocent God-Man sacrificing His life-blood for the redemption of the world. All of the Synoptics agree that at the sixth hour darkness covered the whole land until the ninth hour. Luke adds that the sun failed and the temple curtain was torn in two.

Luke reports that women who had followed Jesus from Galilee witnessed from a distance. Matthew names the women as Mary Magdalene, Mary the mother of James and Joseph, and the mother of the sons of Zebedee (Matthew 27:56), while Mark identifies the women as "Mary Magdalene, and Mary the mother of James the younger and of Joses, and Salome" (Mark 15:40). Mark adds that many other women came up with Him to Jerusalem. The women of Jerusalem on the Way of the Cross represent the faithful of the Church. These people have the same compassionate love for Jesus as He has for them.

None of the Synoptics mention the soldier piercing the side of Jesus. Only John the Beloved offers this additional piece of information to us (John 19:31–37). Only John was there to witness the horror of the soldier piercing the side of our Lord with blood and water pouring forth.

Theological Reflections on the Crucifixion of Jesus ~ Matthew views the crucifixion of Jesus in anticipation of His Resurrection (Matthew 27:51–53), in which the mystery of death is swallowed up by the victory of life (1 Corinthians 15). Mark focuses on the reality that Jesus offered His suffering and death for the salvation of each individual. The highlight of Mark's account comes in the confession of the centurion recognizing the true identity of Jesus: "Truly this man was the Son of God" (Mark 15:39). Luke contemplates the return of Jesus to His Father in view of the Church, born in the mystery of the Passion. Through conversion, the life of each one of us may return to God.

The Way of the Cross in Jerusalem, this ancient expression of Christian piety, demonstrates the longing of the human soul to identify itself with the sufferings of Christ. Simon of Cyrene, the women of Jerusalem, the soldiers, and thieves represent different human attitudes toward encountering God. No death was more shameful than the public horror of crucifixion. For unbelievers, Jesus on the way to Calvary was a criminal sentenced to die. For believers, the Way of the Cross represents the march of the King on His way to victory over evil and to His throne.

There may be many Cyrenians in the world: the exploited masses, the poor, the sick, prisoners, slaves of sin, victims of injustice, the lonely, and abandoned. All of these may carry their crosses for Christ. Like Simon of Cyrene, they can participate in Christ's great triumph over death by bearing the ultimate emblem of victory, the Cross. The weight of the Cross is meant to transform our faith. The faithful, as well as the good thief on the cross, are drawn to the mystery of God's mercy for those who sincerely repent and accept eternal salvation.

The two thieves represent the entire human race facing death. We all are evildoers because we do bad things to others and we fail to do the good that we could do for the love of God and our fellow man. We are dry wood destined to be burned unless we repent and convert like the good thief that Jesus saves because of his plea to God. The good thief recognizes that Jesus is the King of eternal love and did not cease being Son of God on the Cross. This thief, whom tradition calls Dismas, was elevated to the glory of heaven because of his hope in grace that is beyond human understanding. He is the thief who stole heaven.

Only the new Adam, Jesus Christ, true God and true man, could restore lost humanity to its original condition. Only Jesus could restore our relationship with the Father. A great temptation is to think that we can achieve salvation by ourselves, without reconciliation and absolution. Abandon this false perception and recognize the need for redemption. The penitent thief's confession of sin and humble faith shows the proper response to Jesus' mercy. Jesus took your sin, my sin, and the sins of the whole world upon Himself. Heaven requires our sober look at the price Jesus paid for our sins. Ponder the meaning of Jesus' love on the Cross, for the Cross is the key that opens the gates to Paradise.

1. Read Isaiah 53 and list as many verses as you can find that foretell the suffering Servant.

2. How did people react to Jesus on His way to Golgotha?

Matthew 27:29	" *Mockery by the soldiers*
Mark 15:16–20	
Luke 23:26–27	

3. Compare the following verses.

Isaiah 50:6	*I gave my back to those beat me*
Matthew 27:30	"
Mark 15:19–20	*striking his head spitting*

4. Describe the encounter in Luke 23:27–31.

the way of the cross

5. Read Psalm 22 in entirety and write the verses that could describe Jesus on the Cross.

Save me from the lion's mouth, my poor life from the horns of wild bulls

6. How would you explain Psalm 22:30–31?

I will live for the Lord

7. Why did Jesus die on the Cross? CCC 601–603

8. Compare the following scenario from each Synoptic account.

Matthew 27:38–44	Mark 15:32	Luke 23:39–43.

9. What significance do the following verses provide?

Psalm 22:18	
Mark 15:24	

10. Write the last seven words (phrases) of Christ.

Luke 23:34	
Luke 23:43	
John 19:26–27	
Matthew 27:46	
John 19:28	
John 19:30	
Luke 23:46	

11. What words identified Jesus on the Cross?

Matthew 27:37	Mark 15:26	John 19:19

12. What attempt was made to quench Jesus' thirst? Matthew 27:48, Mark 15:36

13. What was the sky like on Good Friday? Matthew 27:45

14. What do the following verses confirm?

Matthew 27:50	
Mark 15:37	
Luke 23:46	
John 19:30	

15. Who stayed with Jesus at the foot of the Cross?

Matthew 27:55–56	Mark 15:40–41	John 19:25–27

16. Read Psalm 31 and write some verses that could apply to Jesus on the Cross.

17. What happened when Jesus died? Matthew 27:51–54

18. What conclusions did these eyewitnesses to Jesus' crucifixion reach?

Matthew 27:54	
Mark 15:39	
Luke 23:47	

19. What did Jesus' death on the Cross accomplish? 1 Corinthians 15:54–57

20. What did Jesus demonstrate in accepting crucifixion for our sins? Philippians 2:5–11

** Meditate on the crucifixion of our Lord and share a favorite hymn that comes to mind.

CHAPTER 22

The Resurrection of Jesus

Matthew 27:57–28:20, Mark 15:42–16:20, Luke 23:50–24:52

He is not here, for he has risen, as he said. (Matthew 28:6)

The place of the Resurrection of Jesus of Nazareth, located in the Basilica of the Holy Sepulcher in Jerusalem just of a few feet from Golgotha, is the most venerated site in all of Christianity. Why was the burial place of Jesus such a short distance from the place of the crucifixion? Recall that at the time of Jesus, Golgotha was an abandoned stone quarry that was also used as a burial ground, since tombs at that time were hewn in rock. The burial place was outside the city walls because no tombs were allowed inside the city walls. Today there are still tombs visible behind the tomb of Jesus. Had not Joseph of Arimathea given his brand-new tomb for the burial of Jesus, our Lord would probably have been buried in the public cemetery in the Kidron valley.

Divine providence arranged that the sites of the crucifixion and burial of Jesus would be very close in proximity. When the Christians in Jerusalem read "that Christ died for our sins in accordance with the scriptures, that he was buried, that he was raised on the third day in accordance with the scriptures" (1 Corinthians 15:3–4), they understood that these greatest events of the Christian faith occurred at a single place in the Holy City. Many skeptics ask whether the Basilica of the Holy Sepulcher is the real place of the burial and Resurrection of Jesus. The answer is a definitive "Yes."

Along with the proof of the tombs, this site corresponds to the topographical description provided in the Gospels. Jesus was crucified on a skull-shaped rock outside the city (John 19:17), with graves nearby (John 19:41–42). The early Christian community in Jerusalem held liturgical celebrations at this site until the siege and destruction of Jerusalem in 70 AD, providing more evidence for the authenticity of this site. Historically, although Hadrian obliterated all Jewish and Judeo-Christian presence in the city in 135 AD and built a shrine to Aphrodite over this site, it was later recovered, and the Christian presence was restored by Constantine.

Eusebius describes the recovery of the Sepulcher of Jesus when Constantine restored the Christian presence in Jerusalem. "At once the work was carried out, and as layer after layer of the subsoil came into view, the venerable and most holy memorial of the Savior's Resurrection, beyond all our hopes came into view" (*Life of Constantine*, 3.28). Eusebius calls the place where Constantine built the sanctuary in 335 AD "the most blessed place," the "saving cave," the "most holy cave and the most marvelous place in the world" (*Life of Constantine*, 3.31). For the first Christians, the tomb of Christ was the sign of the triumph of the Cross and the hope of our personal resurrection to new life after death. The early Church Fathers considered the tomb of Jesus the center of the earth.

Tradition holds that this may also be Paradise, the place where Adam returned and was buried after repenting of his sin of disobedience. According to the Fathers, the new mystical tree of life blossomed at the place where it was planted by the blood of Christ. Adam and all humanity were redeemed from their sins at Calvary. Another reason that the Fathers considered this site to be Paradise are the words of Saint John from his Gospel; "Now in the place where he was crucified there was a garden, and in the garden was a new tomb where no one had ever been laid" (John 19:41). Later, Mary Magdalene mistakes Jesus for a "gardener" (John 20:16). For the early Church Fathers, this place also corresponds to Mount Moriah where Abraham prepared to sacrifice his beloved son, Isaac (Genesis 22:2).

In the theology of the Fathers, the *Anastasis*, the place of Resurrection, became the center of the universe, the heavenly throne where Christ will return in glory for the Last Judgment. Eusebius uses the tomb of Christ as a metaphor of a river that flows from the center of the city bringing salvation to the world, corresponding to the river of the water of life flowing from the throne of God in the New Jerusalem (Revelation 22:1–2). The Fathers propose this memorial of the Savior's Resurrection as the new temple open for every worshiper.

Today, the pilgrim may be dismayed by the cacophony in the Holy Sepulcher basilica. Perhaps the atmosphere of prayer and piety absent today reflects the atmosphere as it was in the time of Jesus in the temple of Jerusalem. Still this is a place of Christian worship where everyone is invited to reflect that our own body is the temple of the Holy Spirit (1 Corinthians 6:19). Saint Paul's admonition to "glorify God in your body" (1 Corinthians 6:20) would not be possible had Jesus not glorified His body at Calvary and in *Anastasis*. Both the death and Resurrection of Jesus enable us to grasp the majesty of God's glory in personal perspective.

Literary Criticism of the Biblical Account ~ Mark provides the most detail of the Synoptic accounts of Christ's burial, including that Joseph of Arimathea was "a respected member of the council" (Mark 15:43). Matthew adds that Joseph was a rich man and Luke describes him as "a good and righteous man" (Luke 23:51). Only Matthew describes Joseph as a disciple of Jesus, while Luke says that Joseph was "looking for the kingdom of God" (Luke 23:51).

Only Mark divulges that Pilate inquired about the death of Jesus (Mark 15:44). Matthew describes Joseph of Arimathea offering his own new tomb and a clean linen shroud for burial. Luke adds that no one had ever been laid in that tomb. Matthew and Mark both describe the large stone rolled against the door of the tomb. Matthew provides the solitary information about the Pharisees asking Pilate to post guards at the tomb and Pilate's acquiescence to their request, securing the sepulcher with a stone and guards (Matthew 27:62–66).

The Resurrection event itself is not described in any of the Gospels, since no one was there to see the most spectacular event of human history. The Synoptics report what was seen and heard. Some see only the empty tomb, some see an angel, and later others see the Risen Christ Himself:

✝ Women find the tomb empty. (Matthew 28:1–8, Mark 16:1–8, Luke 24:1–12, John 20:1–13)
✝ Jesus later appears to the women. (Matthew 28:9–10, Mark 16:9–11)
✝ Jesus appears to the disciples. (Matthew 28:16–20, Mark 16:14–18, Luke 24:36–53)

The theme of the women at the tomb after the Resurrection is tied to their presence at the burial of Christ (Matthew 27:61, Mark 15:47, Luke 23:55). The names of the women in the Gospels stimulate the imagination. Matthew and Mark speak about Mary Magdalene and Mary the mother of Joses. Mark 16:1 adds Salome to Mary Magdalene and Mary, the mother of James. Luke informs the reader that the women were "Mary Magdalene and Joanna and Mary the mother of James and the other women with them" (Luke 24:10). Luke bridges the events between the burial of Jesus and His Resurrection by mentioning twice that the women took spices with them to the tomb. Matthew, Mark, and Luke offer different expressions of time to indicate Easter morning. Mark reports a very large stone and the quandary of the women: "Who will roll away the stone for us from the door of the tomb?" (Mark 16:3).

Matthew reports a great earthquake and reveals that an angel of the Lord descended from heaven to roll back the stone and sit upon it (28:2). Mark confirms the angel's appearance as "a young man," while Luke mentions two men. Mark describes the reaction of the women as amazement, whereas Luke speaks about their awe and fright, as they bow their faces to the ground. Matthew reveals the fear of the guards (28:4). In Matthew and Mark the angel speaks to the women about Jesus who was crucified, whereas Luke describes Jesus as the "living among the dead" (24:5). All three Synoptics confirm the essential historical fact that *Jesus has risen*. Luke recalls Jesus' earlier prophecy regarding His crucifixion and Resurrection on the third day.

After the angel invites the women to inspect the empty tomb, Matthew and Mark describe the angel commissioning the women to tell the disciples to meet Jesus in Galilee (Matthew 28:7, Mark 16:7). Matthew describes the women departing in fear and great joy, while Mark observes their trembling and astonishment. Matthew and Luke confirm that the women told all this to the disciples.

The Synoptic authors convey essentially the same message, choosing to emphasize different details to give a full description of the amazing events. Jesus is risen from the dead! Jesus is the Victor over sin and death proved by His Resurrection after His brutal crucifixion and death on the Cross. This theological truth is the basis for the radical Christian hope of personal resurrection for those who accept and proclaim their faith in Jesus Christ, the Son of God. Paul explains this conviction; "[I]f Christ has not been raised, our preaching is in vain and your faith is in vain" (1 Corinthians 15:14).

---

† Matthew lists thirteen witnesses to the risen Lord: Mary Magdalene, the other Mary, and the eleven apostles.
† Mark lists fourteen witnesses: Mary Magdalene, the two walking in the country, the eleven at table including Peter, Mark's witness.
† Luke has a list of thirteen witnesses, three of whom see Jesus twice: Cleopas and another disciple on the road to Emmaus, Simon, and the eleven.
† John lists twelve or more witnesses, at least five of whom see Jesus three times.
† Paul lists at least 513 witnesses: Cephas, the twelve, more than 500 brethren at one time, James, all the apostles, last of all Paul (1 Corinthians 15:5–8).

Combining the five lists in the box above we arrive at a grand total of 516 or more witnesses to the risen Lord. "Therefore, since we are surrounded by so great a cloud of witnesses, let us also lay aside every weight, and sin which clings so closely, and let us run with perseverance the race that is set before us, looking to Jesus the pioneer and perfecter of our faith, who for the joy that was set before him endured the cross, despising the shame, and is seated at the right hand of the throne of God" (Hebrews 12:1–2). Despite their differences, all five lists take care to confirm the eleven apostles. The very essence of an apostle is one who testifies to the risen Lord. That is why Thomas was being difficult. Until he had seen the risen Lord, he was not on the same experiential level as the other apostles.

Matthew, Mark, and John report Mary Magdalene seeing the risen Lord before anyone else. Catholics have great devotion to Saint Mary Magdalene. A large church in Paris is the Madeleine (1842), and Salt Lake City recently has tastefully restored the Cathedral of the Madeleine (1915). Unfortunately there has been much needless confusion, some of recent origin, about her identity. Here are the things the Gospels tell with certitude about Mary Magdalene:

✝ Mary was from the Galilean shore town of Magdala. (Matthew 15:39)
✝ She was exorcized of seven demons. (Luke 8:2)
✝ Mary Magdalene was present at Calvary. (Matthew 27:56, Mark 15:40, John 19:25)
✝ Mary witnessed the burial of Jesus. (Matthew 27:61, Mark 15:47)
✝ She saw the empty tomb. (Matthew 28:2, Mark 16:4, Luke 24:10, John 20:1)
✝ Mary Magdalene saw the angel. (Matthew 28:2, Mark 16:5, Luke 24:10, John 20:14)
✝ She saw the risen Lord Himself. (Matthew 28:9, Mark 16:9, John 20:14)
✝ Jesus called her "Mary" and she called Him "Rabboni." (John 20:16)
✝ She reported back to the apostles. (John 20:18)

Some people have misidentified Mary Magdalene with two other New Testament women:

1) Mary the sister of Martha and Lazarus of Bethany (John 11) is clearly a different person because the forceful Magdalene of Easter morning has a completely different personality than the shy sister of Bethany. Interestingly, the Benedictine order celebrates the three siblings of Bethany together on the traditional feast day of Saint Martha, who offered hospitality to Christ, as the rule of Benedict exhorts monasteries to do.

2) The penitent woman of Luke 7:36–50 is mentioned in an adjacent chapter to Mary Magdalene (Luke 7 and 8). The failure of their stories to match up on even one particular point makes the identification quite unlikely. No one prior to the 6th century makes this connection.

If tradition has needlessly confused the Magdalene with other women in the New Testament, popular culture has fabricated a mythical Magdalene. The Magdalene of contemporary fiction has no correlation with the historical reality or the biblical truths that define Mary Magdalene and her relationship to Christ fairly and truthfully. Perhaps the seven demons that were expelled from her are still roaming around trying to destroy her reputation. Since Mary Magdalene is the *testis princeps* of the Resurrection, any attack on the Magdalene is an attack on Easter itself. The Dominican liturgy bestows upon her the title "apostle to the apostles." Before Matthew, Mark, Luke, or John, Mary Magdalene sees and testifies that Jesus is alive again and goes before us.

The Gospels convey the greatest truth of all human history: Jesus Christ has risen from the dead and conquered death. And, through His Resurrection Jesus identifies Himself with us. Two caves embrace his life, one of His nativity, the other of His burial. Every human fate is similar. We all originate on this earth and to this earth we shall all return. The liturgy of Ash Wednesday reminds us of this truth, when ashes are marked in a cross on the forehead with the words "Remember man you are dust and to dust you shall return" (cf. Job 34:15). May our love for God and the study of His Word prepare us for the time when we hope to see Him face to face!

1. What happened after Jesus died?

Matthew 27:57–61	Mark 15:42–47	Luke 23:50–56

2. What eyewitness evidence proves that Jesus really died? John 19:31–37

3. Whose idea was it to put a guard at the tomb and why was it necessary? Matthew 27:62–66

the pharisess gatheo and made that desition to prove Jesus was impost

4. How was the stone moved away from the opening to the sepulcher? Matthew 28:1–4

Judas give back the money he was sorry but for betraying Jesus

5. Who was the first eyewitness to the Resurrection of our Lord? Mark 16:9

the appearance to mary

6. Compare the following accounts of the Resurrection of Jesus.

Matthew 28:1–10	Mark 16:1–8	Luke 24:1–12
mary Magdalene came to the Tomb it was earthquakd	it was abat Baptizing man y father son y holy spirit	visiting th Tomb.

7. Defend the Resurrection of Christ as an historical event. CCC 639

8. Explain the Resurrection as a transcendent event. CCC 647

9. Describe the events in Luke 24:13–32.

10. When did the disciples on the road to Emmaus recognize the Lord? Luke 24:30–32

11. What evidence can you cite that Jesus had a real resurrected body? Luke 24:33–43

12. Why did Jesus suffer and die? Luke 24:46–49

13. Where did Jesus go when He left the disciples and what did they do? Luke 24:50–53

14. Who saw Jesus in His resurrected body? 1 Corinthians 15:3–9

15. Who would want to cover-up our Lord's Resurrection? Matthew 28:11–15

16. What significance does the Resurrection have in these verses?

Romans 5:6–21	
1 Corinthians 15:12–28	
Colossians 3:1–4	
1 Thessalonians 4:13–18	

17. What does Saint Peter offer as the foundation of Christian hope? 1 Peter 1:3–12

18. What does Saint Paul aspire to attain? Philippians 3:7–11

19. Jesus has a glorified body. What can we hope for? Philippians 3:20–21

20. What final words did Jesus offer?

Matthew 28:16–20	Mark 16:15–20

** Share one way in which you can share the Good News—Jesus Lives!

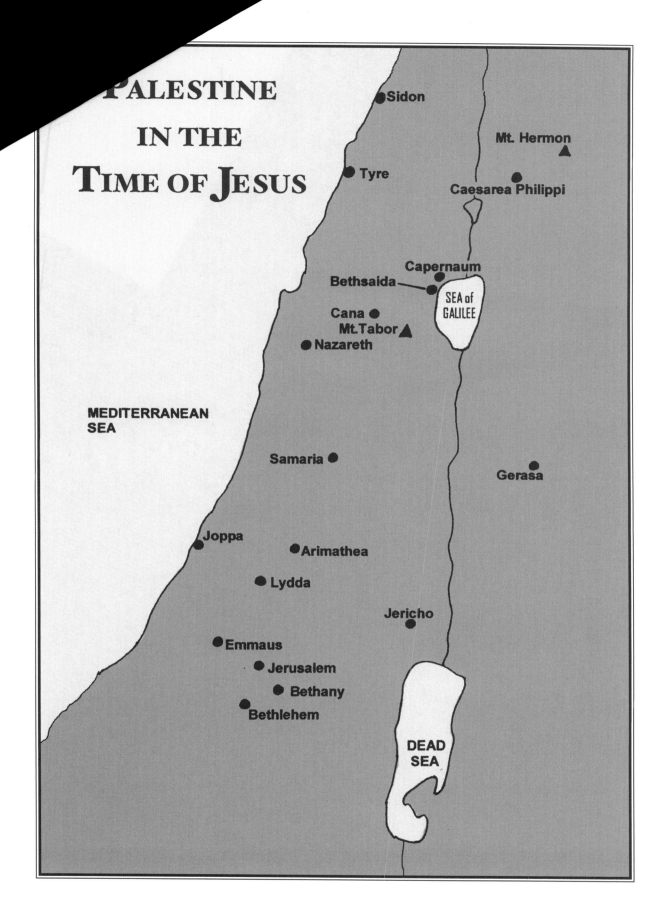

PALESTINE IN THE TIME OF JESUS

Sidon

Mt. Hermon

Tyre

Caesarea Philippi

Capernaum

Bethsaida

SEA of GALILEE

Cana

Mt. Tabor

Nazareth

MEDITERRANEAN SEA

Samaria

Gerasa

Joppa

Arimathea

Lydda

Jericho

Emmaus

Jerusalem

Bethany

Bethlehem

DEAD SEA

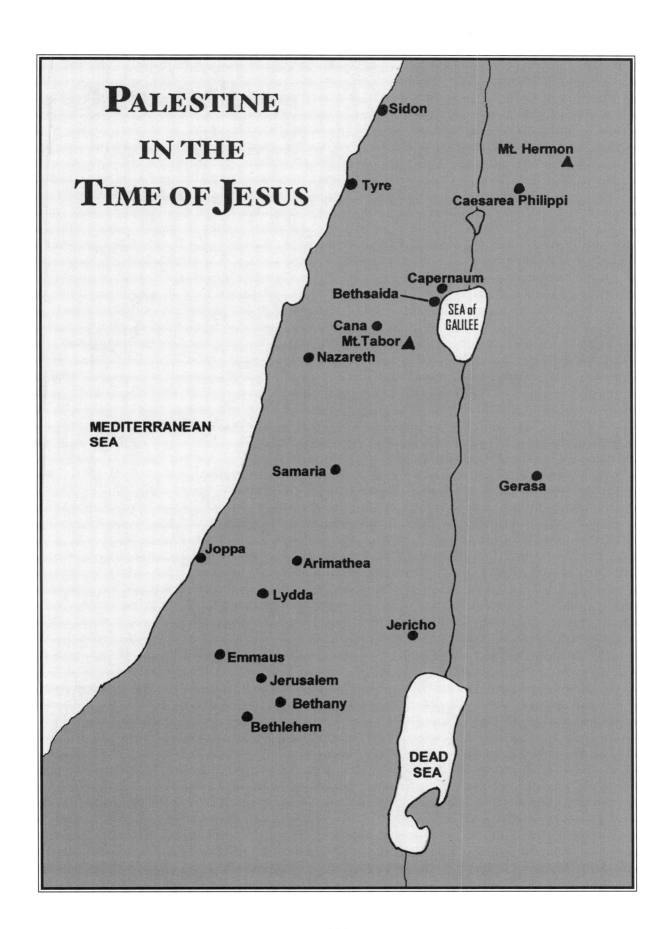

PALESTINE IN THE TIME OF JESUS

Sidon

Mt. Hermon

Tyre

Caesarea Philippi

Capernaum

Bethsaida

SEA of GALILEE

Cana

Mt. Tabor

Nazareth

MEDITERRANEAN SEA

Samaria

Gerasa

Joppa

Arimathea

Lydda

Jericho

Emmaus

Jerusalem

Bethany

Bethlehem

DEAD SEA